INCREASING ACCESS TO COLLEGE

SUNY series

FRONTIERS IN EDUCATION

Philip G. Altbach, Editor

The Frontiers in Education Series draws upon a range of disciplines and approaches in the analysis of contemporary educational issues and concerns. Books in the series help to reinterpret established fields of scholarship in education by encouraging the latest synthesis and research. A special focus highlights educational policy issues from a multidisciplinary perspective. The series is published in cooperation with the School of Education, Boston College. A complete listing of books in the series can be found at the end of this volume.

INCREASING ACCESS
TO COLLEGE

EXTENDING POSSIBILITIES FOR ALL STUDENTS

Edited by

WILLIAM G. TIERNEY AND
LINDA SERRA HAGEDORN

STATE UNIVERSITY OF NEW YORK PRESS

Published by
State University of New York Press, Albany

© 2002 State University of New York

For information, address State University of New York Press,
90 State Street, Suite 700, Albany, NY 12207

Production by Cathleen Collins
Marketing by Patrick Durocher

Library of Congress Cataloging-in-Publication Data

Increasing access to college : extending possibilities for all students / edited by William
G. Tierney and Linda Serra Hagedorn.
    p. cm. — (SUNY series, frontiers in education)
    Includes bibliographical references and index.
    ISBN 0-7914-5363-4 (alk. paper) — ISBN 0-7914-5364-2 (pbk. : alk. paper)
    1. Educational equalization—United States. 2. College preparation programs—United
States. 3. College attendance—United States. 4. Education, Higher—United States. I
Tierney, William G. II. Hagedorn, Linda Serra. III. Series.

LC213.2 .I42 2002
378.1'61—dc21
                                                                    2001042917

10 9 8 7 6 5 4 3 2 1

Contents

Introduction

Cultural Capital and the Struggle for Educational Equity

LINDA SERRA HAGEDORN AND WILLIAM G. TIERNEY

Education has long been called "the great equalizer." We are well aware that the delivery of quality elementary and secondary education combined with college access in ways that are blind to student ethnicity and income status will not only benefit the students themselves, but will also benefit society in general. Yet intuitive awareness has not given birth to programs that have exacted fundamental educational change. Even in the twenty-first century, "the great equalizer" remains a theory —abstract and theoretical. The chapters in this book begin to chip away at the divide between theory and practice. They address programs that attempt and sometimes succeed at increasing the quality of elementary and secondary education and/or paving roads to college access.

Historically, special programs and policies generally have assumed a deficit model and have centered on enabling students to overcome: (a) insufficient funds to pay for college, (b) insufficient academic preparation, and (c) insufficient understanding of the world of higher education. Despite what might be termed "gallant efforts" by some programs there has not been a dramatic increase in college attendance, retention, and graduation for low income and minority youth. First generation African American, Hispanic, and Native American youth still lag behind the college-going rates of their white and Asian American counterparts. Present practices have neither ameliorated nor quashed the academic divide. Although the status quo is unacceptable on many levels, we find it especially objectionable for the following reasons:

- Those who would most directly benefit from a postsecondary education— low income and minority youth are not receiving appropriate service.

1

- Public postsecondary institutions increasingly are unwilling and/or unable to provide services for remedial education; of consequence, effective college preparation programs take on increased importance.
- If the United States is to maintain a competitive edge in the present era of the "global economy," an educated workforce is more important than at any other time in our history.

As American schools in general, and urban schools in particular, continue to grapple with a myriad of apparent long-term structural problems, educators and policy makers have turned to discrete solutions that offer an immediate chance for success for today's students. College preparation programs are one of those purported solutions. Our assumption is that if fundamental changes for *all* school children cannot be realized immediately, then college preparation programs might serve as demonstrations to point out ways to succeed, and in doing so, also help *some* children who otherwise would not have gone to college.

For the purposes of this book, we define college preparation programs as enhancement programs that supplement a school's regular activities and are aimed at low-income youth who otherwise might not be able to attend college. More specifically, we are not interested in programs aimed at high achievers (i.e., programs for the gifted) who will likely go to college, or at students who attend private academies or live in upper income neighborhoods. Thus we are not addressing advance placement courses or the equivalent of programs serving neighborhoods like Beverly Hills or Chappaqua. Instead, we are interested in initiatives on local, state, and federal levels that try to increase access for low-income urban youth. Some of these programs may begin in the elementary school years and others might not occur until the senior year of high school; and still others occur at a college, community agency, or housing project. Appendices 1, 2, and 3 sketch a taxonomy of the kind of programs that exist and delineate programmatic goals. A brief glance at the abundance of programs and multitude of goals highlights a basic tension of the programs: How might one decide which programs are most appropriate for particular kinds of students? Even more fundamental, we are concerned that the very logic behind college preparation programs may have deep wrinkles. As indicated in the chapter by William Tierney, we have neither a good sense of which programs are effective nor have we identified the characteristics of successful programs. Thus in our present state of knowledge we are unable to replicate success nor eliminate ineffective practices.

In this book we provide a way to think about the range of options that exist, we offer some solutions about defining what counts for success, and we underscore the importance and difficulty of defining problems and solutions.

In what follows we sketch the parameters of the book and tie the various chapters together.

Experimentation and Integration

A college degree can no longer be considered a luxury, but is rather a necessary passport to the middle class. In response, we have witnessed a burgeoning array of college preparation programs. For example, there are numerous school-college partnerships seeking to create opportunities and incentives for precollege students to achieve academically, to "test the waters" before full-time college study, to explore various career options, and to understand the commitment necessary to be successful in a given field (Wilbur, et al., 1987; Stoel et al., 1992). Important objectives of most programs are the smoothing of the transition from school to college, improvement of study habits, increase of general academic readiness, and expansion of academic options. Many programs also include counseling (both personal and academic) and remedial assistance. Other programs may include objectives to provide students with realistic job experiences and to improve attitudes about work. Some projects employ a variety of rewards and incentives to encourage students to elect and successfully complete the necessary academic subjects that will allow them to pursue the widest range of career options, an especially important concern in the mathematical, science, engineering and technical fields.

Finally, there are "articulation" programs that exist primarily for the purpose of smoothing the transition for students moving from high school to college and universities, to community colleges, and to vocational and technical programs. Many programs include careful attention to student guidance, advisement services, and the improvement of curriculum and instructional support services. Also included are collaborative arrangements that expand the academic options for students, reduce curriculum duplication, and credit transfer difficulties, encourage acceleration, and address the needs of special groups (e.g., second language learners).

Although a vast array of programs exist, we agree with Ann Coles and others that "it is surprising how little empirical data exists about program effectiveness in terms of college participation rates or strategies that make the most difference" (1993, p. 25). In short, there is not a sufficient knowledge base to decide which ones are effective and which are not. In the recent past we have made great strides in understanding the dynamics of effective schooling. We know, for example, what the determinants are of effective preschool programs for students at risk. Researchers have shown the kinds of programs and practices that create an effective environment for kindergartners (Slavin, et al., 1994). We have a better understanding of class size on student learning, and how one-on-one instruction can enhance student abilities (Slavin, 1989).

Until recently, however, most of the information that we have had available as indicators of success about college preparation programs are anecdotal stories of individuals, or brief project summaries by those who have conducted a particular study. Indeed, as Clifford Adelman and Scott Swail and Laura Perna point out in their chapters, even the conceptual terrain has been murky. We also know that the educational world has changed. A degree of experimentation with options such as charter schools, vouchers, and different teaching methods has created a climate for innovation and change in American public education.

College preparation programs are an additional response for the climate of innovation and experimentation that currently exists. Although some programs such as Upward Bound have existed for a generation, others initiatives such as the federal government's *Gear-Up* are relatively new. The underlying assumption of these programs is relatively straightforward. Regardless of structure or format, individuals assume that students who participate in an enhancement program are more likely to go to college than if they did not. Further, individuals usually assume that these programs will be able to serve as models and be integrated into the core activities of a school. Unfortunately, we are not yet able to say convincingly that all such programs are successful, and in reality, very few programs have become models for best practice, or integrated into the general fabric of a school.

The overarching goal of this book is to provide a channel of integrative ideas, theories, models, and concepts about enhancement programs to enable researchers, policy analysts, practitioners, and others to think through some of the more thorny issues that confront college preparation programs. The book compiles and entwines the various recent research projects of the authors. Throughout this book the authors work either explicitly or implicitly from three primary perspectives: a theoretical framework pertaining to cultural capital, an individualistic framework pertaining to cultural integrity, and a social framework pertaining to the idea of merit.

Cultural Capital

Many college preparation programs implicitly or explicitly accept the role of cultural capital in creating the appropriate environment for college attendance. In its simplest terms, one might think of college preparation programs as a structural response to low-income children's deficit of cultural capital—a response that simulates the conditions to deliver the social and academic capital necessary to succeed in college. Several of the authors (Makeba Jones and her colleagues, Patricia Gándara, and Linda Hagedorn and Shereen Fogel) cite Pierre Bourdieu's work and use his theories as central to their chapters. As a whole, the book extends Bourdieu's notion and stretches the definition in several ways. First, cultural capital is not viewed as unidimensional. Unlike fiscal capital that can be measured in one currency (for example, American dollars), cultural capital is convoluted and consists of multiple denominations that cannot be interchanged. In the chapter by Amaury Nora as well as that by Tierney, it is clear that even if programs were able to equip children with the capital that delivers them to the college door, they often do not have the requisite capital to actually graduate from college. Simply stated, the academic capital that brings a student to the college door may not accrue the requisite interest to sustain him/her through until college graduation. Thus there is the need for structural changes to take place to create closer working relationships between schools and postsecondary institutions. We must cultivate the kind of cultural capital that will not only sustain students *to* college, but will evolve and grow to nurture students *through* college.

An additional way to think of cultural capital is less by way of equipping children with capital but instead how to engage those institutions and groups that hold capital to become more responsive to the needs of their constituencies. In this light, colleges and universities are akin to banks where administrators and faculty are the bankers. The Jones and Oakes chapters outline the challenges that need to be confronted when essentially conservative institutions are met with needs from low-income youth. How might we equip such institutions so that they become more responsive? Rather than banks that seek to preserve capital and have little interest in spending finite resources, we need to think of postsecondary institutions more as lending libraries that seek to increase academic capital. Unfortunately, as our colleagues point out, such a notion will not easily take place. Faculty are surely not a monolith who all think alike, but they also for the most part are neither ready nor rewarded for greater engagement with local communities.

One danger of using the notion of cultural capital as a driving framework is that it can be wrongly viewed as little more than assimilationist. One might assume that cultural capital is simply a warmed over culture of poverty framework. Proponents of such a notion assume that poor people live impoverished lives—economically and culturally—and the role of educational and social agencies is to help them assimilate into the mainstream. Our approach is decidedly different.

Cultural Integrity

As Jeannie Oakes and her colleagues point out, rather than insist on all students assimilating into the mainstream, the approach suggested here takes into account the cultures that students bring with them. It is incorrect to imagine that low-income students come devoid of culture, allowing schools and programs to fill empty vessels with mainstream traditions. Rather, all students regardless of income, race, or other criteria are surrounded by a culture, which may differ from that promoted by the mainstream. We promote a sense of cultural integrity that honors, affirms, and acknowledges the diverse identities that account for America within multiple educational practices.

As Adelman is quick to point out, high academic standards (academic capital) are the clearest indicators about whether children will go on to a postsecondary institution. However, as Michelle Knight and Heather Oesterreich suggest, such standards need to come framed in meaningful ways to those who are being educated (cultural integrity). Without cultural integrity, students will not respond either because the programs do not meet their specific needs, or because they do not feel the programs are actually designed for them. Students approach school with multiple identities and if programs are to be successful they need to honor those identities in culturally specific ways so that learning fits.

Education and Merit

There are two implicit assumptions in the very existence of college preparation programs:

1. Schools are failing to adequately prepare students for college. The need for such programs extends from the inability of schools to properly execute their function. Thus school reform is needed (although there is little consensus about what those reforms should be).
2. Public postsecondary institutions and systems seek to enroll the types of students who have traditionally been left out of the system.

The second assumption in large part speaks to the nation's commitment to access. In a postsecondary system as diverse as that existing in the United States, the manner in which a commitment to access has been operationalized is in large part defined by state policies. Community colleges, state universities, and to an extent, public research universities have as one of their basic tenets access for the broad public.

True, public higher education is not as tightly defined as K–12 public education, but throughout the nineteenth and twentieth centuries there was a broad commitment to increased access. The land grant movement, the false deflation of tuition, the GI Bill, and various federal and state loan and grant policies all have been geared to enable individuals who otherwise could not go to college, to get a college education. Underlying such policies was the idea that public education should be open to everyone, not just the wealthy few.

Over the last decade, however, there has been increased discussion about an alternative public policy that pertains to the idea of merit. Who merits entrance to college? Of course, when capacity is sizable and demand is low, those who merit admission are those who apply. When capacity is confined, however, and other policies have increased demand, then questions and debates come into play with regard to who merits admission to a public institution.

We raise this issue here because college preparation programs may be involved in an increasingly impossible undertaking, no matter how effective and successful they become, if those who work from a strict constructionist interpretation of what constitutes a meritocracy prevail. Our simple point here is that merit is a socially constructed idea; We work from the notion that those who merit a postsecondary education has more to do with the capacity of the state to provide viable postsecondary options to its citizenry than with an individual's test scores. As long as public funding to public higher education decreases, we will face increasingly complex and controversial discussions about who deserves entry to a postsecondary institution.

Our modest proposal instead is that two major sea changes take place in the public arena. First, as Oakes and her colleagues suggest, there needs to be a reinvigorated dialogue about expanding access to public higher education via increased, stable, long-term public funding. Second, those who are involved in activities such as enhancement programs need to do a better job of assessing and determining the elements of effectiveness. As Hagedorn and Fogel demonstrate, not all activities are equally promising. Thus on the one hand we call for cost containment and effectiveness, and on the other, we suggest an expansion of the public sector's commitment to postsecondary education and a movement away from what we see as unhelpful arguments about who merits a college education.

Hans Christian Andersen's famous fairy tale of the *Emperor's New Clothes* provides a suitable closing metaphor. The present system of postsecondary instruction can be likened to that vain emperor who mistakenly believed that tailors could construct a cloth so perfect and exquisite that it would be visible *only* by those sufficiently intelligent and competent to appreciate its quality. Without checking their credentials, the emperor paid the tailors to produce their magical cloth. Thus the sham continued and the emperor soon was dressed in cloth made of nothing but air and paraded before his people. Despite the emperor's nakedness, his people did not speak out in fear of being labeled as foolish or incompetent. Finally, a young boy spoke the words that all were thinking: "The Emperor is naked."

Like the tale, inherent to our postsecondary education system is the assumption of its perfection—that those who criticize it are not sufficiently intelligent or competent to appreciate its quality. Further, expensive college preparation programs abound without appropriate check of their credentials. Few speak out about the lack of testing of these expensive programs because they do not want to be labeled as foolish or incompetent.

In this book, we play the role of the boy who spoke out and announced what he saw. We leave it to you, the reader, to finish the metaphor.

References

Coles, A. (1993). *School to College Transition Programs for Low Income and Minority Youth.* Unpublished manuscript.

Slavin, R. E., Karweit, N. L. & Waskik, B. A. (Eds.). (1994). *Preventing Early School Failure.* Boston: Allyn and Bacon.

Slavin, R. E., Karweit, N. L. & Madden, N. A. (Eds.). (1989). *Effective Programs for Students at Risk.* Boston: Allyn and Bacon.

Stoel, C., Togneri, W., & Brown, P. (1992). *What Works: School/College Partnerships to Improve Poor and Minority Student Achievement.* Washington, D.C.: American Association of Higher Education.

Wilber, F. B. Lambert, L. M., & Young, M. J. (Eds.). (1987). *National Directory of School-College Partnerships.* Washington, D.C.: American Association for Higher Education.

Appendix 1.
Model of College Preparation Program Effectiveness

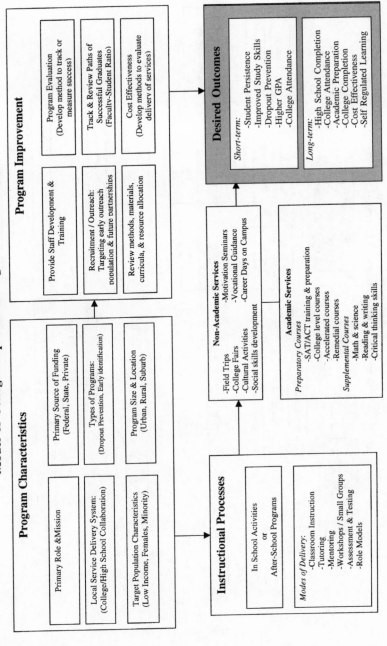

Appendix 2.
College Preparation Programs Overview

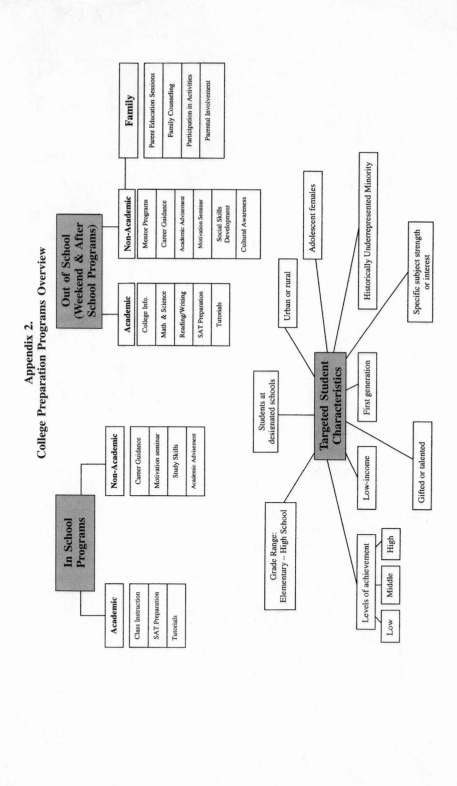

Appendix 3.
General Characteristics of Programs Nationnwide

Funding Sources

- Private Funds
  - Tuition-Driven
  - Institutional Funds
- Federal Funds
- Local/Community
- State Funds

Various Missions & Goals of Programs

- Improve and increase access of postsecondary education for academically gifted yet historically underrepresented youth
- Ensure that underachieving students with academic potential will succeed.
- Assist schools to engage in school-based change.

- Foster partnerships between school districts and four-year colleges to improve learning.
- Reduce number of high-risk students with college potential to finish without high school diplomas.
- Preparation for college admissions and placement tests.

Primary Objectives of Precollegiate Programs

- High School Graduation
- College Completion
- College Attendance
- General Academic Skills
- Other (social service oriented programs)

PART I

The Landscape of College Access

CHAPTER 1

Pre-College Outreach Programs

A National Perspective

WATSON SCOTT SWAIL AND LAURA W. PERNA

Introduction

As the other chapters in this volume attest, despite dramatic increases in postsecondary enrollments at American colleges and universities gaps still exist in who goes to college and who ultimately succeeds. Low-income, African American, Hispanic, and Native American populations continue to be underrepresented at institutions of higher education relative to their representation in the traditional college-age population (Nettles, Perna, & Freeman, 1999). Yet billions of federal, state, and private dollars have been spent to close the enrollment and degree attainment gaps (Gladieux & Swail, 1998).

One reason for the persisting gaps may be that traditional approaches to increasing college access (e.g., student financial aid programs) have focused too narrowly on the issue of college enrollment, without sufficient attention to the steps required to be academically, socially, and psychologically prepared to enter and succeed in college. Achieving the goal of increasing college success for underrepresented students is a complex task, particularly in consideration of the many confounding factors that have an impact on a student's potential to succeed. Our ability to further improve the college-going and college-completion rates for our most disadvantaged students is based on the involvement of stakeholders from all areas of society. Success certainly is a concern for our elementary and secondary levels of education, because they are responsible for cultivating the academic potential within students. Success certainly must concern the colleges, for they are responsible for shepherding students through higher education. Yet success is ultimately dependent upon the ability of our society at large to address inequities that affect education and opportunity for all groups.

15

Working within the constraints of our decentralized system of education only serves to complicate the process. While our entire system of education is arguably the best in the world, there is some noise in the machine that has reduced our ability to better address the needs of education's underclass.

In response to these concerns, policy makers have begun to look at nontraditional mechanisms to improve the education of our students. Three mechanisms in particular sit at the forefront of this policy movement. First, charter schools have become the lightning rod for the conservative movement in education and are the main avenue traveled by many states and localities to foster a sea change in public schooling. But the capacity of charters to have broad structural and systematic impact on the system as a whole is unlikely. The second mechanism is the push for school vouchers. Similar in many ways to the charter concept, voucher programs allow families to choose to enroll their children in a particular public or private school. In addition to providing a choice for families, voucher proponents also share the charter premise that increased competition will ultimately push all schools to change. While some gains may be made through this strategy, it is important to understand that education is very much a closed system. In the voucher-school model, one child's gain may result in another child's loss.

The third focus of policy makers is to look at programs designed to supplement school-based learning. These early intervention programs—designed to improve the academic preparation and college readiness of under-represented groups—do not necessarily have an impact on the systemic problems within our schools. They do provide a safety net for thousands of students who do not get the level of support—academic and social—within their current educational environment to become college ready. Federal and state governments, along with some private organizations, have sponsored these types of programs since the mid-1960s. The most widely known is the Federal TRIO program, established as part of the Johnson administration's War on Poverty. The recent establishment of GEAR UP (Gaining Early Awareness and Readiness through Undergraduate Preparation) extended the federal government's role in early intervention. As well, several states established their own early intervention programs during the 1990s (Perna, 1999), the most publicized being the huge support thrown behind pre-college outreach in the State of California in an attempt to counteract the negative effects on campus diversity associated with the ban on affirmative action established by Proposition 209 (see chapters 7 by Jones, Yonezawa, and Mehan; 6 by Oakes, and 4 by Gandara for more discussion).

Despite the focus and resources devoted to early intervention programs by both the public and private sectors, only minimal data and information are available to describe these programs. Our knowledge is largely based on examinations of the federal TRIO Programs, particularly Upward Bound, and other high-profile programs, such as I Have a Dream, MESA, and AVID.

Even for these programs, however, surprising little is known about program outcomes and effectiveness (see Tierney chapter 10). Moreover, we know virtually nothing about the thousands of other programs that are currently operating across the nation. We don't know how many there are, where they are, what they do, whom they serve, and what impact they have on the educational opportunity and success of the students they serve. Clearly our capacity to make prudent programmatic and funding decisions is restricted by this lack of knowledge.

In an attempt to reduce this information and knowledge gap, the College Board, in association with The Education Resources Institute (TERI) and the Council for Opportunity in Education, conducted a national study in 1999–2000 to identify and collect information from all types of early intervention programs operating nationwide. To supplement the survey data, a series of focus groups were conducted with program directors and administrators over the same period. We briefly describe the history of programs designed to increase college access and success and describe the characteristics of programs currently in operation, based on analyses of the data and information obtained from the survey and focus groups.

A Brief History

Over the past thirty years, the doors of opportunity through postsecondary education have opened dramatically for all groups in the United States. More than 14 million students were enrolled in colleges and universities nationwide in fall 1996, a more than twofold increase since 1967 and tenfold increase since the mid-1940s (NCES, 1999). Growth has occurred at both two-year and four-year colleges and universities and among all racial/ethnic and income groups. The number and representation of African American, Hispanic, and low-income undergraduates attending the nation's colleges and universities are higher today than ever before.

Despite this dramatic increase in access to American colleges and universities, underrepresentation continues. African Americans represented 11.3 percent of first-time, full-time freshmen attending four-year colleges and universities in 1996 but 14.3 percent of the traditional college-age population (18–24 years). Only 6.0 percent of first-time, full-time freshmen attending four-year institutions were Hispanic in 1996, compared with 13.7 percent of the traditional college-age population. The gaps are even more dramatic among bachelor's degree recipients. In 1996 only 7.7 percent of bachelor's degree recipients were African American and 4.9 percent were Hispanic (Nettles, Perna, & Freeman, 1999).

Historically, federal intervention at the postsecondary level has focused primarily on reducing economic barriers to higher education to ensure that no academically qualified citizen is denied access to college for financial reasons. In 1998–1999, $43.6 billion of the $64 billion in financial aid awarded to students from all sources was from the federal government and represents about two-thirds of all federal on-budget outlays for postsecondary education (The College Board, 1999; Hoffman, 1997).

The continued gaps in college enrollment and degree completion despite the dedication of such large amounts of resources suggest that a more comprehensive approach to college access and success is needed. Merely making financial aid available for students to attend college is not enough to ensure that all students have equal access to the benefits associated with earning a college degree (Gladieux & Swail, 1998). A variety of factors influence college enrollment behavior, including educational expectations and plans, academic ability and preparation, information about college options, availability of financial aid, and support from teachers, counselors, family members, and peers (see for example Perna, 2000).

The Federal Approach

The federal government has played a critical role in the development of pre-college outreach and early intervention programs. The federal approach to increasing access to colleges has historically focused on making financial aid available to students through the Pell Grant, campus-based, and subsidized- and unsubsidized-loan programs. More comprehensive programs aimed at increasing postsecondary educational opportunity for educationally and economically disadvantaged students have recently taken on more importance.

As mandated by Congress, two-thirds of the students served by TRIO programs must come from families with incomes below $24,000. Upward Bound, authorized by Congress in 1964 as part of the Educational Opportunity Act, provides students with academic instruction on college campuses after school, on Saturdays, and during the summer. Over 700 Upward Bound programs are operating around the country. One-third of all TRIO funding in 1998 ($600 million) was dedicated to Upward Bound ($220 million) and Upward Bound Mathematics and Science ($20.1 million).

Talent Search and the Student Support Services programs were added to Upward Bound to form the core of the TRIO programs during the authorization of the Higher Education Act of 1965. In 1992 the federal government expanded its commitment to early intervention–type programs by authorizing the National Early Intervention Scholarship Program (NEISP). This program offers matching grants to states for programs providing financial incentives, academic support services and counseling, and college-related information to disadvantaged students and their parents. Funding for the NEISP was $200 million in 1993 and nearly $400 million in 1994, but was reduced to just $3.1 million in 1995, $3.6 million in 1997, and $3.6 million in 1998. Nine state programs have been funded under the NEISP at an average of $500,000 (Fenske, Geranios, Keller, & Moore, 1997).

As part of the 1998 reauthorization of the Higher Education Act, Congress established a new program, Gaining Early Awareness and Readiness for Undergraduate Programs (GEAR UP),[1] to supercede the 1992 NEISP. GEAR UP grants are available not only to state governments, but also to partnerships composed of: (a) one or more local educational agency representing at least one elementary and one secondary school; (b) one institution of higher education; and (c) at least two community organizations, which may include businesses, philanthropic organizations, or other community-based entities. The GEAR UP legislation also includes the "21st Century Scholars Certificate" program. This program, later endorsed and retitled by President Clinton as the "High Hopes" program, notifies low-income sixth to twelfth grade students of their expected eligibility for federal financial assistance under the Pell Grant program. Congress appropriated $120 million for GEAR UP in 1999 and $200 million for 2000—a substantial increase over the $3.6 million provided for NEISP in 1998. More than 670 partnerships applied for the first GEAR UP grants in 1999, and 180 awards were made.

Nongovernment Programs

Early intervention programs are also sponsored by nongovernment entities, including private organizations, foundations, and colleges and universities. Perhaps the most prominent private early intervention program is the I Have a Dream (IHAD) Program, established in 1981. Now almost a part of popular American folklore, the program originated when Eugene Lang, a New York businessman, made a visit to his former East Harlem elementary school and guaranteed the 61 students in his presence the financial resources for college if they graduated from high school. That promise has expanded to 180 projects in over 60 cities across the nation, serving more than 13,000 students, and has doubtless led other philanthropists and agencies to establish similar programs.

Other large-scale programs have shown success in serving needy students. The MESA (Mathematics, Engineering, and Science Achievement), MSEN (Math Science Education Network), and Puente Programs are examples of efforts that have been replicated across the nation to form networks of programs.

There are hundreds of other examples of programs around the country that provide support via some outreach mechanism. Colleges and universities sponsor outreach programs, many supported by TRIO and GEAR UP, but others on their own account or by the support of corporate sponsors or nonprofit organizations (e.g., National Action Council for Minority Engineers).

A National Survey

In 1999, the College Board, in association with The Education Resources Institute (TERI) and the Council for Opportunity in Education (COE), designed and administered the National Survey of Outreach Programs.[2] The survey was designed to provide detailed information about all types of early intervention programs. This information is expected to help practitioners, researchers, policy makers, and philanthropists better understand the programs that are currently serving students around the country. Second, the survey was also intended to provide the backbone for a web-based searchable database system for public use. This system will not only assist practitioners, researchers, policy makers, and philanthropists, but will also help build a network that can be used to develop and strengthen partnerships between programs.

In addition to the survey, a series of focus groups were held around the country with program administrators to provide a more focused discussion with program directors and other personnel about the issues and challenges facing education and early intervention programs. Together, the information regarding early intervention programs provides a unique perspective on the landscape of programs across the nation.

Describing the Landscape

The survey yielded usable responses from 1,110 programs nationwide, with programs from all 50 states, the District of Columbia, Puerto Rico, Guam, and Micronesia.

Of the respondents to the survey, federal TRIO programs (Upward Bound and Talent Search) account for one-third ($N = 363$), while GEAR UP programs account for 9 percent ($N = 102$). In addition, about one-fifth of the programs completing the survey are sponsored by businesses, private organizations, or individuals (see Table 1.1; TRIO programs are, on average, much older than other programs, with an average age of 16 years).

Financial Support

The most common source of financial support for early intervention programs is the federal government. About half of the responding programs

TABLE 1.1

Distribution of Survey Respondents by Program Type, Average Year of First Operation and Average Number of Students Served

Characteristic	Total	TRIO	Gear Up	IHAD	Other Federal	State Funded	University Funded	Other
Number of programs	1,110	363	102	26	137	166	97	219
Percent of respondents	100%	33%	9%	2%	12%	15%	9%	20%
Year first operated	1989	1984	1998	1992	1989	1989	1989	1991
Numbers of students served 1998–1999	827	425	2,585	121	748	1,203	717	1,264

Note: Other includes programs funded by businesses, private organizations and individuals.

receive financial support from the federal government, about one-fourth receive financial support from state governments, and one-fourth receive financial support from colleges and universities.

Most programs receive financial support from more than one source. For example, one-half of the non-TRIO, non-GEAR UP, and non-IHAD programs that received federal funding also received financial support from a state government. More than one-fourth of these programs received financial support from a college or university, and one-fourth received financial support from business or industry. About one-half of the non-TRIO, non-GEAR UP, and non-IHAD programs that received state funding also received financial support from a college or university. A higher share of IHAD programs than of other responding programs appear to receive financial support from AmeriCorps, community organizations, business or industry, private foundations, and fundraising. Colleges and universities are an important source of in-kind support for about one-half of TRIO, GEAR UP, other federal, and state-funded programs. Community organizations are an important source of in-kind support for GEAR UP and IHAD programs. About one-third of responding programs received in-kind support from local school systems.

Program Location

More than one-half (57 percent) of the responding programs are based at a college or university, 16 percent at a school, and 13 percent within the community (See Table 1.2). TRIO programs are generally based at postsecondary institutions (80 percent), while GEAR UP programs tend to operate from schools (39 percent), and IHAD programs are largely community-based (69 percent). The majority of other federally and non-federally funded programs are based on college campuses.

TABLE 1.2
Distribution of Programs by Organization or Institution Housing the Program

Program type	Total %	TRIO %	Gear Up %	IHAD %	Other Federal %	State Funded %	University Funded %	Other %
Total	100.0	100.0	100.0	100.0	100.0	100.0	100.0	100.0
College/univeristy	57.2	79.9	28.4	—	48.2	54.8	69.1	42.0
School	15.6	7.7	39.2	19.2	17.5	15.1	10.3	18.7
Community	13.4	8.8	6.9	69.2	16.1	11.4	6.2	20.5
Other	13.8	3.6	25.5	11.5	18.2	18.7	14.4	18.7

Note: Other includes programs with more than one base.

TABLE 1.3
Distribution of Programs by Primary Location of Services

Location	Total %	TRIO %	Gear Up %	IHAD %	Other Federal %	State Funded %	University Funded %	Other %
Total	100.0	100.0	100.0	100.0	100.0	100.0	100.0	100.0
College campus	45.5	54.0	7.8		46.7	47.6	62.9	44.3
Elementary/secondary school	34.7	34.2	80.4	46.2	28.5	33.7	21.5	21.5
Students' homes	0.3	—	—	7.7	—	—	—	0.5
Community center	5.6	4.4	2.0	23.1	4.4	4.2	4.1	9.6
Other	13.9	7.4	9.8	23.1	20.4	14.5	7.2	24.2

For nearly one-half of all programs, the primary location of program services (which may be different from where a program is located or housed) is a college campus. For GEAR UP programs, however, services are typically delivered at an elementary or secondary school. Elementary and secondary schools are also the primary location of services for about one-half of IHAD programs, one-third of TRIO and state-funded programs, and one-fifth of university funded programs, suggesting that a substantial number of programs have strong ties to K–12 schools and school systems. About one-half of all programs serve students of a particular school or school district, and one-fourth target a particular community. The majority of TRIO, GEAR UP, and IHAD programs target services toward students attending a particular school or school district.

Program Goals and Services

As other research (Perna, Fenske, & Swail, on press) has concluded, the most commonly stated goal of early intervention programs is to increase college enrollment rates. Among the three most common goals of the responding programs are to promote college attendance, college awareness, and college exposure, with about 90 percent of programs reporting each of these goals (See Figure 1.1). These goals appear to be relatively more common for TRIO and GEAR UP programs, likely because both programs were explicitly created to focus on college access. Building college awareness and college exposure is likely to be associated with higher educational aspirations, one of the most important predictors of college enrollment (Hossler, Braxton, & Coopersmith, 1989; Hossler, Schmit, & Vesper, 1999; Perna, 2000).

Building student self-esteem and providing role models are also common goals. As Levine and Nidiffer (1996) concluded, support and encouragement from a mentor, whether a parent, relative, or empathetic member of the community, can play a critical role in college enrollment for students from low-income families. Role modeling is a particularly highly ranked goal for the GEAR UP programs, likely because mentoring strategies are emphasized in the evaluation of program proposals. Other common goals include increasing college completion, increasing high school retention and reducing dropouts, and involving parents.

Improving academic skills was also among the most frequently reported goals, likely reflecting the research showing that academic achievement and preparation are important predictors of both predisposition toward and actual enrollment in a college or university (See Adelman chapter 2; Hagedorn & Fogel chapter 8; Hossler, Braxton, & Coopersmith, 1989; Manski & Wise,

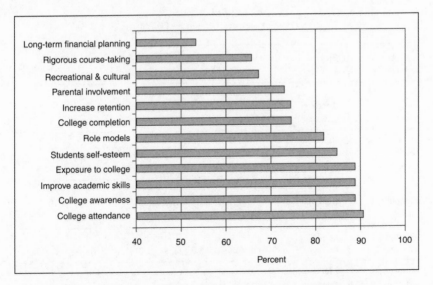

Figure 1.1. Most common goals of early intervention programs

1983; Perna, 2000; St. John, 1991; Hossler, Schmit & Vesper, 1999). Nonetheless, the goal of promoting rigorous course taking is less common, ranking only eleventh out of 14. This may suggest a potential weakness of some programs, given that researchers have shown that the quality and intensity of the high school curriculum is a more important predictor of bachelor's degree completion than test scores or class rank, particularly for African American and Latino students (Adelman, 1999) and that taking at least one advanced mathematics course is associated with a higher probability of enrolling in a four-year college or university among students who are at risk of dropping out of high school after controlling for other variables (Horn, 1998). Slightly more than one-third (37 percent) of the responding programs specified a particular academic focus. The most common areas of focus are science, mathematics, and technology.

To some extent, the particular services offered mirror the reported program goals. Table 4 shows that the most common service is college awareness, reported by 86 percent of the programs. Other relatively common activities that are related to college awareness include campus visits and meetings with college faculty and students.

Services that may help students acquire some of the noncognitive skills that are important to the successful integration of students into campus life are also relatively common. Such services include social skill development, cultural activities, and leadership development.

TABLE 1.4
Program Services Offered by Quintile

Top Quintile service	%	Second Quintile service	%	Middle Quintile service	%	Fourth Quintile service	%	Bottom Quintile service	%
College awareness	85.8	Academic advising	70.9	Meetings college faculty	66.4	Computer-skills training	56.2	Remedial instruction	33.7
Social skills development	79.1	Career counseling	70.6	Reading & writing	62.8	Preparatory courses	54.2	Employability skills	25.9
Campus visits	76.8	Critical thinking skills	69.4	Grade monitoring	60.1	SAT/ACT training	54.1	Accelerated courses	25.5
Cultural activities	75.3	Leadership development	68.9	Personal counseling	56.8	College fairs	47.7	College-level courses	23.3
Study-skills training	71.9	Math/science instruction	67.6	Academic enrichment	56.7	Career days	41.2	Job placement	17.4

Most programs also provide services to develop the academic skills and preparation required to enter and succeed in college. These services include critical thinking skills, study-skills training, mathematics and science instruction, reading and writing instruction, grade and attendance monitoring, and academic enrichment. Again, despite research showing the relationship between high quality coursework and college enrollment, only about one-fourth of all responding programs offer accelerated courses and/or college-level courses.

Program services are delivered via a variety of instructional approaches. About three-fourths of all programs utilize workshops and classroom instruction. Role modeling, tutoring, and mentoring are also frequently used by all types of programs, but particularly by IHAD programs. More than one-half of all programs also use assessment and testing practice for their students (60 percent) or peer group learning groups, a well-documented approach to academic and social development among underrepresented populations (Fullilove & Treisman, 1990).

Working with Parents

Parental involvement was a common theme emerging from the focus groups. Research supports the often heard perception that parental involvement is critical (Hossler, Braxton, & Coopersmith, 1989; Hossler, Schmit, & Vesper, 1999). Some evidence suggests that parental support and encouragement is the single most important predictor of postsecondary educational plans (Jun & Colyar, Chapter 9; Hossler, Schmit & Vesper, 1999). Nonetheless, focus group participants were equally quick to note that effectively involving parents is quite challenging, especially when family and social stresses are intertwined with low income.

The survey data showed that most programs do try to involve parents. More than two-thirds (69 percent) of all programs offer a parental component, while about one-fifth (22 percent) of all programs mandate parental involvement. Parental involvement is very common in GEAR UP and IHAD programs (more than 90 percent of these programs include a parental component). Nearly one-half of the GEAR UP, programs have a mandatory parental component. About one-half (46 percent) of all programs require parents to sign a contract in order for their children to begin participating in the program. Parental contracts are most common among TRIO programs (71 percent) and least common among GEAR UP programs (19 percent).

Because many of the students participating in early intervention programs have parents with no postsecondary experience, a primary function of about one-half (58 percent) of the parental programs is to provide opportunities for parents to learn about college and realize that college is possible for their child. About one-half (51 percent) of the programs request parents to participate in activities with the student. Other services designed to increase knowledge and information about college are financial aid guidance, campus visitations, and meetings with college faculty and students. About 16 percent of parental programs offer instructional programs to parents, giving them the chance to develop their own academic skills. As Hoover-Dempsey and Sandler (1997) have argued, improving parents' sense of efficacy for helping their children succeed in school may increase their level of involvement in the child's education.

Learning ways to effectively coordinate with parents appears to be a challenge many programs are facing. About one-fourth (27 percent) of all programs, and 40 percent of all GEAR UP programs, reported that coordination with parents was at least somewhat of a problem or area requiring additional resources.

Program Operation

About two–thirds (67 percent) of responding programs provide services to students year round. Four out of five TRIO, GEAR UP, and IHAD programs report that they are year round, compared with only one in three

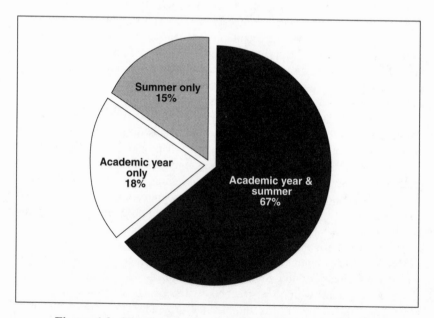

Figure 1.2. Distribution of programs by period of operation

university-funded programs. About one-fifth (18 percent) of all programs operate specifically during the school year and 15 percent operate summer-only programs. About 38 percent of university-funded programs offer services only during the summer.

About one-half (53 percent) of all programs offer services to students both during school hours and after school. More than one-half (60 percent) of all programs offer services on the weekends. The duration of program services varies, with some programs offered for a few days and others for several years. Program capacity also varies, averaging 636 students and ranging up to the tens of thousands (e.g., large, state-wide programs). About one-half (46 percent) of all programs are capable of serving fewer than 100 students per year, one-fourth have a capacity between 100 and 500 students, and one-fourth have a capacity of more than 500 students.

Targeting Students

Early intervention programs generally focus on "educationally or economically disadvantaged students." About two-thirds (62 percent) of all programs report that they target students with certain characteristics. Targeting of services based on economic disadvantage appears to be more common than targeting of services based on educational disadvantage. About three-fourths (80 percent) of survey respondents indicate that their program specifically targets low-income students. The extent to which services are targeted toward low-income students varies by program sponsor, ranging from 70 percent of university and state-funded programs to 99 percent of TRIO programs. Minority and potential first-generation college students are also common target populations for early intervention programs (69 percent and 71 percent, respectively).

Only about one-third of all programs report targeting students at risk of dropping out of high school (36 percent) or students of low academic ability or achievement (38 percent). More than one-third (39 percent) of all programs target students of high academic ability or achievement, and one-fifth (22 percent) of the programs target gifted and talented students.

An underlying premise of early intervention programs is that support services and information about college and financial aid are provided to students and their parents early enough in their schooling so as to influence educational outcomes. Data from the National Center for Educational Statistics (1999) suggest that most of the damage (educationally speaking) to student opportunity has largely occurred by the eighth grade. Students who score poorly on standardized mathematics and reading tests in the eighth grade are unlikely to improve during the course of the next four years. Nonetheless, the survey data suggest that only 10 percent of all programs (but 81 percent of

IHAD programs) first offer services to students while they are attending elementary school, and about one-third of all programs (but 87 percent of GEAR UP programs) begin program services during the middle school years. The tendency of GEAR UP programs to begin services during middle school years is not surprising given that in order to be eligible under the federal GEAR UP program, counseling and other support services must be provided to at least one grade level of students beginning no later than the 7th grade and continuing through the twelfth grade. For about one-half (58 percent) of all programs (but 76 percent of TRIO programs) services are first offered to students during the high school years. For many of these programs, when they start and who they target depends largely upon the original mission and goals of the program. While we now understand more clearly the importance of starting early, many programs were designed to specifically target high school or middle school students.

Incentives for Participation

The most common external reward provided to program participants is a certificate of recognition, used by 69 percent of survey respondents. While all programs receiving funding under the federal National Early Intervention Scholarship Program must guarantee that all eligible low-income participants will receive the financial assistance necessary to attend college, the extent to which other early intervention programs use financial benefits appears to vary by program sponsor. About 89 percent of IHAD programs offer college scholarships, compared with only one-fourth of TRIO programs and 41 percent of GEAR UP programs. More than one-half (60 percent) of all TRIO programs offer a cash stipend for participation, compared with only 14 percent of GEAR UP programs and university funded programs. About one-third of TRIO programs offer reimbursement for tuition and fees, compared with only about 10 percent of GEAR UP, state-funded, and university-funded programs. About one-fifth (21 percent) of all responding programs offer participants academic credit.

Program Staffing and Training

About 87 percent of responding programs indicated that they had at least one paid staff member. Seventy-nine percent employ full-time staff and 67 percent employ part-time staff. More than one-half of all programs (57 percent) employ college students. Nearly one-half (43 percent) of all responding programs use volunteers.

Most programs (79 percent) require an average of 17 hours of pre-service training for staff members. Pre-service training appears to be more common among TRIO programs. Nearly all (95 percent) of all programs hold regular meetings between program staff and coordinators.

Program respondents generally report being very satisfied with their ability to recruit, train, and monitor staff. Only 12 percent of all programs reported that program staff recruitment or staff training is a problem or needs additional resources (rated 4 or 5 on scale of 1 to 5). Given that GEAR UP is a newer program, it is not surprising that a higher share of GEAR UP programs reported that staff training (22 percent) is a "problem" area. Only 6 percent of all programs report that staff monitoring is a problem.

Program Evaluation

Almost all (94 percent) responding programs reported conducting program evaluations. About three-fourths (75 percent) report that they track program completion and 64 percent report that they track high school graduation. Only 29 percent of all programs report tracking graduation from college. Just 17 percent of all responding programs indicated that program evaluation was a somewhat or high problem area.

Although these rates of evaluation are very high, we know from experience that evaluations of these programs are generally weak (see Tierney, chapter 10). Programs have few funds to hire external evaluators to conduct regular evaluations, and most have little or no expertise to conduct their own data collection and analysis. This is a major problem area for most programs, as they have little to present to the public and their funders about successes, apart from anecdotal information.

Conclusions and Implications

The data and information presented in this chapter provide a picture of the number, types, and variety of early intervention programs that are currently operating across the nation. The results of this descriptive study suggest that early intervention programs do not necessarily follow any particular model, but still gravitate to many similar strategies, services, and concepts. Some of the programs are managed and organized in a very corporate manner, with efficient centralized control. The success or failure of other programs sometimes falls on the back of one person. What is most striking in talking with program directors throughout the nation is the shared commitment of staff to the students they are trying to serve. For most, it is a labor of love.

The National Survey of Outreach Programs does not answer all of our questions about early intervention programs. It is not evaluative, only descriptive. The landscape provided by the survey may help us better understand the programs and perhaps design large-scale evaluations to determine best practices for particular audiences. As a conclusion to this chapter, we thought it was important to share the viewpoints of program directors from our focus group sessions. In the half-dozen focus groups, involving over a hundred program directors across the nation, these themes consistently came up when talking about essential elements of successful outreach endeavors. It is our hope that future research may focus on testing these perceptions with actual program outcomes.

1. *Clear, focused mission and vision.* Early intervention programs need to be clear about the desired outcomes of student participation. Because of limited budgets, staffing, and other resources, one program simply can't do it all. Consequently, programs must be tightly focused and operate in a systematic, efficient manner to maximize their effect on student learning and preparation.

2. *Start early.* As Levine and Nidiffer (1996) recommended, programs need to start early, well before high school if possible. A review of racial/ethnic group differences in NAEP scores suggests the challenges associated with inadequate academic preparation exist as early as the fourth grade (Nettles & Perna, 1997). While specific interventions are appropriate during high school and between high school graduation and college matriculation, intervention must begin by at least middle school.

3. *Motivate students.* Students must be motivated and committed to work hard. Perhaps the most critical intervention a program can make is to orient youth to long-term goals and the importance of a strong work ethic. Financial incentives sometimes work, but as Levine and Nidiffer (1996) concluded, the sound advice of a trusted mentor or tutor will often make the difference.

4. *Involve parents.* Parent involvement sends a clear message to the student:"This matters, and so do you." Unfortunately, the most at-risk populations appear to have the least support at home. Participants consistently described the challenges associated with their parental programs, particularly with regard to keeping parents interested and involved. Despite these challenges, practitioners consistently pointed to the importance of parental involvement in their intervention efforts.

5. *Collaborate.* Programs that work in a vacuum don't succeed in the long run. The best run programs are those that work closely with

school and district administrators to link the programs with school curricula and schedules. Programs that work with business and industry, community organizations, and all levels of educational institutions appear to be more stable and effective. Leveraging external support also helps broaden both program accountability and responsibility.

6. *Sustain funding.* Emphasis on national standards, school reform, and accountability has changed attitudes about program funding and operation. Public and private funders are asking for evidence from programs that show progress toward specific goals. Understanding the nexus between funding and programming philosophies is also important. Whereas funders are interested in providing enough funding for programs to become stable and self sufficient, program administrators are interested in extending their external funding as long as possible. Building a more compatible and cooperative alliance between funders and programs may help ameliorate these inconsistent attitudes.

7. *Practice professionalism and personal development.* Program staffing is critical to successful practice. Programs need to have effective hiring strategies to support the mission and goals of the organization. Programs must also provide ongoing professional development to build and keep the staff. Many programs, especially the smaller programs, have high staff turnover rates, in part because of limited salaries and opportunities for professional advancement.

8. *Use proven practices.* While research continues to provide updated information on "best practices" in pre-college outreach, experience is the primary source of information on what works. A higher level of services is offered to students when programs collaborate or learn from one another. Programs should not try to reinvent the wheel, but adapt proven strategies that fit the mission and goals of their program.

9. *Rely on standardized processes.* Stable programs rely on standardized processes and content, such as standardized curricula. Programs should be developed based on the identified needs of the students, school and community.

10. *Incorporate technology.* Mirroring the growing importance of technology within society, the knowledge and use of computers and other modern technologies is an emerging issue for many programs. Programs need to build strategic plans for purchasing, upgrading, and effectively utilizing technology. Although most outreach programs focus on developing academic skills, more attention must be given to developing the technological capacity that complements knowledge acquisition.

Some may argue that early intervention programs are too expensive, serve too few students, and are too inefficient with respect to program dropout rate. Nonetheless, because they appear to have the components that the literature suggests are important to promote college access and degree attainment, we remain optimistic about their role. If society could regenerate the school systems, early intervention and pre-college outreach programs would not be needed. But the reality is that schools are failing and children are falling through the cracks without even being noticed. At a minimum, these programs provide a lifeline to those students who have the potential but aren't getting served as serious contenders. Indeed, many feel that programs need to do a better job of working within the construct of school reform as a partner, not as an accessory.

Thus, a challenge is placed on the table. To proponents of early intervention programs, provide us more systematic evidence of the positive impact you suggest is occurring through these programs. And to critics—show us alternatives that better meet the needs of our underrepresented populations.

Notes

1. See www.ed.gov/offices/OPE/gearup.
2. The National Survey of Outreach Programs was directed by Dr. Swail while at the College Board. Both authors were responsible for the design of the survey and subsequent data analysis. Further information on the National Survey, including a more elaborate analysis and presentation of data, as well as the web-based program directory, may be found at www.collegeboard.org.

References

Adelman, C. (1999). *Answers in the tool box: Academic intensity, attendance patterns, and bachelor's degree attainment.* Washington, DC: U.S. Department of Education, Office of Educational Research and Improvement.
The College Board. (1999). *Trends in student aid 1999.* New York: Author.
Fenske, R. H., Geranios, C. A., Keller, J. E., & Moore, D. E. (1997). *Early intervention programs: Opening the door to higher education.* ASHE-ERIC Higher Education Report (Vol. 25, No. 6). Washington, DC: The George Washington University Graduate School of Education and Human Development.
Fullilove, R. E., & Treisman, P. U. (1990). Mathematics achievement among African American undergraduates at the University of California, Ber-

keley: An evaluation of the mathematics workshop program. *Journal of Negro Education, 59* (3), 463–78.

Gladieux, L. E., & Swail, W. S. (1998, Summer). Financial aid is not enough: Improving the odds of college success. *The College Board Review, 185,* 16–21, 30–31.

Horn, L. & Chen, X. (1998). *Toward resiliency: "At-risk" students who make it to college.* Washington, DC: U.S. Department of Education, Office of Educational Research and Improvement. (Postsecondary Education Descriptive Analysis Reports).

Hoffman, C. M. (1997). *Federal support for education: Fiscal years 1980 to 1996.* Washington, DC: U.S. Department of Education, National Center for Education Statistics (NCES 97-384).

Hoover-Dempsey, K., & Sandler, H. (1997). Why do parents become involved in their children's education? *Review of Educational Research, 67* (1), 3–42.

Hossler, D., Braxton, J. & Coopersmith, G. (1989). Understanding student college choice In J. C. Smart (Ed.), *Higher education: Handbook of theory and research, vol. 5.* (pp. 231–288). New York: Agathon Press.

Hossler, D., Schmit, J., & Vesper, N. (1999). *Going to college: How social, economic, and educational factors influence the decisions students make.* Baltimore, MD: Johns Hopkins University Press.

Levine, A., & Nidiffer, J. (1996). *Beating the odds: How the poor get to college.* San Francisco, CA: Jossey-Bass, Inc., Publishers.

Manski, C. F. & Wise, D. A. (1983). *College choice in America.* Cambridge, MA: Harvard University Press.

National Center for Education Statistics (1999). *Digest of education statistics.* Washington, DC: Author.

Nettles, M. T., Perna, L. W., & Freeman, K. E. (1999). *Two decades of progress: African Americans moving forward in higher education.* Fairfax, VA: Frederick D. Patterson Research Institute.

Nettles, M. T., & Perna, L.W. (1997). *The African American education data book, volume 1, higher and adult education.* Fairfax, VA: Frederick D. Patterson Research Institute.

Perna, L. W. (1999). Early intervention programs: A new approach to increasing college access. *Advances in Education Research, 4* (Winter). Washington DC: Office of Educational Research and Improvement, National Library of Education.

Perna, L. W. (2000). Difference in the decision to attend college among African Americans, Hispanics, and Whites. *Journal of Higher Education, 71* (2), 117–141.

Perna, L. W., Fenske, R., Swail, W. S., (on press). Overview of early intervention programs. In C. Boston (Ed.), ERIC Review Themed Journal

Early Intervention for College Programs. Washington, DC: ERIC Clearinghouse for Higher Education.

St. John, E. P. (1991). What really influences minority attendance? Sequential analyses of the high school and beyond sophomore cohort. *Research in Higher Education, 32* (2), 141–158.

CHAPTER 2

The Relationship between Urbanicity
and Educational Outcomes

CLIFFORD ADELMAN

Introduction

This chapter will provide a targeted portrait of disadvantaged students, whose educational fates can be affected by pre-collegiate outreach programs. The chapter offers some speculations and cautions on program practice and evaluation based on the three degrees of urbanicity (urban, suburban, and rural) within the nine geographic divisions used by the Census.[1] The chapter focuses exclusively on traditional age students because they are the tractable target of pre-collegiate outreach programs.

We must face the choice of confining the analysis to those who actually graduate from high school (including "event" dropouts, those who graduate later than scheduled, and those who earn GEDs or other forms of high school equivalency certificates) or also including those who wind up as permanent ("status") dropouts at age 30. Using the currently available data from the National Education Longitudinal Study of 1988 (hereafter referred to as the NELS-88) and matching data from the decade-earlier cohort of the High School & Beyond/Sophomores (the HS&B/So), Table 2.1 demonstrates the magnitude of the problem. The core of NELS-88 data in the table comes from Berkner and Chavez, 1997 (p. 17), to which I have added urbanicity of high school origins variables and their intersection with the lowest quartile of family income. I have also added HS&B/So enrollment data from post-secondary transcripts, and the parameters of these were matched to the NELS categories as closely as possible.[2]

Table 2.1 tells a number of stories. First, by the early 1990s virtually everybody who graduated from high school planned additional education. Unlike the situation a decade earlier, there are no differences by race or income, and only minor differences by urbanicity (involving students from

CLIFFORD ADELMAN

rural areas and small towns). Second, when one considers generalized plans versus concrete plans to enter postsecondary education directly from high school, the differences are greater by family income than by race/ethnicity, a phenomenon that held for both high school graduating classes. Third, the most significant inter-cohort change in the "plans" variables by race/ethnicity involves Latino high school graduates, whose educational expectations have risen to match those of others.

TABLE 2.1

Comparison of Plans for Postsecondary Education (PSE) and Early Enrollment History: 1992 and 1982 High School Graduates

Percent of 1992 and 1982 High School Graduates Who . . .

	Planned to attend PSE at some time		Planned to attend directly after HS		Enrolled in PSE directly after HS		Enrolled in PSE by 2 years after HS		Planned to attend right after HS and enrolled within 2 yrs	
	1992	1982	1992	1982	1992	1982	1992	1982	1992	1982
All 1992 Graduates:	96.8	76.6	79.4	65.7	65.3	52.1	75.2	57.8	88.6	77.5
Race/Ethnicity:										
White	96.7	77.2	79.7	65.6	66.5	55.0	75.9	60.5	89.6	81.0
Black	96.4	77.4	78.1	68.2	59.5	41.7	71.3	47.9	83.6	62.9
Latino	97.2	67.5	76.4	57.9	57.6	37.9	70.6	43.3	84.3	63.1
Asian/PI	98.1	90.4	84.1	86.6	78.1	73.3	86.2	77.9	93.8	83.6
Family Income										
Lowest quartile	94.3	70.4	70.4	58.2	53.0	42.1	63.5	48.9	83.0	70.2
Mid 2 quartiles	97.4	79.1	81.8	66.5	69.3	53.2	79.3	60.0	89.8	77.5
Highest quartile	99.3	86.0	92.4	77.4	86.9	68.5	93.1	72.7	96.2	86.3
Urbanicity										
Urban	96.9	79.7	81.8	67.4	69.6	48.3	80.7	55.0	91.0	72.4
Suburban	96.8	78.5	81.6	68.8	67.5	56.2	77.9	61.7	89.5	80.3
Rural	92.8	71.8	74.4	59.6	59.4	48.0	68.9	53.4	86.6	76.1
Low Income										
Urban	96.6	73.7	77.6	61.9	59.3	41.6	72.9	49.3	86.0	65.7
Suburban	94.0	70.1	70.2	59.3	52.6	42.6	65.0	48.6	84.8	70.8
Rural	89.4	68.8	63.4	54.8	45.7	42.0	55.9	48.8	78.9	72.4

Notes: (1) *Class of 1982* enrollment data are based on received transcripts. Class of 1992 enrollment data are self-reported.
Source: National Center for Education Statistics: National Education Longitudinal Study (NELS-88), Data Analysis System.

Fourth, comparing the two cohorts when one moves to either enrollment directly following high school or enrollment within two years of high school graduation, the gaps by family income widened in the early 1990s, while those by race/ethnicity contracted. A brief illustration, using enrollment within two years of on-time high school graduation, illustrates this point:

	1982 Gap	1992 Gap	Change
Lowest-Highest income quartile	23.8%	29.6%	+5.8%
White v. Black	12.6	4.6	–8.0
White v. Latino	17.2	5.3	–11.9

But the most revealing and perhaps counterintuitive feature of these data lies in the category of urbanicity, and urbanicity within the lowest family income quartile. Urban high school graduates, regardless of family income, now enter postsecondary education rates equivalent to those of their suburban counterparts (the differences are not statistically significant). This was not true for the Class of 1982 (the HS&B/So). Graduates of *rural* high schools, on the other hand—and poor rural students in particular—evidenced the *lowest* rates of participation in the NELS-88 cohort, whereas there were no differences in the enrollment behavior of low-income students by urbanicity a decade earlier.

Six other comments related to Table 1 are in order at this point. First, all the numbers for the 1992 class (NELS) seem very high, but credible. The proportion enrolling directly after high school graduation (65.3 percent) was fairly close to the estimate for 1992 as computed by the American College Testing Service (61.7 percent), which is diluted somewhat by the inclusion of students who delayed graduation up to the age of 24, whereas a tiny percentage of the NELS high school graduates of 1992 were over the age of 20. This benchmark is the link around which the other data can be judged.

Second, if 75 percent of high school graduates are continuing their education as young adults, one wonders how high the percentage can be pushed? There is little question that if we are to improve these rates, we must concentrate on rural/small town areas and among low-income students (see Smith, Beaulieu, & Seraphine, 1995). Third, these numbers are silent about *where* students first enter postsecondary education, how they attend, and what happens to them. Fourth, according to the Schools & Staffing Survey for 1993, the urban public high school graduation rate is the lowest and the rural high school graduation rate the highest (Snyder, 2000, table 188). In the case of urban high school graduates, this will inflate the continuation rate, while it deflates it for rural high school graduates. Fifth, among the key factors producing higher rates of post-secondary participation among urban students is proximity. That is, there are far more institutions of postsecondary education accessible to urban students—and by public transportation—than to students in less concentrated settlements. When the opportunity is a pervasive physical presence, it is hard to avoid the invitation (Lynch and Associates, 1994; Richardson and Bender, 1987).

Last, the NELS data on postsecondary participation by 1994 (the most recent accounting available at this time) are self-reported. The postsecondary transcripts (to be gathered by January 2001) will provide a more accurate story. In the High School & Beyond/Sophomore cohort history we found that for about 6 percent of the students who claimed postsecondary attendance, the claim seems to have been based on a marginal understanding of what "postsecondary education" means.[3] For the balance of this paper, the High School & Beyond/Sophomore transcript-based history will thus be the principal analytical tool.

Limitations of the Literature

The analytic literature on the paths of economically disadvantaged students to and through postsecondary education is both vast and formulaic. That is, while there are hundreds of studies, the majority does little more than shuffle the same variables in different combinations with different data sets and different statistical techniques. Rarely types of initial enrollment are included (see, e.g., Hearn, 1992), and sometimes (ever more rarely) degree completion in the context of attendance patterns joins the club of dependent variables (e.g., Carroll, 1989; Camburn, 1990).

The public policy–oriented strain of this literature tosses in changes in tuition and fees and levels and packaging of financial aid (St. John, 1990; Kane and Spizman, 1994), the attitudes and responsibilities of parents (Steelman and Powell, 1993), and can be fairly sophisticated in analyses of parents' prior experience in financing higher education (Flint, 1997), or of academic/occupational track choices of students in higher education in relation to changes in net costs (Ordovensky, 1995). At times, this policy literature acknowledges the different modes of "access" in the postsecondary universe (see, e.g., Hearn, 1988).

What I call the "propagandistic" strains of this literature focus only on entry to highly selective or selective colleges, leaving the impression that unless students are admitted to Harvard, or, at worst, Wisconsin, they didn't really have "access" to higher education (see, e.g., Karen, 1991; Persell, Catsambis, and Cookson, 1992; Bowen and Bok, 1998). The "Harvards" of this world enroll about 5 percent of four-year college students (who, in turn, constitute half of all entering postsecondary students), and the "Wisconsins" bring the proportion up to about 15 percent. Since none of these institutions is about to double the size of their entering classes, the intimations of the propaganda are neither wise nor kind to those who struggle against considerable odds to reach the threshold of higher learning (Horn & Chen, 1999), let alone to the masses who attend institutions in which the very notion of "selection" is moot.

One is never sure of the practical implications of these analyses for our daily work. The variables are generalized concepts, usually accepted from received data sets without question. Rarely does a contractor for NCES return to the data elements for which composites were built to test their validity, accuracy, and true usefulness. For decades we have conceived programs and policies around variables that purportedly express student educational "aspirations," variables built from student responses to one snapshot question (the wording of which does not elicit "aspirations"[4]) asked at a moment in time and/or in circumstances that produce socially acceptable answers. All that is to say that while part of the problem lies in the limitations of the data sets, the greater problem is that of analysts' unquestioning acceptance of inherited composite variables. This book's chapter by Nora also comments on this limitation.

What the "Tool Box" Said

In a previous study, *Answers in the Tool Box: Academic Intensity, Attendance Patterns, and Bachelor's Degree Attainment* (Adelman, 1999), I confronted the variables commonly used in these analyses, and demonstrated their fragility. *Tool Box* substituted a far more detailed set of variables for the reflex collection, and was able to refine and isolate the factors that made the greatest difference among traditional age students, not merely for entering higher education, or for "persisting" to a second year of study, but for completing bachelor's degrees by age 30.

The *Tool Box* study utilized 26 variables entered in a 5-stage logistic regression that paralleled students' educational histories in the High School & Beyond/Sophomore Cohort:

1. Pre-collegiate (academic resources, educational "anticipations," demographics)

2. Pre-collegiate plus modes of financial aid
3. Pre-collegiate plus financial aid plus attendance patterns
4. Pre-collegiate plus financial aid plus attendance Patterns plus first-year performance
5. Pre-collegiate plus financial aid plus patterns plus first-year plus extended performance

The most consistent and persuasive independent variables to emerge from this analysis as making a true difference in degree completion were the following:

1. "Academic resources," a composite index of pre-collegiate preparation that is dominated by the *academic intensity and quality of one's high school curriculum.* Test scores and class rank/GPA play lesser roles in the index.
2. Whether the student became a parent by age 20 (the only "demographic" variable that counts). The impact is negative.
3. Continuous enrollment in postsecondary education, whether full time or part time, and no matter how many institutions one attended. The definition of continuous enrollment allowed for one semester (or its equivalent) of stop-out.
4. Transfer from a two-year to a four-year college, a true act of persistence.
5. First year grades, and, more important, the *trend* in one's grades after matriculation.
6. Credit momentum—earning fewer than 20 credits in the first calendar year of enrollment in higher education. The impact is negative.
7. "DWI Index." The proportion of courses from which the student withdrew without penalty, left incomplete, or took as a "no-credit repeat."

The above factors provide very practical guidance to educational planners, administrators, and practitioners. We can actually do something about secondary school curriculum (opportunity-to-learn), ensuring continuous enrollment, even if it is for only one course in a term, ensuring more effective vertical transfer, practicing academic advisement that results in credit momentum in the first year of higher education, and restricting nonpenalty DWIs. The most critical of these policy and practice opportunities are those involving opportunity to learn in pre-collegiate life. That is the setting in which the various types of pre-collegiate outreach efforts play out.

Limitations of the *Tool Box* Analysis

While *Tool Box* paid attention to race/ethnicity in terms of the impact of opportunity to learn, it did not address subpopulations of students in terms of geographic origins: urbanicity and Census division. It also did not hone in on economically disadvantaged students[5] in different environments. Race and socioeconomic status (SES) were among the 26 variables in the multivariate analyses. The former holds a marginal position in the equations through the attendance pattern iteration, then disappears statistically once first-year performance variables enter. SES, on the other hand, plays a minor but consistent role in explaining degree completion. Like race, however, its initially modest power declines as students' educational histories unfold.

The current study was originally designed to extend the analysis with these populations as the primary universe. But here, again, the analyst must clean up some basic categories of analysis that the literature accepts without a moment's hesitation. For immediately, there is a problem in defining students in terms of the urbanicity of the high school they attended when they were first sampled in the tenth grade,[6] let alone in terms of "low income" (see p. 60).

The Fallacy of a Monolithic "Urban" Universe

Students of community and city planning know that "urbanicity" is a variable concept, one that transcends population density (Kurtz, 1973). We have suburban areas in the United States, e.g., in northern New Jersey and Southern California, with higher population densities than some of the urban districts they surround. We know that urban populations in one location look and behave very differently from urban populations in another location. Somehow these commonsense observations seem to escape analysts of educational phenomena, who like to have their populations neatly packaged: urban means poor and minority; suburban means middle class and white; rural is a mystery, and most analysts would prefer to leave it all that way.

Table 2.2 provides some hints about how interventions will fail if they accept the undiscriminating nostrums of most educational research on this matter, and in many ways reinforces the national lessons from Table 2.1. I've taken the 13 high schools in the Washington, D.C. metropolitan area with the highest rates of poverty (defined by the proportion of students on subsidized lunch), and indicated their minority proportions and the college-going rates

CLIFFORD ADELMAN

TABLE 2.2
1996/7 College Access Rates for Graduates of the 13 Washington, D.C., Area High Schools
with the Highest Concentrations of Poverty

School	State	Classified urbanicity	On Lunch subsidy %	Black %	Latino	Going to 2/4-year college %
Bladensburg	MD	suburban	62	77	n.a.	41
Woodson	DC	urban	59	100	—	57
Anacostia	DC	urban	58	100	—	62
Northwestern	MD	suburban	55	71	n.a.	44
Stuart	VA	suburban	54	12	33	81
High Point	MD	suburban	54	52	n.a.	60
Eastern	DC	urban	52	99	1	63
Potomac	MD	suburban	49	99	n.a.	43
Wakefield	VA	suburban	48	29	36	70
Forestville	MD	suburban	47	99	n.a.	65
Parkdale	MD	suburban	47	75	n.a.	41
Central	MD	urban	45	86	n.a.	63
Dunbar	DC	urban	43	99	1	68

Source: "Grading the Area High Schools," Washingtonian Magazine, Sept. 1997, pp. 72–74.

of their graduating seniors in 1996. Taking into account student mobility and other factors, those who graduate may not be those who began,[7] but the points should be obvious.

Only 4 of the 13 poorest high schools are in the central city. A minimum of 52 percent of the students is minority. With the exception of the two Virginia high schools in the group, both of which evidence a substantial Latino presence, the highest rates of college-going are for the schools in the central city of Washington, DC. This table upsets much conventional wisdom. One reaction to the presentation in Table 2.2 might be, "Well, that's the Washington, D.C., area, and that's very different." Indeed, all urban areas do not look alike—nor do their students. We cannot assume that students who graduate from high schools in an urban area attend college in the same urban area—let alone any urban area.

To demonstrate this variability, we can take the nine census divisions by three degrees of urbanicity (urban, suburban, and rural), and look at demographic backgrounds, high school performance, and long-term postsecondary history for the most recent traditional-age cohort for which this history is complete, the HS&B/So (1980–1993). Unfortunately, the 27 cells that result in the basic Census division by urbanicity matrix result in untenably low cell sizes when other independent variables are brought into the analysis. For purposes of achieving adequate statistical power in demonstration, and using an urban versus other configuration, I have collapsed the 27 cells as follows:

TABLE 2.3
The Variable Demography of Urbanicity in the Scheduled High School
Graduating Class of 1982 in Grade 10

	Urban			Other		Residual		
	Mid-At %	Pacif %	Other %	Mid-At %	Pacif %	Suburb %	Rural %	% of All
Race/ethn.								
White	43	58	55	89	75	83	82	78
Black	37	15	30	6	5	10	11	12
Latino	15	19	12	3	13	5	5	7
Asian	2	8	1	—	5	1	—	2
Second Language background	18	17	9	4	9	4	3	6
SES quintile								
Highest	13	23	16	22	28	24	15	21
Lowest	26	18	20	12	11	14	22	16

Notes: Weighted N = 3.77M.

1. Urban: Mid-Atlantic
   (New York, New Jersey, Pennsylvania, Delaware)   3.8%
2. Urban: Pacific
   (California, Oregon, Washington, Alaska, Hawaii)   2.7
3. Urban: All Other   14.3
4. Other Mid-Atlantic (suburban and rural)   11.6
5. Other Pacific (suburban and rural)   9.2
6. Suburban in the other 7 Census divisions   32.2
7. Rural/small town in the other 7 Census divisions   26.2

Table 2.3 displays the demographic characteristics of the HS&B/So students in these categories.

Immediately, we note some variability that advises us to be mindful of Census division when building models addressing the factors that make a difference in the fate and success of urban students. The most conspicuous story line in Table 2.3 is that high school students from Pacific urban areas look a lot different from students in other urban areas. Beyond the surprising SES distribution, this is—or should be—elementary textbook material given the numbers of Asian and Pacific Islanders in Los Angeles, San Francisco, Portland, Seattle, and Honolulu, and the Latino proportion of the California population (which dominates the Census division). The influence of these populations is evident in the cross-currents dj`layed in Table 2.4, which presents the high school backgrounds and college-going rates of the HS&B/So students.

TABLE 2.4

The Variable Secondary School Backgrounds and College-Going Rates of the Base Year (grade 10) HS&B/So Students, by Urbanicity/Census Division Aggregates

| | Urban | | | Other | | Residual | | |
	Mid-At	Pacif	Other	Mid-At	Pacif	Suburb	Rural	All
Event Dropout	16%	14%	16%	8%	13%	11%	12%	12%
Math higher than Algebra 2	14	13	12	27	14	18	10	16
Any AP	14	14	13	21	14	17	13	16
Dual-enrollment[8]	2	7	2	2	5	3	3	3
In TRIO or TRIO-type program	7	6	7	4	3	4	4	4
Postsec Ed at any time	54	61	52	60	63	62	55	59
Bachelor's degree, by age 30	23	26	16	32	22	28	22	24

Source: National Center for Education Statistics: High School & Beyond/Sophomore Cohort, NCES CD#98-135.

What does one observe in Table 2.4? A few bullets will highlight a continuing dissonance in the literature's assumptions about a monolithic "urban" student:

- In the Pacific census division, unlike the Mid-Atlantic, nonurban high school event dropout rates were basically the same as those for urban areas.
- Urban students from the Mid-Atlantic Census division had stronger high school curriculum profiles (math and AP) than other urban students, yet were less likely to continue their education after high school than urban students from the Pacific Census division.
- Urban students were more likely to have been involved in TRIO or TRIO-type outreach programs than nonurban students.
- Pacific Census division students from all types of urbanicity backgrounds were more likely to have taken college courses for credit while still enrolled in high school (dual enrollment) than students from any other part of the country.
- Within the Pacific Census division, students of urban origins earned bachelor's degrees at a higher rate than nonurban students.

The variability within urban student populations will cast a cautious context for the multivariate analysis on pp. 51–55. As for rural/small town populations outside the Mid-Atlantic and Pacific Census divisions, we are reminded (by Table 2.3) that the SES distribution looks more like that of urban areas other than those of the Pacific Census division, and (by Table 2.4) that opportunity-to-learn (reflected in the proportion of students who reached a level of mathematics higher than Algebra 2) is even more constricted than it is in urban areas.

"Educational Fate": Setting Up the Dependent Variable

One of the advantages of the NCES age-cohort longitudinal studies is that they present true life histories—at least from adolescence through age 30 or so. And because they include high school and college transcripts, we can construct long-term educational histories. The literature using these data bases tends to treat educational attainment as a binary phenomenon (that is, either something happened or it didn't), hence sets up analyses using logistic regression.

One of the principal methodological reasons for positing a binary dependent variable (initial college attendance, retention [in an institution] persistence [in the system] to the second year, bachelor's degree attainment) is that the metrics of educational attainment are not like those of test scores—it is difficult to establish a continuous variable with standard intervals. Who is to say—and with what authority—how much more an associate's degree is worth versus a postsecondary certificate, for example? On the other hand, we know that a 76 on a test is worth more than a 70. With test scores or grades as the dependent variable, we ask how much of the variance in the results can be accounted for by different configurations of background and behavioral factors. This question usually calls for an Ordinary Least Squares (OLS) regression.

In this exploration, I would like to posit a hierarchy of "educational fates" that would allow for an Ordinary Least Squares (OLS) regression analysis of determinants. Since we are looking at pre-collegiate factors in educational histories, the weights of the analyses are those developed for the base year (grade 10, 1980) of the High School & Beyond/Sophomores, and, unlike the *Tool Box* study, I am not using discrete post-matriculation behavior as independent variables in the analysis of "educational fate." In effect, I am presenting a continuous variable, with seven values:

1. No evidence of college attendance, and in the bottom 60 percent of high school academic resources.[9]
2. No evidence of college attendance, but in the top 40 percent of high school academic resources.

TABLE 2.5
Educational "Fate" to Age 30 for Tenth Graders of the HS&B/So Cohort, by Urbanicity of
High School.

	Urban	Suburban	Rural	All
No PSE, bottom 60%	36%*	28%*	37%*	33%
No PSE, top 40%	2	2	2	2
Incidental PSE students	12*	10	8*	10
PSE: 10–29 Credits	8	10*	7*	8
Certif. or 30–59 credits	10	10	11	10
Assoc. or 60+ credits	13	12	13	12
Bachelor's or higher	18*	29*	22*	24

Note: *Differences in row pair comparisons are significant at $p \leq 05$.
Source: National Center for Education Statistics: High School & Beyond/Sophomore Cohort, NCES CD#98-135.

3. Attended some form of postsecondary education, but either earned 10 or fewer credits by age 30 (incidental students) or presented a record that consisted of nothing but GED-level or basic skills courses.
4. Attended some form of postsecondary education, and earned between 11 and 29 credits, but no degree by age 30.
5. Earned either a postsecondary certificate or between 30 and 59 credits (but no degree) by age 30.
6. Earned either an associate's degree or 60 or more credits (but no degree) by age 30.
7. Earned a bachelor's or higher degree by age 30.

Unlike test scores, the intervals between these values are obviously not regular. In fact, there is no way to determine the precise relative position of these values. At the "lowest" levels, for example, they distinguish between those who never continued their education after high school and offered weak records from those who never continued their education after high school but who had achieved a relatively weighty amount of "academic resources."

Before construction of multivariate analyses, it would be helpful to explore some variables that might make a difference in accounting for "educational fate," and, in the process, to show what happened to the HS&B/So cohort. Table 2.5 lays out the portrait by urbanicity of high school and indicates:

• Both urban and rural students with mediocre/poor high school records are less likely to continue their education than suburban students with the same records.

TABLE 2.6

Near-Term History of Urban High School Sophomore in the 9 Census Divisions, 1980 of Students from Urban High Schools:

	% Urban	Event/status dropouts	Children by age 20	Expect B.A.	Math >Alg2	% of All
New England	18.5%	14.2%	9.4%	41.2	11.5%	6.5%
Mid-Atlantic	28.5	20.4	11.4	44.6	15.0	16.4
East North Central	21.5	24.3	13.2	36.7	13.2	20.2
West North Central	15.8	16.8	13.1	42.1	14.8	7.7
South Atlantic	22.4	19.2	16.5	40.0	6.8	16.6
South East Central	15.9	21.8	11.9	46.2	7.4	5.4
South West Central	24.7	22.4	15.4	48.6	11.8	10.3
Mountain	14.0	17.4	18.8	41.5	18.4	4.9
Pacific	21.4	22.9	9.1	49.7	12.5	12.1

Notes: (1) Weighted $N = 3.77$M.
Source: National Center for Education Statistics: High School & Beyond/Sophomore Cohort, NCES CD#98-135.

- The proportion of students who do not continue their education despite strong high school records does not differ by urbanicity.
- The real differences in educational "fate," by urbanicity of origin, are seen only at the bachelor's degree level.

Even at this point, we need another layer of information to weave into the background tapestry to help us explain educational fate and the potential role of pre-collegiate outreach and early intervention programs in improving the lot of disadvantaged students. For this information, we return to the Census division analysis. Table 2.6 demonstrates some key variances.

One immediately notices that the dropout rate (both event and status) reflects the behavior of roughly one out of five urban high school students, and in Census divisions in which the rate is comparatively low (New England, West North Central), the suburban and rural dropout rates are also low. One notices, too, an extraordinarily low percentage of students from both the South Atlantic and South East Central Census divisions who complete a mathematics course beyond Algebra 2. This provides clear directions—of all secondary school curriculum components, the highest level of mathematics one studies provides the strongest momentum into and through a collegiate education (see Adelman, *Answers in the Tool Box*, Table 6, p.17). And yet another clue for focusing early intervention efforts lies in the comparatively low "expectations" of students in East North Central urban high schools.

Independent Variables in the Analysis

Since we are interested in pre-collegiate histories in relation to postsecondary participation and completion, the independent variables in our multivariate analyses are all prematriculation phenomena. In addition to race/ethnicity (African-American/Latino/American Indian versus White and Asian/PI) and gender, there are seven such variables in this analysis. A brief description of each follows:

1. *Socioeconomic Status (SES)*. While I have used family income to illustrate divergent trends in access to postsecondary education, the problem with this variable in any pre-1996 NCES data set[10] is that the data are self-reported, and when experts have been called in to determine what cases are either not credible or out-of-scope, we lose a significant portion of the universe.

   The family income variable, taken alone, is problematic unless one can accurately determine family size and present convincing criteria and benchmarks for "low income." Choy (2000) used 125 percent of the federally defined poverty threshold by family size and student dependency status, an appropriate, accessible, and persuasive configuration given her data source in the NPSAS-96. A single independent student, an only child who lived with her mother, and another student from a household with two parents and three other siblings—all with family income of $25,000—are not all "low income." Only the large household can be classified as "low income" by the 125 percent by family size criteria (Choy, 2000, p. 3). One can estimate household size for the NELS-88, but not for the High School & Beyond/So because the student was not asked for the *number* of siblings.

   Under these circumstances, the SES composite becomes the variable of preference (Alexander, Pallas, and Holupka, 1987). The SES variable in the NCES longitudinal studies has two virtues: (a) the composite washes out some of the discrepancies and anomalies of its components, and (b) we lose only 5 percent of the cases in the HS&B/So (versus 25 percent if we use the best of the family income variables). The correlation between SES and income in the HS&B/So is .544 and that between SES and an adjusted parental education variable[11] is .649, whereas the correlation between family income and parental education is a comparatively weak .373 (all these estimates are significant at $p \leq 001$).

2. *Outreach*. Participation in pre-collegiate outreach programs of any type, TRIO (Upward Bound, Talent Search) or their equivalents. In

the HS&B/So, students were first asked whether they had "ever heard" of these programs, and then, whether they participated. Students who had never heard of these programs in either grade 10 or grade 12, but whose files contain complete high school transcript records, were assumed to be nonparticipants.

3. *Language.* A "dummy" variable indicating whether or not the student was a native speaker of English. For the HS&B/So, the variable was constructed from a special language supplement file, from high school transcripts that indicated ESL courses, from college transcripts indicating that the student took a course in Spanish for Native Speakers, and from a flag that indicated the student filled out the Spanish-language version of the base year questionnaire in grade 10.

4. *Children.* A "dummy" variable indicating early parenthood (e.g., becoming a parent by age 20). The variable first includes those who indicated that they were parents or lived with their children in either the base year (1980) or the first follow-up year (1982). It then adds those who, in 1984, indicated that they were parents of children born in 1983 or earlier. Parenthood includes both men and women.

5. *Dropout.* One can discern four types of dropout histories in the HS&B/So, the only NCES longitudinal study in which long-term high school dropout status can be determined:

- Left high school sometime after grade 10 and returned at some time (event dropout) but did not graduate or receive an equivalency certificate by age 29 (status dropout);
- Left high school sometime after grade 10, never returned, and did not receive an equivalency certificate by age 29 (status dropout only);
- Left high school sometime after grade 10 but returned (event dropout) and either graduated later than scheduled (1982) or received a GED or other equivalency certificate by age 29. These students are event dropouts only.
- Left high school sometime between grade 10 and grade 12, but returned and graduated on schedule (1982). Again, these students are event dropouts only.

Table 2.7 presents a distribution of these dropout histories by urbanicity of high school and early parenthood. The urban dropout rate is higher than the rates in other types of communities. But there are no easy conclusions, hence one would not be surprised to find a comparatively low correlation between early parenthood and dropout in multivariate analyses. What we lack in longitudinal studies that begin even in grade 8 (NELS-88) let alone grade 10 (HS&B/So) are proven precursors of dropout such as retention in grades

TABLE 2.7
Types of Dropout Histories in the Scheduled High School Graduating Class of 1982, to Age 28/29 (1992), by Urbanicity of High School Community and Early Parenthood Status

	Event and status %	Status only %	Event & late grad %	Event & on-time grad %	No drop %
Urban	6.3	5.4	4.5	4.7	79.1
Suburban	4.4	2.4	2.7	3.2	87.3
Rural	5.0	2.4	3.8	3.5	85.3
All:	5.0	3.0	3.4	3.6	85.0
% w/children by age 20	29.7	11.0	33.8	28.3	6.8

Note: Urbanicity rows add to 100.0%. Universe includes only base year (1980) students.
Source: National Center for Education Statistics: High School & Beyond/Sophomore Cohort. NCES CD#98-135.

during elementary school and the number of times children changed schools (Temple, Reynolds, and Ou, 2000).

For purposes of the multivariate analysis, *dropout* is a "dummy" variable flagging students in the first three of these groups. Students who were event dropouts but graduated with their class as scheduled in 1982 were *not* considered "dropouts."

6. *Anticipations.* This variable replaces the standard educational "aspirations" or "expectations" variable used in most analyses of access/participation/completion in postsecondary education. While described in detail in *Answers in the Tool Box* (pp. 32–35), the basic principle is worth repeating: constructed from six pairs of questions asked in both grade 10 and grade 12, "anticipations" indicates the *level and consistency* of a student's vision of his/her future education. In a five-step sequence, the highest rung is for those who consistently anticipated earning a bachelor's degree (or higher) and whose concrete plans did not contradict that anticipation in any way. The five levels of "anticipations" were the following:

- bachelor's consistent
- increased to bachelor's between grade 10 and grade 12
- associate's consistent or reduced from bachelor's between grades 10 and 12
- certificate consistent or reduced from associate's between grades 10 and 12
- expected to earn no degree or never knew what degree they might earn

7. *AccPrep.* The "academic resources" (ACRES) variable from the *Tool Box* study. ACRES is a composite built from (a) an index of the academic intensity and quality of a student's high school curriculum, (b) senior year score on the "enhance, mini-SAT" administered to all NCES longitudinal studies participants (and, where missing, an equated substitution of SAT/ACT score where available), and (c) high school class rank quintile (and, where missing, academic GPA quintile). All three elements are in quintiles. Their weights in the composite index, based on a simple multivariate analysis with bachelor's degree attainment as the dependent variable, are: curriculum (41 percent), test scores (30 percent), and class rank/GPA (29 percent). The results of weighting the components are then again set out in quintile presentation.

What Makes a Difference? The Multivariate Analysis

In this section, a series of OLS regressions, with Educational Fate as the dependent variable, are presented and analyzed for different populations by urbanicity of high school. In all cases, three variables stand out as determinants of educational fate regardless of urbanicity: educational expectations, academic preparation, and SES. TRIO/TRIO-type participation (the *outreach* variable) and second language background did not even qualify for inclusion in the equations (with one minor exception for the *outreach* variable). The *dropout* and gender variables move in and out of the equations, and at the margins of significance. Race is a very weak contributor.

TABLE 2.8

Background Model: The Relationship of Basic Pre-college Variables to Educational "Fate" by Age 30 for Students in the HS&B/So Who Were Enrolled in High School in 1982.

Universe: All students for whom complete high school transcripts, class rank/academic GPA, senior year test scores, SES data, and six components of the "anticipations" variable were available, and for whom educational histories to age 30 could be constructed. $N = 10,270$. Weighted $N = 2.65M$. Design effect $= 1.64$.

Variable	Parameter estimate	Adj. s.e.	t	p	Contribution to R^2
Intercept	−0.31363	0.1597	3.16		
Acad prep	0.63876	0.0254	13.9	.001	.4079
Anticipations	0.58175	0.0237	13.6	.001	.0983
SES	0.19842	0.0229	4.78	.05	.0112
Race	−0.23629	0.0748	1.74	—	.0013
Sex	0.17904	0.0551	1.79	—	.0014
				R^2	.5199
				Adjusted R^2	.5197

TABLE 2.9.

Extended Background Model. Relationship of Expanded List of Background Variables to Educational "Fate" by Age 30 for Students in the HS&B/So Who Were Enrolled in High School in 1980.

Universe: All students for whom complete high school transcripts, class rank/academic GPA, senior year test scores, SES data, and six components of the "anticipations" variable were available, and for whom educational histories to age 30 could be constructed. $N = 10{,}270$. Weighted $N = 2.65M$. Design effect $= 1.63$.

Variable	Parameter estimate	Adj. s.e.	t	p	Contribution to R^2
Intercept	1.03489	.2424	2.62		
AcadPrep	0.61652	.0253	14.9	.001	.4089
Anticipations	0.55663	.0235	14.5	.001	.0973
SES	0.19298	.0226	5.83	.01	.0118
Children	−0.63577	.1030	3.78	.02	.0050
Sex	0.22351	.0548	2.50	.05	.0022
Dropout	−0.57033	.1367	2.56	.05	.0021
Race	−0.21309	.0732	1.78	—	.0010
				R^2	.5283
				Adjusted R^2	.5280

Table 2.8 presents the most basic variables in the students' pre-collegiate backgrounds. The equation included *outreach,* but this variable did not meet even a generous statistical selection criterion and hence does not appear in the model.[12] Participation in TRIO or TRIO-type programs plays no role in the explanation of variance in attainment.

Overall, this is a fairly strong model, with the adjusted R^2 indicating that it accounts for about 52 percent of the variance in an educational story line of access, participation, and completion.

The equation for Table 2.9 expanded this background model by adding the variables for second language dominance, early parenthood (both men and women are affected), and dropout status. Of the variables added, early parenthood and dropout evidence modest significance (negative effects). Academic preparation remains at the top of the list of influences, supported by the "anticipations" ladder. The rise in the R^2 is negligible.

I thought that by including status dropouts, the *dropout* variable would be a more significant contributor to the model (albeit with a negative sign). But the correlations between *dropout* and the strongest variables in the set, AcadPrep and Anticipations, are both roughly −.2, and the effects of dropping out are thus attenuated. In thinking ahead to the best target populations for pre-collegiate outreach programs, we would be wise to note that 20 percent of status dropouts never reached the ninth grade and 25 percent attended school outside the United States (McMillen and Kaufman, 1997), both factors putting a large portion of this population beyond the reach of intervention efforts focused on postsecondary access and participation.

We previously observed a number of differences in student characteristics and fate by urbanicity of their high school community, so it may be worth putting this model to the test for the three types of community populations. There are so many cross-currents and so much economic, social, and cultural diversity in communities of a similar type that a single independent variable to which one can attach a transparent "value" and include in a multivariate equation is difficult to defend. Thus, it may be better to use the three degrees of urbanicity as filters on the population, and bring in the full range of pre-collegiate background variables to determine the extent to which the general model holds up in both strength and components. Tables 2.10 through 2.12 execute this strategy.

In the "urban" variation of the model, the overall explanatory power declines. Academic preparation and educational anticipations, while still

TABLE 2.10

Extended Background Model, Urban Variation: Relationship of Expanded List of Background Variables to Educational "Fate" by Age 30 for Students in the High School & Beyond/Sophomore Cohort whose "Referent" High School in Grade 10 (1980) was Located in an Urban Community.

Universe: All students for whom complete high school transcripts, class rank/academic GPA, senior year test scores, SES data, and six components of the "anticipations" variable were available, for whom educational histories to age 30 could be constructed, and who attended high school in an urban area in 1980. $N = 2201$. Weighted $N = 550k$. Design effect = 1.62.

Parameter Variable	Contribution estimate	Adj. s.e.	t	p	to R^2
Intercept	1.08838	.5144	1.31		
AccPrep	0.59215	.0569	6.43	.001	.3640
Anticipations	0.48539	.0526	5.71	.001	.0789
SES	0.23499	.0493	2.94	.05	.0195
Children	−0.65225	.2191	1.84	.10	.0067
Sex	0.25534	.1213	1.30	—	.0032
Race	−0.29304	.1378	1.31	—	.0025
Dropout	−0.47148	.2596	1.12	—	.0021
				R^2	.4768
				Adjusted R^2	.4752

TABLE 2.11

Extended Background Model: Suburban Variation. Relationship of Expanded List
of Background Variables to Educational "Fate" by Age 30 for Students in the High School
& Beyond/Sophomore Cohort whose "Referent" High School in Grade 10 (1980)
was Located in a Suburban Community.

Universe: All students for whom complete high school transcripts, class rank/academic GPA, senior
year test scores, SES data, and 6 components of the "anticipations" variable were available, for
whom educational histories to age 30 could be constructed, and who attended high school in a
suburban area in 1980. $N = 5531$. Weighted $N = 1.4M$. Design effect = 1.67.

Variable	Parameter estimate	Adj. s.e.	t	p	Contribution to R^2
Intercept	0.20144	.3881	.311		
AccPrep	0.66528	.0335	11.9	.001	0.4442
Anticipations	0.56698	.0321	10.6	.001	0.1018
SES	0.20271	.0309	2.93	.02	0.0106
Children	−0.61634	.1606	2.30	.05	0.0034
Sex	0.22759	.0742	1.84	.10	0.0021
Dropout	−0.64926	.2042	1.80	.10	0.0025
Outreach	0.39207	.2021	1.16	—	0.0009
				R^2	.5654
				Adjusted R^2	.5648

dominant, are less overwhelming, while SES and early parenthood move up
slightly in importance. Dropout, race, and sex remain at the periphery. No
other pre-collegiate variables qualify.

In the suburban variation, two slight ripples appear. The overall power of
the model increases, *dropout* becomes statistically significant, and *outreach*
enters the model for the first time, though below the level of statistical
significance.

Why the minor changes? Dropping out has a far more significant impact
in a suburban area than in an urban area, where the dropout rate is much
higher. SES has less of an impact because the suburban variance is less than
the urban variance. And *outreach* at least meets the statistical criteria for
moving forward from a correlation matrix into a regression equation because,
I speculate, that in a suburban area the type of outreach at issue is probably
Talent Search and its imitators (that is, a more selective and different type of
program than Upward Bound).

As for the rural/small town population, there is a change in the strength
of the model's component parts. "Anticipations" replaces academic preparation in the top slot.

TABLE 2.12

Extended Background Model: Rural Variation. Relationship of Expanded List of Background Variables to Educational "Fate" by Age 30 for Students in the High School & Beyond/Sophomore Cohort whose "Referent" High School in Grade 10 (1980) was Located in a Rural/Small Town.

Universe: All students for whom complete high school transcripts, class rank/academic GPA, senior year test scores, SES data, and 6 components of the "anticipations" variable were available, for whom educational histories to age 30 could be constructed, and who attended high school in a rural area in 1980. N = 2730. Weighted N = 933k. Design effect = 1.29.

Variable	*Parameter estimate*	*Adj. s.e.*	*t*	*p*	*Contribution to R^2*
Intercept	1.06453	.3284	2.52		
Anticipations	0.58039	.0362	12.4	.001	.4014
AcadPrep	0.56407	.0397	11.0	.001	.0781
Children	−0.71638	.1441	3.86	.02	.0089
SES	0.17808	.0352	3.93	.02	.0073
Sex	0.22858	.0879	2.02	.05	.0021
Dropout	−0.54515	.2161	1.96	.05	.0019
				R^2	.4997
				Adjusted R^2	.4986

However, both the anticipations and academic preparation variables are strong enough to reinforce each other (co linearity analysis reinforces this observation) and dominate the models for all three types of communities. If one wished to speculate on the minor shift in strength of these two variables, recall (from Table 2.4) that rural students had less opportunity-to-learn (hence could not amass as strong an academic preparation profile) than others. Early parenthood and SES continue to play modest roles (as they did in the suburban model), but in the rural model, race does not even enter the equation even though roughly 25 percent of Latino and African-American students in the HS&B/So lived in rural/small town communities in grade 10.

What Do We Learn?

Looking back over this excursion, it may be helpful to summarize what we learned about pre-college variables that can sharpen our focus on students who either do not attend or do not succeed in postsecondary education. If we need to hone our objectives and target our populations better in outreach programs, what aspects of this learning should we use in program design and evaluation?

- First, the outcome we envision for students must allow for both levels of achievement and time to achieve. The "educational 'fate'" ladder at age 30 is a representation that captures these conditions. It tells us far more than a "dummy" judgment that a student either entered college or not, entered the second year of college or not, or finished a bachelor's degree or not.
- Implications for practice. Long-term tracking of student populations is necessary for evaluation of interventions, and the analytic design for that tracking must have clear and credible benchmarks. The effects of interventions occur in stages, and longitudinal studies can capture the extent to which behavioral responses at one stage influence those at subsequent stages (Nora and Cabrera, 1992).
- Second, participation in pre-college outreach programs currently affects such a small percentage of cohort populations that effects cannot be judged in the context of educational histories. Of course it would be helpful if the volume of pre-collegiate outreach programs and the volume of students participating would rise. But as of 1994, only 32 percent of our two-year and four-year colleges operated outreach programs for disadvantaged students, and these programs served an estimated 317,400 individuals spread throughout the K-12 system (Chaney, Lewis, and Farris, 1995).
- Implications for practice. In the absence of a large national cohort participation rate in outreach programs, evaluations should be conducted only with targeted, large-scale expansions. That is, pick a limited number of school districts with historically low rates of participation in higher education, and triple or quadruple the populations involved in outreach programs so that one can achieve statistical significance in the tracking analysis, given the likelihood of high attrition rates (Myers and Schirm, 1996).
- Third, high school dropout behavior is more complex than single "dummy" variables can or will reveal. Some 20 percent of dropouts never return (among urban students, it's 25 percent), but 25 percent not only return but graduate on-time with regular diplomas.
- Implications for practice. Some triage of populations targeted by pre-collegiate outreach programs is necessary if we are to address "feasible numbers" and have a chance of succeeding. Objectives for students in dropout-prevention programs are different from those for students who complete high school on time but do not either attend or succeed in postsecondary education (Gleason and Dynarski, 1998).
- Urbanicity presents diverse portraits by Census division. There is more diversity in suburban populations than conventional wisdom assumes, hence a larger set of factors casts light on what happens to suburban students than is the case for either urban or rural/small

town populations. Also, the nature of students' use of time in rural places is different from that in urban places.

- Implications for practice. Program designs must be adjusted for regional by urbanicity factors. A program in a rural area where students spend two to four hours a day on school buses is restricted in the ways it can use nonschool time for academic preparation. Evaluation designs must follow suit. No one size fits all.
- While family income bands reveal disparities in school achievement and postsecondary access, SES is a more convincing analytic tool in the consideration of student histories.
- Implications for practice. If we wish to isolate and target truly poor students, we should use more precise measures of economic disadvantage than are currently employed in analyses, and if we wish to bound populations by first-generation-college-student status, then we have to ask the parents—not the student—for their educational histories.
- Academic preparation is, most consistently, the strongest of all momentum builders in pre-collegiate histories. Academic preparation depends on opportunity-to-learn, and students' "anticipations" grow from that preparation.
- Implications for practice. This is the true bottom-line for outreach programs, the challenge of providing content, confidence, and skill development that schools in some areas (urbanicity by Census division) do not provide. The objective, and its evaluation, is easy to incorporate in program design, though often challenging to execute, as it involves either non-school time or alternative uses of school time.
- For example, dual enrollment is the least threatening (to school systems) path to providing opportunity-to-learn, particularly in rural areas where school districts have considerable difficulty in hiring teachers. Dual enrollment is an alternative use of school time. The challenge to colleges and community colleges in such areas is one of creative capacity: how much space can be assembled in different ways (and in different courses) to provide secondary school students with the academic momentum they need to enter, participate, and succeed in postsecondary education?
- Of all populations we examined, high school graduates from rural areas/small towns—and poor students from those areas, in particular—are at the greatest disadvantage in terms of opportunity-to-learn, and consistently evidence the lowest rates of college going. "Anticipations"—more than other pre-college factors—sustain rural/small town students who succeed.
- Implications for practice. There is a "mission population" that needs increased attention in pre-collegiate outreach efforts, one that includes a significant proportion of minority students. The student experience

of time and space in rural/small town environments is very different than that of students in more concentrated settlements (see Lynch, 1972), and the design of outreach efforts must take these factors into account. Dual-enrollment and direct provision of secondary school instruction through creative distance learning offer potentially productive design solutions.

How many students should be involved in quality pre-collegiate outreach efforts? If our only objective were increasing postsecondary participation, we would seek to increase the access rate from 75 percent to perhaps 80 percent, or about 150,000 students in a given scheduled high school graduating class. But the new vision of pre-collegiate outreach programs has to accomplish more in an age when 75 percent of high school graduates continue their education but only 40 percent ultimately earn a degree. That means we are looking at an additional 1 million students annually who need more academic momentum than they currently receive. Of this one million, approximately 400,000 come from the lower-income and lower-SES bands. To provide adequate content and to build consistently high educational expectations, outreach programs do not start and end in the same year. And if, as many suggest, they should begin in the middle school years, the target population swiftly aggregates to over 3 million—ten times the number actually served by pre-collegiate outreach programs in 1994.

Choices, Choices

Can we do it? Perhaps we can do better, but not likely ten times better. The resources—principally human time and effort—of higher education institutions that might join or expand the outreach and early intervention efforts are limited both by quantity and proclivity. Colleges and community colleges thus will want to place the "bets" of their efforts on populations that (a) have the best chance of succeeding, (b) to which they can communicate, and (c) for which they can control the factors that most strongly influence change. Principles of triage operate whether we want to admit it or not. Three reality checks should help define the principles of triage.

First: There are factors beyond our control that have a telling impact on "educational fate," early parenthood being the most obvious (see Akerhielm, Berger, Hooker & Wise, 1997). Colleges engaged in pre-collegiate outreach programs are not disposed to be in the birth-control business, nor in family counseling on a large scale. Colleges also cannot affect the heritage of grade retention in elementary school, lack of parental involvement, and frequent transfer from one school to another in elementary and middle school years (Reynolds, 1999).

Second: The characteristics of populations predisposed to high school dropout are (a) overage for their grade level, which indicates cumulative problems in schooling; and (b) far more likely to exhibit behavior subject to discipline (Dynarski and Gleason, 1998). Colleges and community colleges designing outreach/intervention programs to fill in academic content and skills where schools have left off are not disposed to deal with populations such as these. The dropout-prevention demonstration programs involved alternative schools, residential schools, schools-within-schools, and GED programs, and the evaluations clearly showed an improvement in retention but not in academic achievement, a very sobering conclusion (Dynarski, Gleason, Rangarajan, & Wood, 1998). Colleges and community colleges are not disposed to be in the alternative school business, and, in some states, are precluded from entering that business by laws specifying who may teach.

Third: Colleges and community colleges are best able to assist opportunity-to-learn at the secondary school level. The personnel on which they can draw for outreach efforts focusing on academic preparation are too distant from middle-school level curricula and learning problems. Doable objectives of outreach programs at the middle-school level can focus on information and expectations. That's what GEAR-UP is essentially about. To the extent that GEAR-UP works in different Census divisions by urbanicity environments, its ninth and tenth grade "alumni" will become the responsibility of expanded pre-collegiate preparation efforts.

Notes

1. The nine Census divisions are as follow: New England, Mid-Atlantic, East North Central, West North Central, South Atlantic, East South Central, West South Central, Mountain, and Pacific. The reason for using the Census divisions is that state-level analysis is not available in longitudinal studies of the National Center for Education Statistics (the samples are not large enough for state-level analysis), and the four geographic regions (northeast, southeast, midwest and west) are too generalized.

2. The match is not always exact. For example, the NELS-88 variable for enrolling in postsecondary education directly following on-time (1992) graduation is "Enrolled in October, 1992." The HS&B/So transcript-derived variable is "Enrolled at any time, July, 1982-June, 1983." The NELS-88 variable for enrollment by 2 years after high school graduation uses August (1994) as a censoring date, whereas the HS&B/So variable uses June (1984). The major difference between the two data representations is that because the HS&B/So is transcript-based, students who claimed attendance but for whom we did not

receive transcripts are excluded, as are students for whom transcript records were incomplete in ways that precluded determination of the first date of attendance. The HS&B/So enrollment-rate data are hence slightly understated.

3. The fault lies in the questions asked in survey forms or telephone interviews. All forms of de facto on-the-job-training, civilian and military, get confounded with formal educational history. The transcript files allow us to sort these cases in a more sophisticated manner.

4. The wording used in High School & Beyond, NELS-88, and the Beginning Postsecondary Students studies is: "As things stand now, how far in education do you think you will get?" This is an "expectations"question, not an aspirations question. Only in the NLS-72 did the phrasing unmistakably elicit aspirations: "If there were no barriers, how far in education would you like to get?"

5. The only point in *Answers in the Tool Box* at which family income (as distinct from SES) played a role in the analysis was a section that sought to distinguish the characteristics of students who began their postsecondary careers in community colleges, consistently expected to earn a bachelor's degree, and transferred to a 4-year college from a parallel set of students who did not transfer. While the SES composite played a modest role in explaining the difference, family income did not. See *Answers in the Tool Box*, pp. 57–59.

6. Ironically, in the case of school urbanicity, I accept the variable presented by the NCES contractor, since it was derived from the standard CIC code used by the Census Bureau. The alternative is to take the *student's* answer to the question asked (variable #FY100, NCES CD#95–361) in the 1982 survey: "Which of the following best describes the place where you lived the first week of February, 1982?:

A rural or farming community
A small city or town of fewer than 50,000 people that is not a suburb of a larger place
A medium-sized city (50,000–100,00 people)
A suburb of a medium-sized city
A large city (100,000–500,000 people)
A suburb of a large city
A very large city (over 500,000 people)
A suburb of a very large city
A military base or station"

But if one uses the responses to this question, one loses nonparticipants in FU1 (about 10 percent of the group), another 3 percent who skipped the question or provided multiple responses, and 1 percent who lived on military bases in areas not defined by urbanicity. That's too big a loss for analytical purposes, and besides, (a) students don't always know how many people live in their community and (b) some of these categories are highly ambiguous in terms of urbanicity.

7. The event dropout rate for the District of Columbia in 1994–1995 was 10.6 percent (McMillen and Kaufman, 1997, Table 3, p.11).

8. Based on examination of transcript records, the student was enrolled for college courses prior to graduation from high school.

9. "Academic resources" is a construct developed in the *Answers in the Tool Box* study. It is a composite of three secondary school performance indicators: intensity and quality of curriculum (41%), senior year test scores (30%), and class rank/academic GPA (29 percent). The composite index is a proxy for the academic momentum a study brings forward from high school.

10. The National Postsecondary Student Aid Study of 1996 and its subset, the Beginning Postsecondary Students longitudinal study of 1995–1996, were the first to draw family income data from both FAFSA financial aid forms (aid applicants only), and from the National Student Loan Data System (for federal loan recipients). The unobtrusive nature of these sources renders them more accurate than self-reported (by the student) family income.

11. In approximately 3 percent of the HS&B/So cases, there was a blatant contradiction between student accounts of parental occupation and student accounts of the highest level of parental education. For example, we have schoolteachers whose highest level of education was reported as "high school graduate," lawyers whose highest level of education was "some college," etc. Since late adolescents tend to know more about what their parents do for a living than they do about their parents' education, these cases were adjusted with reference to the reported occupation. Thus, for example, the schoolteacher was given a bachelor's degree and the lawyer was given a graduate degree. The resulting variable, PARED2, reflects the highest level of education reached by either parent.

12. The variables in a regression equation are drawn from a correlation matrix. To qualify for entering the regression equation, a variable must meet a criterion for statistical significance in the correlation matrix. The default setting for this criterion in most statistical software packages is $p \leq .05$, but the analyst can be more generous, and I set the criterion at $p \leq .2$.

References

Adelman, C. (1999). *Answers in the Tool Box: Academic intensity, attendance patterns, and bachelor's degree attainment*. Washington, DC: U.S. Department of Education.

Akerheilm, K., Berger, J., Hooker, M., & Wise, D. (1997). *Analysis of NELS:88 follow-up data: Factors that affect college enrollment*. Washington, DC: U.S. Department of Education (Final report, Contract #EA94078001).

Alexander, K., Pallas, A., & Holupka, S. (1987). Consistency and change in educational stratification: Recent trends regarding social background and college access. *Research in Social Stratification and Mobility, 6,* 161–185.

Bowen, W. G. & Bok, D. (1998). *The shape of the river: Long-term consequences of considering race in college and university admissions.* Princeton, NJ: Princeton University Press.

Camburn, E. M. (1990). College completion among students from high schools located in large metropolitan areas. *American Journal of Education, 98,* no.4, 551–569.

Carroll, C. D. (1989). *College persistence and degree attainment for 1980 high school graduates: Hazards for transfers, stopouts, and part-timers.* Washington, DC: National Center for Education Statistics.

Choy, S. (2000). *Low-income students: Who they are and how they pay for their education.* Washington, DC: National Center for Education Statistics.

Dynarski, M. & Gleason, P. (1998). *How can we help? What we have learned from evaluations of federal dropout-prevention programs.* Washington, DC: U.S. Department of Education, Planning and Evaluation Service.

Dynarski, M., Gleason, P., Rangarahan, A., & Wood, R. (1998). *Impacts of dropout prevention programs.* Washington, DC: U.S. Department of Education, Planning and Evaluation Service Final Report. Contract # LC91015001).

Flint, T. A. (1997). Intergenerational effects of paying for college. *Research in Higher Education 38* (3), 313–344.

Gleason, P. & Dynarski, M. (1998). Do we know whom to serve?: *Issues in using risk factors to identify dropouts.* Princeton, NJ: Mathematica Policy Research.

Hearn, J. C. (1988). Determinants of postsecondary education attendance: Some implications of alternative specifications of enrollment. *Educational Evaluation and Policy Analysis, 10* (2), 182–185.

Hearn, J. C. (1992). Emerging variation in postsecondary attendance patterns: An investigation of part-time, delayed, and non-degree enrollment. *Research in Higher Education, 33* (6), 657–687.

Horn, L. & Chen, X. (1999). *Toward resiliency: At-risk students who make it to college.* Washington, DC: U.S. Department of Education.

Kane, J. & Spizman, L. M. (1994). Race, financial aid awards and college attendance: Parents and geography matter. *American Journal of Economics and Sociology, 53* (1), 85–97.

Karen, D. (1991). Politics of class, race, and gender: Access to higher education in the United States, 1960–86. *American Journal of Education, 99,* 208–237.

Kurtz, S. A. (1973) *Wasteland: Building the American Dream.* New York: Praeger Publishers.

Lynch, K., and Associates (1977). *Growing up in cities: Studies of the spatial environment of adolescence.* Cambridge, MA: MIT Press.

Lynch, K. (1972). *What time is this place?* Cambridge, MA: MIT Press.

McMillen, M. M. & Kaufman, P. (1997). *Dropout Rates in the United States: 1996.* Washington, DC: National Center for Education Statistics.

Myers, D. & Schirm, A. (1996). *The short-term impact of upward bound: An interim report.* Washington, DC: U.S. Department of Education, Planning & Evaluation Service.

Nora, A. & Cabrera, A. F. (1992). *Measuring program outcomes: What impacts are important to assess and what impacts are possible to measure?* Paper prepared for the Design Conference for the Evaluation of Talent Search, U.S. Department of Education.

Ordovensky, J. F. (1995). Effects of institutional attributes on enrollment choice: Implications for postsecondary vocational education. *Economics of Education Review, 14* (4), 335–350.

Paul, F. G. (1990). Access to college in a public policy environment supporting both opportunity and selectivity. *American Journal of Education, 98* 4, pp. 351–388.

Persell, C. H., Catsambis, S., & Cookson, P. W. (1992). Differential asset conversion: Class and gender pathways to selective colleges. *Sociology of Education, 65* (2), 208–225.

Reynolds, A. J. (Ed.). (1999). Schooling and high-risk populations: the Chicago longitudinal study (special issue). *Journal of School Psychology, 37* (4).

Richardson, R. C. Jr. & Bender, L. W. (1987). *Fostering minority access and Achievement in higher education: The role of urban community colleges and Universities.* San Francisco: Jossey-Bass.

Smith, M. H., Beaulieu, L. J., & Seraphine, A. (1995). Social capital, place of residence and college attendance. *Rural Sociology, 60* (3), 363–380.

Snyder, T. (2000). *Digest of education statistics, 1999.* Washington, DC: National Center for Education Statistics.

St. John, E. P. (1990). Price response in enrollment decisions: An analysis of the high school and beyond sophomore cohort. *Research in Higher Education, 31* (2), 161–176.

Steelman, L. C. & Powell, B. (1993). Doing the right thing: Race and parental locus of responsibility for funding college. *Sociology of Education, 66* (4), 223–244.

Temple, J. A., Reynolds, A. J., & Ou, S. R. (2000). *Grade retention and educational attainment: An explanatory analysis.* Paper presented at the biennial meeting of the Society for Research on Adolescence. Chicago, IL.

CHAPTER 3

A Theoretical and Practical View of Student Adjustment and Academic Achievement

AMAURY NORA

As we now enter the twenty-first century, access to college and to high-level jobs for at-risk groups of students in both urban and suburban areas remains one of the most critical issues facing the nation. In fact, the question of access—who gets into college and who is eligible to fill high-level jobs in a highly competitive job market that rewards the best prepared individuals—is more important than ever. At the center of this issue is a critical question: *What constitutes true access?* Access simply defined as entrance into higher education misses the intent of many research efforts, interventions, grants, and policies. For access without choice and without a connection to any measurable outcomes, be they cognitive or attitudinal, is not true access.

Many programs have tried to address this policy issue through early outreach requiring that institutions of higher education engage in K–12/university partnerships in an effort to increase the number of college-eligible students. Over the past 20 years, those funding systemic change initiatives (local, federal, state, as well as public and private) have been looking for a meaningful answer to the access issue. Considering that we live in an imperfect world, and taking into account a multitude of factors that preclude access, is there some kind of formula that can generate larger numbers of at-risk students who graduate from high school fully eligible to enter college and earn bachelor's degrees? At the heart of this pursuit is the need to build a pathway to college for at-risk students.

Current Theoretical Frameworks: In Pursuit of a Pathway

Concurrent with K–12/university collaborative efforts has been research on student achievement and persistence that has tried to identify specific variables and the interplay among those variables based on theoretical frameworks by researchers. These conceptual frameworks, however, have not gone without some degree of criticism. At the center of this controversy is the argument that "one-model-fits-all" is the underlying assumption among such research endeavors. Further, it is argued that these models were first used to examine the specific behavior of a very homogenous group—white males—and that constructs within those models are not appropriate for other racial/ethnic groups. Along this same line of reasoning is the notion that findings from studies where students with very unique characteristics are used cannot possibly provide a "generalizable" model for all students. These arguments, while giving the impression that they are distinct, have a high degree of overlap and deserve a more in-depth examination into the nature of the assumptions and assertions made.

If it is assumed that the meaning of certain constructs may represent different conceptualizations to different groups, it is also appropriate to assume that these conceptualizations are not generalizable to all student populations. As an example of the first part of this argument, it has been argued that the notion of "social integration" cannot be used to examine withdrawal behavior among minority students, for it is believed that such behavior would mean the acquiescence of cultural differences by minorities (Tierney, 1992). Suffice it to say that the counter-argument focuses on the nature of the social integration of different student populations with very different cultural backgrounds and that the issue is more methodological than conceptual, as is the implementation of interventions based on such research. The manner in which social integration is measured should be different for different subgroups and interventions should focus on those differences. However, to assume that the construct is either inappropriate for minorities or totally lacking is simply not true.

Let us return to the argument that these models are not applicable to all students. If we assume that all models have used the exact same measurements for the various constructs in their underlying frameworks (and a very erroneous assumption to make), when they have repeatedly been validated for different students at different institutions with different characteristics is very telling. Were these models inappropriate for different subgroups in different settings, how does one explain the consistency with which these frameworks have been validated? Perhaps it is a lack of understanding that the results of these studies, while revealing differences in the strength and direction of similar factors, serve to attest to the validity of the use of similar theoretical conceptualizations among different student populations.

Moreover, the question of the generalizability of most persistence studies has also lead to the conventional, and somewhat misguided, view that the only way to determine what factors affect the underrepresentation of minorities in degree attainment, the high levels of attrition rates, and the lack of adjustment to college is by examining huge databases. How else can any generalizabilities be made to minorities if the findings do not come from an analysis of a larger student population? However, a major problem associated with most national databases is a total conceptual dependency on proxy variables that do not sufficiently capture the important underpinnings of persistence models, consequently lacking in rigor. For example, these larger data sets do not incorporate attitudinal or psychosocial factors in considering the impact of high school factors on subsequent collegiate experiences, achievement, and persistence and are very simplistic in nature.

The Question of Generalizability:
A Distinction between *Outputs* v. *Outcomes*

In examining the links among K–12 experiences, college performance and "success" through the evaluation of collaborative efforts and interventions, it is important to establish the distinction between merely identifying and profiling indicators of student progress and a true outcomes assessment. According to Shadish, Cook, and Leviton (1991), evaluation theory has evolved to reflect accumulating practical experience. Rather than rely exclusively on studying outcomes, there is now concern with examining the quality of program implementation and causal processes that mediate program impacts (Shadish et al., 1991). Exclusive reliance on outcomes and outputs has yielded to more productive and informative quantitative and qualitative assessment that focuses on process (the links between the different aspects of programming and specific outcomes). The overreliance on program outcomes has lead to the misconception that current models of student adjustment and achievement are not applicable to students in general. The confusion comes in the perception that the use of performance indicators truly reflect or capture programmatic efforts or interventions. A simple view that focuses only on outcomes, however, does not uncover the underlying processes incorporated in student attitudes and behaviors. The interplay among these important factors that leads to specific outcomes cannot be revealed through the examination of large databases that profile outputs more than they capture the nature of student ways of thinking and behaving.

Assessing K–12/University Partnerships

The assessment of many reform initiatives that examine factors throughout the K–16 educational system requires program monitoring and data collection designed to provide an evaluation of the effectiveness of those efforts. In addition to establishing performance indicators of the overall progress of students at different levels, two other phases of assessment should be conducted on all collaboratives. One phase should consist of the *assessment of systemic reform* initiated by the partnership between schools and postsecondary institutions. The second phase should consist of the *assessment of interventions/ practices/policies* on specific outcomes at different sites and local levels.

Teachers, administrators, parents, and students should be involved in all aspects of assessment. Moreover, different stakeholders should be consulted to provide appropriate direction with regard to cultural and racial/ethnic differences among students or any other considerations that must be taken into account in the assessment of different reform-related activities. As previously mentioned, it is the intent of assessment to examine the processes underlying all intervention strategies or efforts in an attempt at linking those features of the intervention that are provided to students with specific outcomes. Isolated outcomes merely provide a baseline by which gains can be estimated. Without examining the *why* or the *how* associated with reform activities, data collection and analysis are not very productive.

Assessments of collaborative efforts, as well as local interventions, should utilize both quantitative and qualitative approaches/techniques. Be it the evaluation of outcomes or processes associated with systemic reform or those associated with the local programs/practices, both areas must be examined qualitatively and quantitatively. It is important to note that process does not refer to outputs. That is, the things that intervention provides (e.g., computer-assisted instruction, curricular reform) are not representative of the underlying mental and behavioral processes that students undergo as they make use of those interventions. It is the behavior, attitudes, perceptions, and cognitive skills that are affected by a specific teaching or mentoring approach and ultimately have an impact on student outcomes. For this reason, in-depth qualitative techniques and sophisticated quantitative methodologies are necessary to capture the link between process and outcomes.

Implications for Practice: Whose Responsibility Is It to Make Sense of Findings?

Over the years the assumption has been made that the final responsibility of converting empirical findings into sensible, pragmatic, and institution-specific interventions rests squarely on the backs of researchers. Part of this argument intuitively makes sense, for whom else but the researcher is familiar and knowledgeable of what all those quantitative parameters mean? However, even if a researcher engages in the identification and testing of factors as predictors of various outcomes at a specific institution, the burden of providing a definitive plan of action for immediate student "success" should involve both the researcher and those administrators, practitioners, faculty, and staff who are necessary to link what the data is indicating to the most appropriate action to be taken on that specific campus. The notion that along with the presentation of findings researchers must provide a "blueprint" of what is necessary to address all problems on a campus is simply asking too much.

The Relationship Between High School and Collegiate Experiences and Their Subsequent Impact on College Outcomes

A considerable amount of evidence indicates that if first-year students become involved in one or another aspects of their new college communities, that is, if the transition from high school to college can be negotiated successfully, the likelihood of persistence is significantly increased (Pascarella & Terenzini, 1991). Significant involvement and satisfaction with relationships have been found to predict persistence (Padilla, Trevino, & Gonzalez, 1998). Yet, not all students become involved (Astin, 1984) or feel that they are part of a social or learning community within a university setting (Tinto, 1998; Cabrera, Nora, Pascarella, Terenzini, & Hagedorn, 1999; Nora, Cabrera, Hagedorn, & Pascarella, 1999). While persistence and retention literature has grown dramatically in the last twenty years, the complexity of the process remains to be fully developed. The graduation rate for first-time, full-time, first-year students measured over a six-year period continues to be less than 40 percent (College Board, 1999). Nationally, less than 20 percent of the total population hold a Bachelor's degree or higher (Chronicle of Higher Education, 1999). An additional 25 percent enter higher education but never complete degrees (Chronicle of Higher Education, 1999). Nearly 50 percent of these students drop out during their first year. Before researchers and practitioners conclude that the issue of retention is no longer as salient as in years past, these dropout and graduation rates must reflect the perception that enough has been investigated in the area to influence practice.

Further research is still needed to uncover even more of what shapes the involvement and attitudes that so dramatically influence a student's decision to quit attending college. One area so desperately overlooked in the persistence literature is the impact of a student's psychosocial factors developed during his or her pre-college years. Perhaps these factors have been slighted because of the misinterpretation of what is considered the need for a disengagement from past communities before a student can truly become academically and socially integrated into his or her new environment (Tinto, 1987, 1993; Nora & Cabrera, 1996; Cabrera, Nora, Pascarella, Terenzini, & Hagedorn, 1999). More recent research (Nora & Lang, 2000), however, has begun to examine what personal, background, and other pre-college experiences and attitudes of students are related to their involvement and social integration during their first year in college and what should be appropriate measures for those constructs. The remainder of this chapter will focus on this study that identified and defined scales that capture the psychosocial constructs of pre-college first-year students and explored their relationships within current persistence models. The intent of this discussion is to begin to explore the links between high school experiences/activities/behavior and subsequent integration and adjustment in college as is often reflected in K–12/ university partnership programs and to examine the implications for practice.

Persistence models have often included the notion that pre-college academic ability has a direct influence on college academic achievement and, therefore, indirectly on persistence decisions (Nora, Castaneda, & Cabrera, 1992; Nora & Cabrera, 1996; Pascarella & Terenzini, 1980). Studies have also included extrinsic pre-college characteristics or factors such as work experience and family educational level that students bring with them to college, which have also been found to be influential in determining the likelihood of persisting to the second year in college (Nora, Cabrera, Hagedorn, & Pascarella, 1996). Many of the models include pre-college academic abilities and demographic variables; however, few encompass a wide range of pre-college psychosocial constructs such as self-efficacy, anticipatory attitudes, intimacy motivation, introversion, extroversion, leadership, involvement, friendship support, parental support, and explanatory styles. These attributes provide a much better profile of those factors developed during a student's formative years that also play a much greater role on a student's persistence process.

Researchers have relied on Tinto's (1975, 1987, 1993) *Student Integration Model* and others (Bean, 1983, 1985; Pascarella & Terenzini, 1985) as platforms to replicate and test persistence theory. Although with some mixed results, under given constraints these models have been validated and demonstrate predictive value (Pascarella & Terenzini, 1983, 1991). More recently, Nora and associates (1996, 1999) developed a more comprehensive *Student Adjustment Model* that conceptually and methodologically increases understanding of the persistence process. All of these persistence theories have incorporated pre-college academic and background variables as well as constructs that convey the significant impact of a student's socialization to the campus in the persistence process, yet none of the models explore the pre-college or high school psychosocial factors that might affect a student's ability to become involved and ultimately persist in college.

Upon closer examination of the literature (e.g., Bandura, 1977, 1982; Christie & Dinham, 1991; Jones & Carpenter, 1986; McAdams & Vailant, 1982; Nora & Cabrera, 1996; Paul & Kelleher, 1995; Seligman, 1970; Tomlinson-Clarke & Clarke, 1994), several psychosocial constructs can be identified that are believed to shape a student's attitudes, perceptions, and behavior not only during his or her high school years but are also believed to carry over to their postsecondary experiences and have an impact on academic and social experiences in college.

Bandura's (1977, p. 193) view of self-efficacy as the belief that one can successfully carry out a behavior that is required to produce a specific outcome is believed to be applicable within the persistence process. For high school students who have made a decision to attend college, it is also believed that they develop different anticipatory levels of confidence or efficacy related to their expectations of future academic and social experiences. Coupled with this view is the assumption that pride in their past successes would further support their confidence in their future successes.

As with Bandura's (1977) premise, Christie and Dinham (1991) posit that an individual's anticipation of a new environmental setting can affect the coping strategies that they choose to employ upon encountering that environment. An individual will either assess a new situation as a challenge while another individual will evaluate the new situation as a threat, converting those assessments into positive or negative expectations. In the Nora and Lang (2000) study, it was believed that the anticipatory attitudes of entering first-year students would outline the coping strategies that they utilize in their new college settings.

The notion put forward was that a belief in one's ability to perform well in anticipated circumstances (or environments) was grounded in past behavior and attitudes. As with former expectations (or anticipatory attitudes), an individual's preferences at a prior point in time may be just as influential in determining one's current behavior and decision making. McAdams and Vailant (1982) make reference to an individual's desire for intimacy, which they referred to as "Intimacy Motivation." An individual's personality was conceptualized as a recurrent preference for warm, close relationships with others. It was believed that this psychosocial factor developed prior to college attendance would bear not only on a student's social involvements in a postsecondary setting but would also color a student's decision to withdraw from or remain in college.

Another high school, psychosocial attribute believed to exert an influence during a student's first year in college was introversion. Although intervallic introversion was to be expected of individuals and considered as normal, Jones and Carpenter (1986) found that shyness could be converted into a chronic difficulty that limits full, satisfying relationships. Nora and Lang (2000) believed that a student's shyness could be captured as a sense of interpersonal limitations, a diminished self-esteem in comparison to other students, perceived limited social skills, and a history of few intimate relationships. All of these aspects of shyness were hypothesized to limit the academic and social experiences of students and ultimately to influence a student's withdrawal decision in college.

Involvement in the social scene in college has been repeatedly found to be related to increased persistence and achievement (Pascarella & Terenzini,

1991; Nora & Cabrera, 1996; Cabrera, Nora, Hagedorn, & Pascarella, 1999; Nora, Cabrera, Pascarella, Terenzini, & Hagedorn, 1996). An extension in this line of thought is the assumption that students who have held high school leadership roles or who have been involved in civic activities during their high school years are better prepared to engage their social environment during their college years, specifically during their first year when all surroundings and situations are new (Tomlinson-Clarke & Clarke, 1994).

Seligman (1970) makes note of an individual's instinctive nature to explain events in specific patterns, particularly those that are perceived as negative experiences. These explanatory styles that individuals possess are composed of multiple dimensions. Individuals perceive actions taken by one or others as either being internally or externally motivated. Consequences triggered by specific actions are perceived as brought on by behavior initiated by one or caused by circumstances not under one's control. Seligman also proposes that events in one's life can be viewed as being global or specific in nature, and as being either unstable or stable. It was believed that the first dimension, internal versus external viewpoint, could be used to capture the degree to which a student attributed outcomes to something or someone else during his pre-college schooling. The authors hypothesized that the student's view of outcomes as either internal or external developed prior to attending college would also exert an influence on a student's integration and subsequently on his or her decision to drop out of college.

All of these pre-college facets were hypothesized to be related to integration and persistence during the initial college transition period. Nora and Lang (2000) based their conceptual framework on Nora's (2000) comprehensive model as a theoretical framework with the reconceptualization of pre-college factors.

Evidence of the Relationships Between High School and College Behavior: A Case for Engaging in Collaborative Initiatives

Educators should not be totally surprised by the finding that skills and attitudes developed prior to enrollment in higher education have an impact on a student's transition to a college environment and a student's decision to remain enrolled in college or drop out. Previous studies (e.g., Pascarella & Terenzini, 1985; Nora & Cabrera, 1996; Cabrera, Nora, Pascarella, Terenzini, & Hagedorn, 1999) that incorporated pre-college factors as conceptualized by persistence theories and found limited influences on a student's academic and social adjustment and on his or her reenrollment may have misspecified the conceptualization of those pre-college factors. This oversight, coupled with the results of recent studies (Cabrera, Nora, Pascarella, Terenzini, & Hagedorn, 1999; Nora & Cabrera, 1996) that establish the importance of parental support systems and past communities, makes it necessary to revisit the role of high school psychosocial factors within the persistence process and establish the need for educational partnerships (see Jun & Colyar, chapter 9). Development of appropriate intervention and support systems informed by the results may help to nurture students successfully through their first year in college and foster the skills necessary to become involved in the college process and persist to completion.

The results revealed four major areas for intervention by higher education institutions: mentoring services, faculty and staff development, student activities/residence hall programming, and counseling initiatives. Mentoring programs, staffed by both students and faculty, should develop strategies that focus on successfully engaging the student in positive academic experiences, alleviating fears that students might have with regard to their ability to succeed during their first year, and providing realistic feedback to students so that they can make informed decisions. Coupled with these strategies are efforts by the institution to provide an early systematic approach at identifying students who are in need of counseling, either personal or academic. Anticipatory fears, unrealistic self-expectations, and alienation are very real to students and a sense of isolation or not belonging has been found to affect persistence negatively (Cabrera & Nora, 1994; Nora & Cabrera, 1996). Counseling initiatives at both the secondary and postsecondary levels must be carefully planned so that they not only address these issues but also allow early identification of those needing the service.

Faculty sensitivity and awareness of the negative impact of some psychosocial factors could be raised through faculty and staff development. That is not to say that faculty must assume the role of counselors. Rather, the intent of this professional development is to heighten the faculty's awareness of the validation of students in the classroom (Rendon, 1994), to enhance the degree and nature of their interaction with students, and to participate in the overall mentoring experience of students. Faculty participation in orientation programs and in social activities designed to bring faculty and students together is highly suggested. Collaborative learning experiences in the classroom have been found to enhance the interchange of values and attitudes among students and to affect the academic achievement of some students (Cabrera, Nora, Bernal, Butts, Terenzini, & Pascarella, 1998). Among those conversations and discussions engaged by students in those specific types of learning communities is the possibility of a student processing anticipatory issues as well as issues related to self-efficacy.

As part of institutional responsibilities (of middle schools, high schools, and colleges) to also focus on these psychosocial factors, encouragement of active participation in student activities through a wide array of social activities and student governance structures will not only provide the means by which students can engage in leadership roles but where social interaction among peers is an expected outcome. In this manner, issues related to shyness, fear of failure, and intimacy may be dispelled or, at a minimum, drawn out for discussion. Moreover, institutional efforts should attempt to provide a systematic approach at involving parents in different activities. The vast majority of the research on persistence has established the influence of parental support prior to the students enrolling in college (e.g., Nora & Cabrera, 1996; Nora, Rendon, & Cuadraz, 1999; Cabrera, Nora, & Castaneda, 1993; Rendon, 1994; Nora, 1987; Nora, 1993).

Additional initiatives by higher education institutions might include building better bridges between secondary and postsecondary education systems. Both higher education and secondary administrators and counselors could play a key role in nurturing the psychosocial factors that facilitate student success at higher levels.

Concluding Remarks

There are those who might believe that there has been a saturation of interventions and initiatives (everything from local efforts to federally funded programs), that there is no further need for additional projects or studies associated with those labors, that we have learned as much as we need to know about partnerships, and that all we need to do is identify best practices across the country. While it is true that much is to be found in the literature focusing on collaboratives, systemic reform, and academic achievement, dropout rates continue to haunt administrators and educators at all levels of the educational pipeline. Some increases in persistence rates have been identified across the country and sometimes among different units at a single institution. The truth is that there remains much more to be uncovered. Whether it is to be found in classroom activities, in instructional approaches, in the academic and social engagement of the student, in systemic reform, in the area of pre-college psychosocial factors, or even in K–16 initiatives, research must address the question of why students forego their educational hopes and desires.

References

Astin, A. (1984). Student involvement: A developmental theory for higher education. *Journal of College Student Personnel, 25,* 297–308.

Bandura, A. (1977). Self-efficacy: Toward a unifying theory of behavior change. *Psychology Review, 84,* 191–215.

Bandura, A. (1982). Self-efficacy mechanism in human agency. *American Psychologist, 37,* 122–147.

Bean, J. P. (1983). The application of a model of turnover in work organizations to the student attrition process. *Research in Higher Education, 6* (2), 129–148.

Bean, J. P. (1985). Interaction effects based on class level in an exploratory model of college student dropout syndrome. *American Education Research Journal, 22* (1), 35–64.

Cabrera, A. F., & Nora, A. (1994). College students' perceptions of prejudice and discrimination and their feelings of alienation. *Review of Education, Pedagogy, and Cultural Studies, 16,* 387–409.

Cabrera, A. F., Nora, A., Bernal, E. M., Butts, L., Terenzini, P. T., & Pascarella, E. T. (1998, November). *Collaborative learning: Preferences, gains in cognitive and affective outcomes, and openness to diversity among college students.* Paper presented at the annual meeting of the Association for the Study of Higher Education.

Cabrera, A. F., Nora, A., & Castaneda, M. B. (1993). College persistence: Structural equations modeling test of an integrated model of student retention. *Journal of Higher Education, 64* (2), 123–139.

Cabrera, A. F., Nora, A., Terenzini, P. T., Pascarella, E. T., & Hagedorn, L. S. (1999). Campus racial climate and the adjustment of students to college: A comparison between White students and African American students. *Journal of Higher Education, 70* (2), 134–160.

College Board. (1999). *Reaching the Top.* New York: The College Board. The Chronicle of Higher Education. (1999). *1999–2000 Almanac Issue, SLV.*

Christie, N., & Dinham, S. (1991). Institutional and external influences on social integration in the freshman year. *Journal of Higher Education, 62* (4), 412–436.

Jones, W., & Carpenter, B. (1986). Shyness, social behavior, and relationships. In W. Jones, J. Cheek, & S. Briggs (Eds.), *Shyness: Perspectives on research and treatment* (pp. 227–228). New York: Plenium.

McAdams, D. P., & Vailant, G. E. (1982). Intimacy motivation and psychosocial adjustment: A longitudinal study. *Journal of Personality, 46,* 586–593.

Nora, A. (1987). Determinants of retention among Chicano college students: A structural model. *Research in Higher Education, 26,* 31–51.

Nora, A., & Cabrera, A. F. (1993). The construct validity of institutional commitment: A confirmatory factor analysis. *Research in Higher Education, 34,* 243–263.

Nora, A., & Cabrera, A. F. (1996). The role of perceptions of prejudice and discrimination on the adjustment of minority students to college. *Journal of Higher Education, 76* (2), 119–148.

Nora, A., & Lang, D. (1999, November). *The impact of psychosocial factors on the achievement, academic and social adjustment, and persistence of college students.* Paper presented at the annual meeting of the Association for the Study of Higher Education. San Antonio, TX.

Nora, A., Castaneda, M. B., & Cabrera, A. F. (1992, November). *Student persistence: The testing of a comprehensive structural model of retention.* Paper presented at the annual conference of the Association for the Study of Higher Education. Minneapolis, MN.

Nora, A., Cabrera, A. F., Hagedorn, L. S., & Pascarella, E. T. (1996). Differential impacts of academic and social experiences on college-related behavioral outcomes across different ethnic and gender groups at four-year institutions. *Research in Higher Education, 37* (4), 427–451.

Nora, A., Rendon, L. I., & Cuadraz, G. (1999). Access, choice, and outcomes: A profile of Hispanic students in higher education. In A. Taskakkori & S.H. Ochoa (Eds.), *Readings on Equal Education, Education of Hispanics in the United Sates: Politics, Policies, and Outcomes, 16,* 175–200.

Padilla, R. V., Trevino, J., & Gonzalez, I. (1997). Developing local models of minority student success in college. *Journal of College Student Development, 38,* 125–135.

Pascarella, E. T., & Terenzini, P. T. (1980). Predicting freshman persistence and voluntary dropout decisions from a theoretical model. *Journal of Higher Education, 51* (1), 60–75.

Pascarella, E. T., & Terenzini, P. T. (1991). *How college affects students: Findings and insights from twenty years of research.* San Francisco: Jossey-Bass Publishers.

Pascarella, E. T., & Terenzini, P. T. (1983). Predicting voluntary freshman year persistence/withdrawal behavior in a residential university: A path analytic validation of Tinto's model. *Journal of Educational Psychology, 75* (2), 215–226.

Paul, E. L., & Kelleher, M. (1995). Precollege concerns about losing and making friends in college: Implications for friendship satisfaction and self-esteem during the college transition. *Journal of College Student Development, 36 (6),* 513–521.

Rendon, L. I. (1994). Validating culturally diverse students: Toward a new model of learning and student development. *Innovative Higher Education, 19* (1), 23–32.

Seligman, M. E. P. (1970). On the generality of the laws of learning. *Psychological Review, 77,* 406–418.

Shadish, W. R., Cook, D. T., & Leviton, L. C. (1991, December). *Foundation of program evaluation.* Thousand Oaks, CA: Sage Publications.

Tierney, W. (1992). An anthropological analysis of student participation in college. *Journal of Higher Education, 63* (6), 603–618.

Tinto, V. (1987). *Leaving college: Rethinking the causes and cures of student attrition.* Chicago: The University of Chicago Press.

Tinto, V. (1993). *Leaving college: Rethinking the causes and cures of student attrition* (2nd ed.). Chicago: The University of Chicago Press.

Tinto, V. (1998). Colleges as communities: Taking research on student persistence seriously. *The Review of Higher Education, 21* (2), 167–177.

Tomlinson-Clarke, S., & Clarke, D. (1994). Predicting social adjustment and academic achievement for college women with and without precollege leadership. *Journal of College Student Development, 35* (2), 120–124.

PART II

The Real World of College Preparation Programs

CHAPTER 4

Meeting Common Goals

Linking K–12 and College Interventions

PATRICIA GÁNDARA

For the last several decades there has been widespread consensus that something is wrong with the pipeline that leads to and through higher education for minority students. Nationwide, 93.6 percent of caucasian students in the 25–29-year-old category had received a high school diploma or GED certificate in 1998. However, this figure was only 88.2 percent for African Americans, and 62.8 percent for Latinos. In spite of the discrepancies among ethnic groups, this represents considerable progress over a period of three decades. In 1971, 81.7 percent of Whites held a diploma or GED, but only 58.8 percent of Blacks and 48.3 percent of Latinos had achieved this educational goal. (See Table 4.1.)

College attendance has increased dramatically over the last three decades as well—from 6.9 million students in 1967 to 14.3 million in 1997 (NCES, 1999). Nonetheless, the gaps in access to higher education among students of different racial/ethnic and socioeconomic groups are large. African American, Latino, and Native American students begin school behind their White and Asian classmates, and this gap continues to grow throughout their years of schooling (NCES, 2000a; 2000b), resulting in relatively small percentages of Blacks, Latinos, and Native Americans going on to four-year colleges, and fewer still represented among college graduates. For example, African Americans were only 11 percent of all college students in 1997–1998 while they comprised 14.3 percent of the college-age population, and Latinos held only 8.6 percent of the seats in higher education institutions, although they comprised a similar percentage (14.4) of the college-age population. Moreover, students who go directly to four-year colleges are significantly more likely to complete their degrees than those who matriculate into two-year colleges initially (Rendon & Garza, 1996).

TABLE 4.1
Percent 25–29-year-olds Completing High School or GED by Ethnicity, 1971 and 1998

Ethnic Group	1971	1998
White	81.7	93.6
Black	58.8	88.2
Latino	48.3	62.8

Source: National Center for Education Statistics, 2000

TABLE 4.2
College Enrollment by Ethnicity, 1997–1998

	Percent of 18–24-year-olds	Percent of total college enrollment	Percent of 2-year college enrollment	Percent of 4-year college enrollment
White	66.3	73.2	68.2	76.3
Black	14.3	11.0	11.8	10.5
Hispanic*	14.4	8.6	12.5	6.2
Asian	3.9	6.1	6.2	6.1
Native Am	1.0	.9	1.3	.8

* Includes Hispanics of all racial groups
Source: National Center for Education Statistics, U.S. Bureau of the Census, Population Tables

However, Latino students, in particular, are much more likely to attend two-year colleges than other groups. (See Table 4.2.)

College enrollment rates also vary by family income and parents' level of education. Among high-income students, 77 percent enroll in four-year college or university within two years of graduation, compared with only 33 percent low-income students. Likewise, 71 percent of students whose parents are college graduates enroll in a four-year college or university, compared with only 26 percent of students whose parents have no more than a high school diploma (Perna & Swail, 1998). Only 17.9 percent of African Americans and 16.5 percent of Latinos had obtained a Bachelor of Arts degree in 1998, compared to 34.5 percent of White individuals (NCES, 1999). Thus, while both African Americans and Latinos have been closing the enormous gap that divided them from Whites with respect to high school completion three decades earlier, White students are still twice as likely to complete a college degree as either Blacks or Latinos. This very large difference in academic attainment spells significant differences in lifetime opportunity and well-being.

In a study of the costs and benefits of closing the education gap for minorities, Vernez (1999) found that the *public benefit* gained from increased education outweighs its costs in all cases. For example, if Blacks and Latinos were educated at the same level as Whites, every additional dollar spent on

TABLE 4.3
Median Annual Household Income, by Educational Attainment of the Householder, 1998

Ninth Grade	$15,541
H.S. Diploma	19,851
H.S. Graduate	33,779
Some college	40,015
A.A. Degree	45,258
Bachelors Degree	59,048
Masters Degree	68,115
Doctoral Degree	87,232
Professional Degree	92,228

Source: The College Board, 1999

education would save the state about $1.90. About one-third of this savings would come from public expenditures and two-thirds from increased taxes on earnings. When *societal benefits* are computed—public benefits plus the increased disposable income that accrues to individuals—benefits increase to more than $4 for every dollar spent on education (Vernez, 1999). This is consistent with national data that show the increase in income for individuals by education in 1998. Each level of increased education confers substantial additional income benefits.

As important as it is to have a strong economy, there are other compelling reasons to increase minority access to higher education. Beyond the pecuniary benefits of a college education are numerous social benefits to increasing the education levels of underrepresented groups. Persons with higher levels of education enjoy better health and longer lives (Perna & Swail, 1998), are more likely to attend cultural arts activities, to vote, and to provide leadership in their communities (Mortensen, 1997).

Diversity within educational settings has also been shown to confer cognitive advantages on those students schooled in such settings, especially when this occurs in late adolescence. Thus, not only do underrepresented students obtain benefit from access to higher education, but their nonminority classmates can be expected to benefit cognitively as well. For example, Gurin (1999) examined multi-institutional national data, an extensive survey of students at the University of Michigan, and data drawn from a specific program at the University of Michigan. Based on these analyses, she concluded that

interaction with peers from diverse racial backgrounds, both in the classroom and informally, is positively associated with a host of . . . learning outcomes. Students who experienced the most racial and ethnic diversity in classroom settings and in informal interactions with peers showed the greatest engagement in active thinking processes, growth in intellectual engagement and motivation, and growth in intellectual and academic skills.

Notwithstanding the very large benefits associated with closing the education gap among ethnic groups, there is currently a highly polarized national debate about the legitimacy of using race, ethnicity, or gender as factors for consideration in higher education admissions, special programs, or financial aid. In 1994, the U.S. Fourth Circuit Court of Appeals decided in *Podberesky v. Kirwan* that the University of Maryland's Banneker Scholarship for African-Americans was unconstitutional because race was the sole determinant of eligibility. In the same year, the regents of the University of California passed SP-1 and SP-2, two provisions that prohibited the use of race, ethnicity, or gender in hiring, contracting, or college admissions decisions within the university. In 1996, California voters followed suit with Proposition 209, led by one of the UC regents, and outlawed the consideration of race, ethnicity, or gender for admissions, contracting, or hiring decisions throughout the state. In 1997, the Fifth Circuit Court of Appeals ruled in favor of Cheryl Hopwood who had been denied admission to the University of Texas law school. She argued that she was discriminated against because minority applicants who were less qualified than she was had been accepted for admission to the law school. The Court's decision was interpreted by the attorney general of Texas as outlawing the use of race or ethnicity as a factor in admission, financial aid, and retention and recruitment programs in all institutions of higher education within the fifth circuit. Most recently, the state of Washington followed the example of California and passed Initiative 200 barring the consideration of race or ethnicity in college admissions decisions within that state, and similar efforts are underway in other parts of the country. The data suggest that the impact of these events on college-going for minority youth has been considerable.

Restrictions on the use of affirmative action in public institutions have seriously exacerbated the problem of unequal access to higher education in recent years. In 1998, the year after Proposition 209 took effect, 53 percent fewer Latinos and 66 percent fewer African Americans were admitted to the entering freshman class at UC Berkeley, and 33 percent fewer Latinos and 43 percent fewer Blacks were admitted to UCLA. Prior to the passage of Proposition 209, the two flagship campuses of the UC system had the highest percentages of underrepresented students of all the UC campuses. Similarly, the Fall 1997 entering freshman class at the University of Texas, following on the Hopwood decision, included 12 percent fewer African Americans, and 10 percent fewer Latinos, and the law school enrolled only 52 percent of the prior year's proportion of Latinos and 19 percent of African Americans (Chapa, 1997). While the University of Texas undergraduate admissions have returned to pre-Hopwood levels in Texas (Walker, 1999), and University of California schools have begun to recover to pre-1998 levels, discrepancies among ethnic groups remain huge, and the tools to address the problem have been severely limited.

Early Intervention as a Response

Given the declining numbers of underrepresented students who are eligible for admission to some of the nation's most selective public universities, and the continuing challenges to affirmative action practices, many educators and policy makers are placing increased hopes on the potential for early intervention programs to address this crisis. For example, the University of California claims to be spending $250 million annually in outreach-associated efforts to attract, prepare, and retain underrepresented students to its campuses. Texas has also undertaken a large outreach initiative that includes extensive support services on each campus to retain students enrolled under the ten percent plan. Many other states have already launched comprehensive programs to prepare students, especially low-income and minority students, to go on to college, and across the nation there are thousands (Perna & Swail, 1998) of programs dedicated to this task. However, in spite of the scale of these activities, data are generally sparse, and for most, it is difficult to know if they work, or for whom, and under what circumstances. Nonetheless, they represent a significant beacon of hope for many young people, and it is therefore critical that we have a much better understanding of how these programs can work to increase the representation of low income and minority youth in higher education. This chapter reviews the strategies that appear to be working in K–12 and in higher education institutions and suggests where the they may be improved to increase the numbers of underrepresented students successfully completing high school and college.

Key Intervention Strategies in K–12

Early intervention, college access, or university outreach programs—all titles that describe these interventions—can be categorized into two major groups. They may fall into the category of student-centered or school-centered. Student-centered programs focus their resources and activity on individual students who are generally admitted to the program through some kind of selection procedure. The intent of the programs is to foster the fortunes of individual students with the hope that they will succeed in high school and go on to college. School-centered programs, on the other hand, focus on changing schools so that the schools are capable of being the primary vehicle of mobility for students. If this strategy is effective, students throughout the school should be benefited, rather than just the select few who are in a program. The great majority of these programs, however, are student-centered, and for very good reasons. School-centered programs require intensive resources to have an impact, and they require time to take hold. Moreover, they require the sustained cooperation of many people in the school. All of these things are in limited supply in most schools, and it is difficult to engage the cooperation of funders for long-term strategies. While student-centered approaches are also more labor-intensive and costly than many would like to acknowledge, there is at least the likelihood that they will produce a few great "stories"—the poor student who goes to an Ivy League college as the result of the program—that will help sustain the morale and the outside funding even in the relatively short term.

Few programs are actually explicit about their theories of action—the relationship between what they do and the kinds of problems they are attempting to ameliorate—nonetheless it is possible to create logical links by matching known impediments to higher education access with the strategies that programs commonly incorporate. Several major impediments to higher academic achievement among underrepresented students have been identified in the literature. The analysis that follows is an attempt to merge the literature on academic impediments with the existing literature on early intervention strategies. The discussion progresses through concentric rings of influence on students—from neighborhoods to schools, to peers, and finally families.

Inequality of Neighborhood Resources

There is considerable debate in the literature about the relative effects of neighborhood type, as distinct from family or peer influence, on student achievement. However, at least two theoretical models help to explain how neighborhoods can affect the development of youth in ways that in turn have an impact on their schooling outcomes. Neighborhood Resource Theory postulates that the quality of local resources available to families (e.g., parks, libraries, child care facilities) affects child developmental outcomes. Because poor children's neighborhoods have fewer of these supportive resources than neighborhoods in which middle class children grow up, researchers conjecture that they receive less exposure to developmentally enriching activities (Brooks-Gunn, Denner & Kebanov, 1995). Of course, even when such resources are available, a family's access to them is still mediated by the skills (cultural capital) of the parents. More educated, well-informed parents are more likely to use whatever resources exist. Thus, methodologically, there are difficulties in separating the effects of neighborhoods from the effects of parenting.

A second theory, Collective Socialization Theory, argues that more affluent neighborhoods generally provide more successful role models and stronger normative support for the kinds of behavior that are associated with school success (Jarret, 1997). Thus, middle income students are more likely to encounter both adults and peers in their communities who are supportive of high educational goals and can even assist young people in achieving them. This theory, like Neighborhood Resource Theory, is also plagued by methodological problems that make it difficult to prove the independent effects of neighborhoods. For example, Darling and Steinberg (1997) note that it is difficult to separate the influence of peers in these neighborhoods from the effects of the neighborhoods themselves. Thus, neighborhood effects can be confounded with peer influence. Nonetheless, Jessor (1993) has argued strongly for the importance of considering the total ecological context in which a child is raised—families, schools, and communities—as influences on development. A recent report by the National Academy of Sciences on the problems of adolescence points out that too much emphasis has been placed on "high risk" youth, and not enough on the high risk settings in which they live and go to school (National Research Council, Panel on High Risk Youth, 1993). Low-income and minority youth are almost certainly handicapped by neighborhoods that simply hold more risks than those in which middle class White students grow up and go to school.

There are two primary ways that programs attempt to address issues of neighborhood resources. Some early intervention and college access programs provide after school and weekend clubs, homework groups, and other activities to strengthen students' academic skills and to keep them safely out of harm's way during nonschool hours. Others that are rooted in the community provide programming related to community experiences that are taken into the schools. The objective is to increase students' pride in their home culture and expose the entire school community to the strengths and assets that exist in the neighborhood. Some programs draw mentors from the neighboring community and also tap community resources to build a cadre of role models accessible to students within their neighborhoods or local communities. However, another way of acknowledging the shortcomings of some low-income communities is to remove the students from them and transfer them into educational settings where high levels of community resources already exist. This strategy can work for some individual students, but it does nothing for the great majority of students in the neighborhood schools.

Inequalities in K–12 Schools

Quality of instructional offerings. The particular school that a student attends can have a significant impact on his or her academic achievement. Schools in more affluent neighborhoods have been shown to provide more rigorous college preparatory and honors courses than schools in lower income communities that largely serve populations of underrepresented students. For example, in a recent study of California schools, Betts, Rueben and Danenberg, (2000) found that the lowest income schools offered only 52 percent of their classes as meeting college preparatory requirements, while this figure rose to 63 percent in the highest income schools. Similar patterns held up when the analysis was done by percent nonwhite in the school.

Likewise, Betts, et al. found that "the median high SES school has over 50 percent more AP courses than the median low-SES school." Based on analyses of high school and beyond data, Adelman (1999) concluded that the rigor of the curriculum to which students are exposed is more predictive of long-term academic outcomes than even the powerful variable of family socioeconomic status. That is, Adelman argues that the greatest amount of the variance in long-term academic outcomes among ethnic groups can be attributed to the differences in the groups' exposure to high level curricula—most particularly to advanced mathematics, and Black and Latino students are least likely to take advanced mathematics courses.

Quality of teachers. Not only are schools in more affluent areas better organized to provide more rigorous curricula, they also tend to have stronger teachers (Haycock, 1998; Ferguson, 1998). However, Haycock (1998) reviews data that show children of color, regardless of their socioeconomic level, are more likely to be taught by teachers with lower test scores and less academic preparation than White children. And the quality of the teacher, measured by certification, quality of institution from which the teacher received his or her degree, and test scores, has been shown in a number of studies to have a significant impact on student performance. Ferguson (1998) reviewed data from Texas in the 1980s and found that teachers with higher scores on the Texas teachers' test were more likely to produce significant gains in student achievement than their lower scoring counterparts. Goldhaber and Brewer (1996), in an analysis of NELS 88 data, showed a positive relationship between teachers' degrees in technical areas (math and science) and students' achievement. Teachers' expectations of children's abilities can also affect their school performance.

Segregation of minority students within and between schools. Racial and ethnic segregation continue to have an impact on school performance for underrepresented students. Inequalities in educational opportunity between segregated White schools and segregated schools with students of color have been well-documented (Orfield & Eaton, 1996) and served as the catalyst for a decades-long experiment with desegregation and busing. That experiment has largely come to an end. Today, both Black and Latino students attend increasingly segregated schools. Latino segregation has been increasing since data were first collected in the 1960s. In 1997, 35.4 percent of Latino students were attending schools that were 90 to 100 percent minority (Orfield & Yun, 1999). And as Orfield (1996) points out:

> Low-income and minority students are concentrated in schools within metropolitan areas that tend to offer different and inferior courses and levels of competition, creating a situation where the most disadvantaged students receive the least effective preparation for college. A fundamental reason is that schools do not provide a fixed high school curriculum taught at a common depth and

pace. The actual working curriculum of a high school is the result of the ability of teachers, the quality of counseling, and enrollment patterns of students.

Not surprisingly, the research suggests that high achieving Black and Latino students tend to come from more desegregated schools than their lower performing peers (Borman, et al., 2000; Gándara, 1995).

Of course, even within nominally desegregated schools, the organization of schooling often operates to resegregate students by ability track within the school. Thus, minority students are much more likely to be found in the vocational and general education tracks that provide weaker curricula and fail to prepare students for the option of going to college than are White or Asian students (Oakes, 1985).

Most early intervention programs offer some kind of academic enrichment designed to make up for the inequalities in the schools. Many programs provide extensive academic coursework before and after school, on weekends, and in the summer, to augment the public school curriculum. Others provide tutors to help students improve their achievement in regular classes. However, only one program that we (Gándara & Bial, in press) identified specifically targeted the educational system across segments to help strengthen all students' academic experience. This program fundamentally altered the existing curriculum in the schools, though its focus did not extend into the high schools where tracking continues to be a problem (Opuni, 1999).

Poor counseling. High school counseling represents both a problem of quantity and quality. Over the last couple of decades as school budgets have been stretched thin, particularly in some high growth states like California, school counselors have been the target of budget cuts. For example, the average high school counselor in California serves almost 850 students (McDonough, personal communication, 15 May 2000), and an abundance of literature on high school counseling points to the situation that most public school students rarely, if ever, see their counselors, and when they do it is usually for the purpose of routine scheduling of courses (Hutchinson & Reagan, 1989). For low-income and underrepresented students there is the additional problem that many see their counselors not as allies or sources of support, but as gatekeepers who all too often refuse them admission to the courses that would prepare them for college. The bases for these decisions are commonly cited as students having low test scores or being ill-equipped to take on the challenges of more rigorous coursework (Oakes, 1985; Romo & Falbo, 1996). Of course, this is a vicious cycle: once tracked into the slower reading group —or lower math group—it is difficult, if not impossible, for low-tracked students to ever compete with their peers who have become proficient in material to which they have never even been exposed.

Most college access programs offer educational and/or personal counseling. While educational preparation has been shown to be a powerful predictor of postsecondary choices (Adelman, 1999), there is also abundant evidence that counselors who track students into low level courses are responsible, in large part, for the kinds of curriculum to which students are exposed and therefore the kind of preparation that they receive (McDonough, 1997). Hence, to break the back of the underpreparation problem, the kind of counseling that underrepresented students receive is a key site for improved practice. One California consortium[1] introduced a unique approach to comprehensive college counseling. Through its Passport to Education program, the program began the college counseling process at grade four and continued meeting with students at intervals to document their progress on the pathway to college. Each time a benchmark is achieved, the student receives a stamp in his or her passport. In this way students are constantly reminded of the requirements for college, and that others are holding out that expectation for them.

Low expectations and aspirations. While ethnic minority parents may have high aspirations for their children's educational attainment, research also shows that these aspirations are moderated by more realistic expectations of what their children are likely to achieve (Henderson, 1997). Other research also has shown that high school students' postsecondary aspirations are not very good predictors of eventual attainment, but their expectations are indeed good predictors of where they will end up after high school (Adelman, 1999). It appears that both parents and students wish for particular academic outcomes, but that these wishes are tempered by a realistic assessment of the constraints imposed by their educational situation. One important constraint on aspirations is the way in which teachers respond to ethnic minority students.

Teachers can be very effective in sending nonverbal messages to students about the amount of confidence they have in their abilities. For example, not only do teachers call on favorite students more often, research has shown that they wait longer for an answer from a student they believe knows the answer than from one in whom the teacher has little confidence. With the latter, the teacher is more likely to provide the correct answer, or move quickly on to another student (Brophy & Good, 1974). Students have also been shown to be very sensitive to these subtle teacher behaviors and to "read" their teachers' attitudes quite accurately (Weinstein, 1989). In a series of studies conducted by the psychologist Robert Rosenthal, teachers' attitudes toward their students were shown to have a substantial impact on their academic performance. Thus, Sprinthall, Sprinthall & Oja (1998) conclude, "the Rosenthal effect is three-fold: (1) Pupils who are expected to do well tend to show gains; (2) pupils who are not expected to do well tend to do less well than the first group; and (3) pupils who make gains despite expectations to the contrary are regarded negatively by the teacher." In this way, students' assessments of their own abilities can be moderated by teachers' attitudes and beliefs. Unfortunately, teachers are more likely to assess middle class and nonminority students as having higher ability than their low-income and minority peers (Baron, Tom, & Cooper, 1985).

Many programs incorporate activities designed to strengthen students' self-concepts and to raise their aspirations. Some offer regular, motivational speakers, often from the communities from which the students come, who act as role models and provide encouragement to students that they, too, can make it to college and beyond.

Lack of Peer Support

Adolescent peer groups are commonly portrayed as having a negative influence on the values and behavior of youth. Drug and alcohol use, gang membership, and a culture of underachievement are popularly viewed as risks that are associated with peer influence, and with good reason since such risky behaviors have been shown to occur in peer clusters (Henderson, 1997). Peers can, however, also have a positive influence on one another. They can support academic goals and serve as important sources of information for upward mobility (Stanton-Salazar, 1997). For example, Steinberg (1996) presented survey data that showed that Asian peers are more supportive of academic achievement than other groups. Of course, students who hang out with low-performing friends tend to perform at lower levels as well, and those whose friends are dropouts are at higher risk for dropping out themselves (Epstein & Karweit, 1983). Among ethnic minority students from underrepresented groups, however, the issue of academic achievement can be complex.

Steinberg (1996) reports that one in five adolescents says that his or her friends make fun of students who do well in school, and this is particularly true for Black and Hispanic students. Many African American and Latino students who aspire to high achievement report the problem of being accused of "acting White" (Fordham & Ogbu, 1986) and thus being shunned by their lower-performing peers who may be the arbiters of social acceptability in their schools. Because adolescents are confronting the difficult (and self-absorbing) task of establishing a personal identity and forging a place within their social order, peer acceptance is exceptionally important for the healthy development of most adolescents. Thus, it is not difficult to understand why many students succumb to the admonitions of their friends to put aside the schoolbooks and not be a "nerd" or a "schoolboy" or "schoolgirl."

The lack of peer support is consciously countered in some programs that work directly to develop and nurture peer groups from the same backgrounds and communities who mutually support high academic goals. Through joint activities, field trips, and course taking, students come to build supportive friendships; one program we identified built strong peer groups through joint activities and workshops during high school, then sent the group together to college where they support each other during the critical first year away from home (Bowen & Gordon, 1998). These kinds of activities generally fall under the rubric of social integration. Many programs provide some kind of integrating function for students, but most do not attend specifically to their peer groups, and the issues that students face when they choose to excel in a peer culture that is not supportive of academic accomplishment.

Inequalities in Familial Cultural and Social Capital

A number of studies have found that ethnic minority families have uniformly high aspirations for their children (Haro, 1994; Delgado-Gaitán, 1990; Steinberg, 1996). However, not all parents have the skills and resources to help their children realize these aspirations (Lareau, 1987; Steinberg, 1996). Low income and minority parents often lack the *cultural capital*—knowledge of how the system works—and *social capital*—access to important social networks—that play such an important role for middle class White and Asian parents in supporting their children's academic achievement. These concepts are elucidated extensively in the chapters by Yonezawa et al., Hagedorn & Fogel, and Jun & Colyar in this volume.

Cultural capital also takes the form of knowing how to manage public resources, like school curricula, to the advantage of one's children. Lareau (1987) demonstrated how middle-class parents effectively "managed" the school system and its resources through active engagement with school staff to afford the best opportunities for their children, while low-income parents tended to refrain from interactions with teachers and school administrators, accepting the school's decisions at face value. In another study of middle class cultural capital, Useem (1992) showed how well-educated parents, keenly aware of the implications of taking algebra versus basic math in junior high school, actively intervened when they disagreed with their children's placement. In contrast, parents with lower levels of education were largely unaware of the implications of being tracked into a low math course and tended to trust the school personnel's decisions. Even among middle class parents from underrepresented communities of color, cultural capital may be in short supply. Often these families represent the first generation in the middle class and they do not have these middle class experiences in their own backgrounds to draw upon and replicate for their children (Miller, 1995). Attitudes, tastes, and dispositions develop over generations and result from exposure to particular cultural experiences that are unique to class categories (DiMaggio, 1982).

Research has also converged on a particular parenting style that appears to be associated with the majority culture and a middle class orientation. Parents who are classified as *authoritative*—firm in their expectations yet warm in their relationships with their children, and who provide significant autonomy for their progeny—are most likely to have children who do well in school (Baumrind, 1989; Steinberg, 1996). Yet many African Americans and Latinos are accustomed to parenting in a more traditional, authoritarian style that has been adaptive to their own sociocultural circumstances; higher risk urban environments may call for a different parenting style than lower risk suburban neighborhoods (Clark, 1983; Gándara, 1995). Authoritarian parenting, however, may not prepare these students as effectively to compete in the classroom with their European American peers whose parents have emphasized greater autonomy in problem solving (Steinberg, Dornbusch & Brown, 1992).

Programs often attempt to address these inequalities through parent involvement programs that provide parents with critical information about educational opportunities and teach skills to help parents monitor their children's educational progress. Some programs invest substantial resources in developing extensive data and information delivery systems so that parents of first generation college goers can easily gain access to the information they need, including students' records and college requirements, to help support their children's pathway to college. Mentoring is also a strategy that supports the goals of increasing cultural and social capital to students, and sometimes to parents. A primary role of the mentor is to share knowledge and experience gained from having successfully navigated at least some portion of the educational system.

Limited parental financial resources. Even if underrepresented students had no other impediments to obtaining higher education, financial constraints would continue to be a major factor in their postsecondary choices. While there is some debate over the role of financial constraints as a major factor in students leaving college (Tinto, 1987), there is little debate that it is critical in deciding whether or not a young person will go to college at all (Adelman, 1999; Cabrera, Stempen & Hansen, 1992). Low-income students are significantly less likely to attend college than upper income students, even when their test scores are similar. Akerhielm et al. (1998) found that within the top test score group of the NELS:88 achievement test, 75 percent of low-income, 86 percent of middle-income, and 95 percent of high-income students went on to college. Stated differently, one out of every four high school graduates scoring at the top of their class, but coming from a low-income family, did *not* go to college.

The cost of a college education encompasses more than the cost of tuition for young people from low-income families. They must also weigh heavily the costs of forgone income, and that they will not be able to help their families financially while they are in college. Therefore, even if college costs are covered by grants and/or loans, it can be a difficult decision for some low-income youth to forgo helping their families at an age when they can be productive wage earners. In a study of high achieving, low-income Chicano students, Gándara (1995) found that it was relatively common for older siblings to forgo college in favor of work so that younger siblings might have the opportunity to study as family finances were augmented by the incomes of the older siblings.

Although limited financial resources are a major barrier to attending four-year colleges for low-income students, most intervention programs do not directly provide financial support. Many offer information about scholarships that are available and encourage students to seek these scholarships. Provision of financial support is probably not a core aspect of most programs because they do not have the resources to do this. Some states, however, have made large-scale commitments to provide adequate support for all qualified low-income students within their borders. For example, Indiana legislators reasoned that they could provide an assortment of intensive services for some students, or they could take the same resources and provide a state-of-the-art data gathering and information dissemination system and scholarships to ensure that every student who was qualified could go to college in the state. It chose the latter policy option. Some private, nonprofit programs worked to ensure that all children in the program who qualified for college received a scholarship sufficient to cover their costs.

TABLE 4.4
Inequalities and Strategies That Address Them in K–12 Intervention Programs

Inequalities	Impediments	Ameliorating Strategies
Neighborhood resources	Lack of infrastructure—parks, libraries, etc.; lack of role models and normative support for achievement	After-school and weekend programs geared to academics, tapping community "funds of knowledge," stimulating pride in home culture
Unequal schools	Weak curriculum, underprepared teachers, segregation by ethnicity and income, poor counseling, low expectations, academic tracking	Access to high tracked courses, academic enrichment before and after school, weekends, and summers; intensive counseling focused on college
Lack of peer support	Pressure to engage in "risky behavior," culture of low achievement, put-downs for achievement behavior	Provision of high achieving peer groups and activities with these students that build bonds; send cohorts of students to college together
Unequal family resources	Lack of social and cultural capital, parenting styles that do not promote achievement or autonomy, lack of knowledge of how to support students' achievement; lack of financial resources	Parent involvement programs; parent workshops to provide information about postsecondary options, mentors to supplement the parent role; scholarships or financial counseling

How Effective Are K–12 Intervention Strategies?

It is difficult to draw definitive conclusions about the effectiveness of most college access programs, in part because it is rare to encounter an evaluation study that employs true control groups. Most attempt to compare their outcomes with other students in the same schools, district, or state who have not participated in the program. To draw comparisons to other students in the same school district or state ignores the reality that the program participants were usually selected into the program by some process, and were *not* like all other students.

Some programs simply provide information about responses to surveys conducted on selected participants (those they are able to locate and who agree to participate, introducing substantial selection bias). It is often impossible to determine what the response rates are to these surveys, and thus to what extent they may represent a highly skewed sample—only those individuals who were either happy enough with the program, or upset enough with it, to want to "have their say." There is also a troubling lack of specificity of outcomes and measurement. For example, many programs purport to "double" college attendance, but are nonspecific about what they mean by "college." Is this part-time attendance at a community college while holding a full-time job? Is it full-time attendance at a four-year college? Of course, the answer to this question has major implications for the likelihood that the students will persist in college and actually earn a college degree. It is also rare to find programs that measure anything beyond "college going," such as grade point averages or college admissions scores or some other measure of achievement. Thus, it is typically not possible to know whether achievement has been influenced, or if the outcome is simply matriculation in some kind of postsecondary institution. The few studies that do report such data give us reason to believe that affecting achievement is a much more difficult task than affecting college attendance. And since high school achievement is a much stronger predictor of persisting in college and completing a degree than simply matriculating, this is important missing data.

There is sufficient rigorous evaluation data, however, to draw some conclusions about the general effectiveness of K–12 interventions for individual students. There are almost no data that speak to effectiveness of school-centered strategies. Well-implemented, comprehensive programs that extend over a considerable length of time do appear to be able to at least double the rates of students going on to some kind of college. They do not, however, appear to raise grades or test scores, and thus their major impact is getting students who would not otherwise go to any college to go to a community college, or those who would aspire only to a two-year college to go on to a four-year college. It is uncommon for students who are not already reasonably high achievers to become competitively eligible for highly selective schools.

Successful programs work to emulate the features of prep schools that routinely send the children of the upper middle class on to college, but the programs are able to do it only for part of the day, and often outside of school hours. The rest of the time, students are exposed to the same school practices that have been proven to be unsuccessful for them. Thus, the good programs tend to help students raise their aspirations, maximize their assets, and expand their goals, but do not appreciably alter their academic achievement. For this to happen, the schools would need to adopt the practices of these effective interventions into the core of their operations.

College Interventions

Although all of these programs are geared toward increasing college attendance, very few actually find out whether students continue going to college after they initially matriculate, or if they meet with success there. Even first-year persistence rates are rarely reported. This is, however, a widely acknowledged, and heavily funded, concern of the postsecondary institutions. Just as early intervention programs have sprung up in schools and communities across the country, virtually every college campus in the nation has at least one program to help underrepresented students on the campus survive to college completion, and occasionally they are geared to helping these students actually thrive and excel. Gándara and Maxwell-Jolly (1999), in a national review of college-level interventions, identified five core strategies utilized by these programs, and assessed the evidence for their effectiveness. The core strategies included mentoring, academic support, psychosocial support (generally counseling or structured study and social group activities), professional opportunities, and financial aid. With the exception of professional opportunities (where students are placed in internships in their field of study), the other strategies have a great deal of overlap with the strategies used in the K–12 sector. However, the effectiveness of these programs is often difficult to judge because programs are ambiguous about their goals—whether the goal is to simply retain students to graduation, or to help them succeed at higher academic levels. Not unlike the K–12 programs, most of the college programs' focus is on just "keeping the students in the game," so that "success" is often defined as retention—getting students to graduate. In general, little attention is paid to the academic level of the students who receive their degrees. Like the benchmark of "college enrollment," some programs, especially those in the heavily funded science, math, engineering, and technology (SMET) fields, marked their success as graduate or medical school enrollment, which certainly connotes a higher level of academic accomplishment.

Interventions at the level of higher education tend to decouple students from their home backgrounds, and focus more specifically on what are per-

TABLE 4.5
Higher Education Interventions

Perceived Deficit	*Ameliorating Strategies*
Academic weaknesses	Summer bridge programs; tutors, study workshops; peer study groups;
Self-confidence; motivation	Counseling; peer study/social groups; faculty mentors
Career knowledge	Internships, research opportunities; faculty sponsors
Financial resources	Work-study opportunities; internships, scholarships

ceived as deficits in the skills or attitudes that the student brings to the learning situation. Table 4.5 summarizes the strategies that such interventions employ. There is notable overlap with the K–12 strategies, even though the interventions are often based on somewhat different assumptions.

How Effective Are College Level Interventions?

Like the K–12 programs, college interventions suffer from a serious lack of rigorous evaluation, in spite of the millions of dollars that are invested in them annually. However, based on a few careful studies, we are able to conclude that some strategies hold particular promise. Peer study groups that are articulated with a rigorous curriculum and guided by an expert leader appear to be very effective in raising students' achievement. Comprehensive programs that provide a host of supportive services over the entire under-graduate career and incorporate sufficient financial support to allow students to devote themselves to study have also been shown to be effective at raising students' achievement. Summer bridge programs that give students a head start on college work appear to be effective in raising first-year grades, but this is not sustained if the intervention is not also sustained. Programs that provide faculty mentors and laboratory experiences for students in the sciences appear to aid achievement and are especially effective as a retention strategy. It is troubling, however, that while it is clear that a number of the strategies in both K–12 and higher education are similar, there is little col-laboration between the sectors at the point of transition from high school to college.

Higher education partnerships abound in which a college or university works with the K–12 schools to stimulate college attendance abound, but ironically, at the point where students actually enroll in a postsecondary institution, most of these programs end. This is especially ironic given the amount of overlap in the strategies that the programs incorporate. Across both sectors—K–12 and college—the most consistently successful strategies appear to be the following:

- Providing a key person who monitors and guides the student over a long period—sometimes this is a "mentor," program director, faculty member, or guidance counselor.
- Providing high quality instruction either through access to the most challenging courses offered by the institution ("untracking"), through special coursework that supports and augments the regular curricular offerings (tutoring and specially designed summer bridge courses), or by revamping the curriculum to better address the learning needs of the students. At the higher education level, we saw extraordinary examples of unpacking "gatekeeping" curricula for students and redesigning courses to ensure both high standards and high rates of success. This effectively countered the gatekeeping function of some freshman courses, and was perhaps the single most effective strategy we saw in higher education.
- Long-term investments in students rather than short-term interventions. We found repeatedly that the longer students were in a program, the more they tended to benefit from it.
- Paying attention to the cultural background of students and using this as a supportive resource. Many programs reported having greater success with one group of students than another—Latinos, African Americans, women. One suspects that this was related to the background and expertise of the staff and directors, and the kinds of cultural connections they were able to make to students. Of course, this begs the question of whether "color blind" policies in program admissions are always a good idea.
- Providing a supportive peer/study group. At the higher education level, Uri Triesman's (1992) work on calculus study groups has been fairly definitive and we are convinced by the data that the skillful use of peer study groups that incorporate a carefully articulated curriculum can have a significant impact on students' academic achievement. This strategy may very well have an impact at the K–12 level also, but there has been no good test of it outside of the literature on cooperative learning. What does appear to help adolescents is a peer group that supports their academic aspirations and that meets for academic as well as social and emotional support.
- Financial assistance. This is clearly a larger issue at the college level where we know it has an impact on students' decision to attend college as well as affecting the amount of time they have available to study. At the K–12 level, financial assistance is important to pro-

vide access to academic leveling experiences—college visits and SAT preparation courses, for example.

Higher education also shares a similar problem with K–12 in the challenge to embed programs into the core of the institution. Most college-level programs are housed in the student services side of the university—or are perceived to be housed there—and therefore tend to lack credibility with mainstream faculty in the institution. They are often characterized as programs designed to help struggling students, rather than as centers dedicated to achieving educational excellence for high-potential students. In fact, some program directors note that their biggest challenge is not the students, but the attitudes of faculty.

Conclusions

Although the lack of articulation between K–12 and higher education institutions has been identified in numerous studies as a major barrier to the successful transition of underrepresented students from high school to college, programs in the K–12 rarely link with programs in the colleges and universities. Thus, K–12 program directors chart their success on the basis of college matriculation with little knowledge of how their participants fare once they are in college. And college program directors lament the poor K–12 preparation of their students, but seldom communicate their needs or standards to the high schools. Moreover, seldom do they share their expertise and resources with the K–12 schools to help these junior institutions meet the challenges that they face. A good conversation between the two sectors would likely produce the finding that much of what they do in early intervention overlaps, and that common efforts could help both institutions to more effectively meet common goals.

Moreover, the lack of attention that is paid to rigorous evaluation of intervention programs has allowed for the proliferation of such efforts on campuses across the nation with little concern for what works, for whom, and under what circumstances. Although modest, a literature now exists to help guides these efforts. One of the findings in this literature is that some programs do indeed have greater success with some types of students (Gándara & Bial, 1999), and it would behoove programs to attend to issues of goodness of fit. Yet, there is little evidence that most programs even consider this or attempt to determine which types of students yield the greatest successes for the program.

Finally, there is much research left to be done in the area of early intervention. The urgency to find a solution to the serious underrepresentation of some groups among the college-going population has resulted in the funding and growth of programs without thoughtful attention to how they might maximize their resources. It is doubtful that any of these programs actually harm the students who participate in them, but it is also virtually certain that they could meet with much greater success if the research were able to better identify which strategies are most effective for which types of students, under which conditions. A systematic investigation of these efforts could yield such understandings.

Notes

1. The Monterey Bay Education Consortium has offices located at the University of California, Santa Cruz, and organizes the feeder K–12 schools in the region for this program.

References

Akerheilm, K., Berger, J., Hooker, M., & Wise, D. (1998). *Factors related to college enrollment.* Final Report. Mathtech, Inc. Washington, DC: U.S. Department of Education, Office of the Undersecretary.

Baumrind, D. (1989). Rearing competent children. In W. Damon (Ed.), *Child development today and tomorrow (pp. 349–378).* San Francisco, CA: Jossey-Bass.

Betts, J., Rueben, K., & Danenberg, A. (2000). *Equal resources, equal outcomes? The distribution of school resources and student achievement in California.* San Francisco: Public Policy Institute of California.

Borman, G., Stringfield, S., & Rachuba, L. (2000). *Advancing minority high achievement: National trends and promising programs and practices.* New York: The College Board.

Bowen, C., & Gordon, E. (1998). *A connoisseurial evaluation of the posse program.* New Haven: Yale University Press.

Brooks-Gunn, J., Denner, J., & Klebanov, P. (1995). Families and neighborhoods as contexts for education. In E. Flaxman & A. Passow (Eds.), *Changing populations, changing schools: Ninety-fourth yearbook for the National Society for the Study of Education, Part II.* Chicago: National Society for the Study of Education.

Brophy, G., & Good, T. (1974). *Teacher-student relationships: Causes and consequences.* New York: Holt, Rinehart and Winston.

Cabrera, A., Stempen, J., & Hansen W.L., (1990). Exploring the effects of ability to pay on persistence in college, *Review of Higher Education, 13,* 303–313.

California Department of Education (CDE) (1999). *California Basic Educational Data System.* [www.cde.ca.gov/demographics/reports/statewide/sums98.htm]. Sacramento, CA.

Chapa, J. (1998). Hopwood in Texas: The untimely end of affirmative action. In G. Orfield & E. Miller (Eds.), *Chilling admissions.* Cambridge: The Civil Rights Project, Harvard University.

Clark, R. (1983). *Family life and school achievement: Why poor Black children succeed and fail.* Chicago: University of Chicago Press.

Crouse, R., & Trusheim, W. (1988). *The case against the SAT.* Chicago: University of Chicago Press.

Darling, N., & Steinberg, L. (1997). Community influences on adolescent achievement and deviance. In J. Brooks-Gunn, G. Duncan & L. Aber (Eds.), *Neighborhood Poverty. Volume II. Policy Implications in Studying Neighborhoods.* New York: Russell Sage Foundation.

Delgado-Gaitán, C. (1990). *Literacy for empowerment: The role of parents in children's education.* London: Falmer Press.

DiMaggio, P. (1982). Cultural capital and school success: The impact of status culture participation on the grades of U.S. high school students, *American Sociological Review, 47,* 189–201.

Epstein, J. & Karweit, N. (Eds.). (1983). *Friends in school: Patterns of selection and influence in secondary schools.* New York: Academic Press.

Ferguson, R. (1998). Can schools narrow the black-white test score gap? In C. Jencks & M. Phillips (Eds.), *The black-white test score gap.* Washington, DC: The Brookings Institution.

Fordham, S., & Ogbu, J. (1986). Black students' school success: Coping with the burden of "acting white." *Urban Review, 18,* 176–206.

Gándara, P. (1995). *Over the ivy walls: The educational mobility of low-income Chicanos.* Albany, NY: State University of New York Press.

Gándara, P., & Maxwell-Jolly, J. (1999). *Priming the pump. Strategies for increasing the achievement of underrepresented minority undergraduates.* New York: The College Board.

Gándara, P., & Bial, D. (1999). *Paving the way to higher education: K–12 interventions for underrepresented students.* Washington DC: NCES.

Goldhaber, D., & Brewer, D. (1996). *Evaluating the effect of teacher degree level on educational performance.* Rockford, MD: Westat.

Gurin, P. (1999). *Expert Testimony in the Cases Gratz, et al., v Bollinger, et al. and Grutter, et al., v Bollinger, et al.* Ann Arbor: University of Michigan.

Haro, R., Rodríguez, G., & Gonzales, J. (1994). *Latino Persistence in Higher Education: A 1994 survey of University of California and California State University Chicano/Latino students.* San Francisco, CA: Latino Issues Forum.

Haycock, K. (1998, summer). Good teaching matters. How well-qualified teachers can close the gap. *Thinking K–16, 3,* 1–14.

Henderson, R. (1997). Educational and occupational aspirations and expectations among parents of middle school students of Mexican descent: Family resources for academic development and mathematics learning. In R. Taylor & M. Wang (Eds.), *Social and Emotional Adjustment and Family Relations in Ethnic Minority Families.* Mahwah, NJ: Lawrence Erlbaum Associates.

Jarret, R. (1997). Bringing families back in: Neighborhood effects on child development. In J. Brooks-Gunn, G. Duncan & L. Aber, (Eds.), *Neighborhood poverty. Volume II. Policy implications in studying neighborhoods.* New York: Russell Sage Foundation.

Jessor, R. (1993). Successful adolescent development in high risk settings. *American Psychologist, 48,* 117–126.

Lareau, A. (1989). *Home advantage: Social class and parental intervention in elementary education.* London and New York: Falmer Press.

Lee, H. (1998, April 17). Oakland teachers decry UC rebuff of top students. *San Francisco Chronicle,* p. A21.

Lehman, N. (1999). *The big test: The secret history of the American meritocracy.* New York: Farrar, Straus & Giroux.

McDonough, P. (1997). *Choosing colleges. How social class and schools structure opportunity.* Albany, NY: State University of New York Press.

Miller, L.S. (1995). *An American imperative: Accelerating minority educational achievement.* New Haven, CT: Yale University Press.

Mortenson, T. (Ed.) (1999). *Postsecondary Education Opportunity.* Washington, DC. Self-published.

NCES (National Center for Education Statistics) (1999). *Digest of Education Statistics, 1998,* Washington, DC: U. S. Department of Education. Table 105, p. 124.

NCES (2000a). *Condition of Education 1999.* Washington DC: U.S. Department of Education.

NCES (2000b). *Early Childhood Longitudinal Study.* Washington DC: US Department of Education.

National Research Council, Panel on High Risk Youth (1993). *Losing generations: Adolescents in high risk settings.* Washington DC: National Academy Press.

Oakes, J. (1985) *Keeping track: How schools structure inequality.* New Haven, CT: Yale University Press.

Opuni, K. (1998). *Project GRAD. Graduation really achieves dreams, 1997–98. Program evaluation report.* Houston, TX: Project GRAD.

Orfield, G. (1996). The growth of segregation. In G. Orfield, & S. Eaton (Eds.), *Dismantling desegregation. The quiet reversal of Brown vs Board of education.* New York: The New Press.

Orfield, G. & Eaton, S. (Eds.). (1996). *Dismantling desegregation: The quiet reversal of Brown vs the Board of education.* New York: W. W. Norton.

Orfield, G. & Yun, J. (1999). *Resegregation in American schools.* Cambridge, MA: Harvard Civil Rights Project.

Perna, L. & Swail, W.S. (1998). *Early Intervention Programs: How Effective Are They at Increasing Access to College?* Paper presented at the annual meeting of the Association for the Study of Higher Education, Miami, FL.

Rendón L., & Garza, H. (1996). Closing the gap between two- and four-year institutions. In L. Rendón, & R. Hope (Eds.), *Educating a New Majority: Transforming America's Educational System for Diversity* (pp. 289–308). San Francisco, CA: Jossey-Bass.

Robinson, N., Weinberg, R., Redden, D., Ramey, S. & Ramey, C (1998). Family factors associated with high academic competence among former Head Start children, *Gifted Child Quarterly, 42,* 148–56.

Romo, H., & Falbo, T. (1996). *Latino high school graduation. Defying the odds.* Austin, TX: University of Texas Press.

Sprinthall, R., Sprinthall, N. & Oja, S. (1998). *Educational psychology: A developmental approach.* 7th ed. Boston, MA: McGraw Hill.

Stanton-Salazar, R. (1997). A social capital framework for understanding the socialization of racial minority children and youths, *Harvard Educational Review, 67,* 1–40.

Steinberg, L. (1996). *Beyond the classroom: Why school reform has failed and what parents need to do.* New York: Simon & Shuster.

Steinberg, L., Dornbusch, S., & Brown, B. (1992). Ethnic differences in adolescent achievement: An ecological perspective, *American Psychologist, 47,* 723–729.

Tinto, V. (1987). *Leaving college: Rethinking the causes and cures of student attrition.* Chicago: University of Chicago Press.

Treisman, U. (1992). Studying students studying calculus: A look at the lives of minority mathematics students in college. *The College Mathematics Journal, 23,* 362–72.

Useem, Elizabeth L. (1992). Middle Schools and Math Groups: Parents' Involvement in Children's Placement. *Sociology of Education 65,* 263–279.

Vernez, G. (1999). *Closing the education gap.* Santa Monica, CA: RAND Corp.

Weinstein, R. (1989). Perceptions of classroom processes and student motivation: Children's views of self-fulfilling prophecies. In R. Ames & C. Ames (Eds.), *Research on Motivation in Education: Goals and Cognition's, 3* (187–221). New York: Academic Press.

CHAPTER 5

The Social Construction of College Access

Confronting the Technical, Cultural, and Political Barriers to Low-Income Students of Color

JEANNIE OAKES, JOHN ROGERS,
MARTIN LIPTON, AND ERNEST MORRELL

When Californians outlawed affirmative action, the University of California (UC) system launched an "Outreach" initiative aimed at creating a diverse pool of high school graduates who are eligible and competitive for the university in a race-neutral admissions environment. A blue ribbon Task Force outlined a four-pronged approach focused on schools in low-income neighborhoods with a history of sending few students to UC. The approach included (a) student-centered academic development programs; (b) school-centered systemic reforms; (c) recruitment and yield activities, and (d) research and evaluation that would sharpen our understanding of the challenge and suggest new approaches. As Patricia Gándara points out in her chapter, the state legislature, eager to minimize the political fallout of the state's affirmative action ban, funded the Task Force's recommendations rather generously.

However, the funding was tied to a challenging accountability requirement: By 2002, UC would need to demonstrate (a) a 100 percent increase the number of graduates from UC Outreach partner schools who are eligible for admission to UC, and (b) a 50 percent increase in the number of graduates who are competitive enough to gain admission to the system's most selective campuses. To be admitted to a UC campus, students must rank in the top 12.5 percent of the state's high school graduates, as determined by a combination of grade-point averages (GPA) in a set of college-preparatory course requirements and Scholastic Aptitude Test (SAT) scores. Applicants to Berkeley and Los Angeles must satisfy even more rigorous requirements. For freshmen entering UCLA in 2000, for example, being "competitively eligible" meant scoring among the top 25 percent of the nearly 40,000 applicants, most of whom met the basic eligibility requirements. Not surprisingly, few students from "educationally disadvantaged" high schools currently meet this high standard.

In the two years following its launch, the UC Outreach leadership focused its resources and energy designing and implementing programs that enabled more diverse groups of high school graduates to meet the eligibility criteria. However, it has become increasingly clear that Outreach confronts far more than the technical challenges inherent in program development and delivery, as extraordinary as those challenges are. The low UC admission rates among African American and Latino students is a profound social phenomenon that is deeply rooted in politics, norms, and practices that lie far beyond the reach of even the most sophisticated technical strategies.

This chapter uses UCLA's outreach as a case study to illuminate the cultural and political challenges of college preparation programs, as well as their more technical dimensions. Whereas other chapters in this book focus on the dynamics of college preparation programs themselves, we investigate the social and cultural dynamics that surround these programs. We begin by describing UCLA's comprehensive approach and laying out its conceptual underpinnings. We then use social theory to examine the cultural and political challenges that even these well-conceived and generously funded strategies cannot touch. We argue that a lens of social theory helps us see the cultural and political forces that translate conventional conceptions of merit into college eligibility, and enables sharp inquiry into how the ideology of merit holds in place the current, uneven distribution of opportunities to learn.

We also argue that social critique, while liberating, is not in itself a sufficient grounding for new Outreach strategies that construct and support a broadened view of college preparation and merit. Accomplishing a needed reconstruction of merit and the accompanying redistribution (or less threateningly, an even distribution) of high-quality teaching and learning will likely require that social theory be broadly integrated with new understandings of cognitive and sociocultural theories of learning. Those theories permit us to reexamine and redefine what constitutes academic promise, high-quality teaching, high-quality knowledge, and high-quality learning. To illustrate this perspective, we offer an example of an exploratory project at UCLA that tackles the cultural and political dimensions of outreach, alongside its efforts to meet the more technical challenges. We argue that such projects are necessary to stretch the conceptual and programmatic boundaries imposed by the technical emphasis of many current reform and outreach efforts.

We conclude with an additional challenge. Although we applaud the programmatic efforts that we and others in this book discuss, we are also aware that any new construction of college eligibility will inevitably bring enormous political resistance, as California's recent rejection of affirmative action illustrates. Consequently, a penetrating critique and a pedagogy grounded in sociocultural theories of learning, as liberating and educationally enriching as this may be, will do little to expand college access absent a theory for political action. Moreover, such a theory must inform efforts to gain legitimacy for a broadened conception of merit and official recognition of it in the college admissions process.

The Technical Challenge: Implementing a Theory of Action

UCLA Outreach programs touch students in 47 high schools and many of their feeder schools in seven school districts. The bulk of the activities are of two types. As Patricia Gándara points out in her chapter, those activities loosely called "student centered," consist of targeted efforts to help the most promising students in partner schools meet UC requirements and to provide top students with the extra boost they may need to become "competitively eligible" for Berkeley and UCLA. In all 47 schools, selected students receive academic advisement, and those who seem to have strong UC prospects receive an individualized learning plan designed by UC Outreach staff. In a smaller number of schools, the Career Based Outreach Program (CBOP) supports students more intensively as they seek to become eligible and competitive for UC admission. They are mentored by trained UCLA undergraduates (CBOP Fellows) who are themselves students of color seeking to increase their prospects for admission to graduate school. These undergraduate "Fellows" provide CBOP high school "Scholars" instruction in a Personal Academic Learning System (PALS) that teaches learning tools to enable students to be optimal learners in less than optimal schools and helps students realize that they must be responsible for their own learning and pathway to college. Saturday Academies for CBOP Scholars focus on developing critical reading skills, college-level writing competence, math and analytical thinking, computer skills, research in the sciences, and preparing for college entrance exams. Weekend residential programs at UCLA—called "academic boot camps"—engage the CBOP scholars in completing the steps in complex, college-level assignments such as writing a college-level research paper.

The second type of Outreach strategy, called "school centered," seeks to improve the quality of college preparation that a group of designated "partner" K–12 schools provides to *all* students. The Partner schools are high schools and their feeder schools in the low-income neighborhoods of color in Los Angeles, and Partnership activities focus on all grades, K–12. The goal is for UCLA faculty and Outreach staff to work collaboratively with educators at the schools to build school's capacity to ready students for college as well as to work directly with students themselves. So, for example, Outreach's direct work with students overlaps with teachers' professional development.

One strategy, "instructional coaching," brings expert teachers affiliated with UCLA together with teachers at Partnership schools. The coaches work one-on-one with Partnership teachers in their classrooms, helping them hone their knowledge and skills as they work with their students. During summer/intercessions, teachers and their expert partners collaborate to refine the teachers' instructional skills while providing students with academic enrichment and college preparation. In all such activities, the focus on student work is paramount.

Another strategy is to use student work from high-performing schools to calibrate expectations at some of the traditionally low-performing schools. UCLA's Outreach staff also provide assistance to administrators as they develop new programs and change structures that support college preparation—that is, extend school days; expand academic course offerings and requirements; summer bridge programs; and connections with community colleges. Partnership college "coaches" assist counselors and teachers to foster a college-going culture. Data teams at each school examine patterns of course taking and achievement. Parent seminars provide parents with knowledge and skills to help them navigate the college-readiness process with their children.

UCLA grounds this multidimensional set of outreach strategies in a "theory of action" drawn from research about college-readiness and further refined from experience. Specifically, the campus has relied on evidence from research on college-going behavior and on the relationships among school structure and social organization, curriculum, teaching practices, and student achievement. This literature, combined with considerable prior campus experience, led UCLA's outreach leadership to identify six conditions essential for students to gain admission to and success at UCLA:

1. *College-going culture*—where adults and peers see college-going as expected and attainable, and where they see the effort and persistence that preparation for college requires as normal (values, beliefs, and expectations)
2. *Rigorous academic curriculum*—A-G University of California eligibility courses, honors/AP courses, engagement with significant subject matter (access to knowledge)
3. *High-quality teaching*—well-qualified teachers, instruction that engages students in work of high intellectual quality (opportunity to learn)
4. *Intensive academic and college-going support*—academic tutoring, SAT prep, coaching about college admissions and financial aid, support beyond the classroom including access to the "hidden curriculum" of the college track
5. *A multicultural, college-going identity*—confidence and skills to negotiate college without sacrificing one's own identity and connec-

tions with one's home community (bridging students' multiple worlds; identity development).

6. *Parent/community connections re: college going and academics—* parent seminars on curriculum, teaching, and college going (access to knowledge about college preparation and to college-savvy social networks).

Each UCLA outreach activity must show how it contributes to one or more of these six conditions in the schools and communities in which we work.

This is noble work, and certainly it can profoundly affect the schools and students who the programs touch. However, it is becoming increasingly clear that Outreach will not meet its goal of significantly increasing the diversity of the university's study body if it limits its efforts to these interventions— as extraordinary as they may be. Efforts to mold low-income Latino and African American students into applicants who fit the university's current narrow constructions of eligibility are not likely to bring significant new diversity to the university. The prevailing definition of eligibility represents far more than a culturally and politically neutral standard of academic excellence that is operationalized through culturally and politically neutral measures such as course-taking patterns, grades, SAT scores, and so on. At root, eligibility reflects social decisions shaped by cultural traditions and political struggles over how "merit" is defined, what indicators or proxies of such merit are legitimate, and the relevance of merit and its indicators to success in the university and to the larger social good.

Cultural and Political Barriers: Through the Lens of Social Theory

A social theory lens reveals the cultural and political contexts that frustrate and obstruct efforts to increase the capacity of schools in disadvantaged communities and to prepare students at these schools to gain admission to and succeed in the UCs. Among the most salient features of this context is the prevailing and largely unquestioned ideology of merit. Members of privileged groups employ this ideology of merit as the moral and rational foundation and leverage for maintaining their competitive advantage in university admissions. This ideology conflates the ability to profit from educational opportunities with prior achievement in the traditional academic curriculum, as gauged by conventional measures. Moreover, it positions students with this prior achievement as more *deserving* of those opportunities. Thus, not only does the definition of merit advantage youngsters from mainstream cultures and middle-class status, we are arguing that this ideology supports and requires the structural inequalities that plague Outreach schools, including the uneven distribution of curriculum and teaching quality.

The Social Construction of Merit

In this post–affirmative action period, we must decide who is worthy of admission to elite universities according to criteria that give advantage to students lucky enough to be born into privileged families and/or into cultures with long traditions that match traditional definitions of merit. However, because Outreach seeks changes that are fundamentally redistributive—that is, Outreach would reconfigure how the schooling system allocates its most precious resources, opportunities to prepare for college—it challenges, even disputes, traditional and deeply felt beliefs about which students "deserve" the best that schools have to offer and which schools should offer the best opportunities.

A 1999 *New York Times* column (Jensen, A19) asked a number of scholars to define merit in relation to college admissions. Harvard historian Stephan Thernstrom responded with a fairly conventional view:

> There are doubtless many forms of merit in the eyes of God. But selective institutions of higher learning are best advised and best equipped to judge applicants on the basis of academic merit, as measured by grade point averages adjusted for course difficulty, class rank, and scores on standardized tests. These indicators allow us to predict with considerable confidence who will flourish in college or graduate school and who will barely scrape by or drop out. But some groups earn higher grades and have better academic records than others. . . . [g]roups with fewer high achievers will inevitably be underrepresented. Pretending that such applicants have academic skills they lack does nothing to resolve the real problem, and indeed deflects attention from it.

In contrast, UC sociologist Jerome Karabel invoked Michael Young's 1958 British satire, *The Rise of the Meritocracy*, reminding readers that Young argued "the real consequences of meritocracy are to leave intact the vast inequalities of a traditional class society, while convincing both the winners and losers that they deserve their lot in life" (As cited in, "What the Deserving Deserve and Whether They Get It." *New York Times*, 23 October 1999). Karabel also asserted,

> Meritocracy's dirty little secret is that the content of "merit" in any society is defined by the powerful. . . . In the United States today, the prevailing definition of merit is a strange mishmash of grades, test scores (especially standardized multiple choice tests), extracurricular activities and that elusive quality called "character," a criterion that was introduced at America's leading universities only in the 1920's when "too many" Jews succeeded in meeting the academic qualifications. The demise of affirmative action in California and elsewhere has generated calls to redefine merit, and such a reconsideration is long overdue. (*New York Times*, 23 October 1999)

Karabel's rendering of merit reflects assumptions quite different from Thernstrom's about more than just the nature of merit. Karabel's answer reflects a social theory that asserts: (a) that human knowledge of everyday social life is socially constructed, rather than objective scientific fact (Berger & Luckman, 1966); (b) and, specifically, that conceptions of merit are socially constructed and deeply felt cultural ideologies rather than scientific discoveries.

Social theorists argue that ideology refers to the ways in which culturally based meanings serve, in particular circumstances, to establish and sustain asymmetrical relations of power (Gramsci, 1971; Thompson 1990; Lewotin, 1992). When the majority of the people ruling internalize such meanings, they appear as "common-sense." In the case of merit, then, common-sense notions explain what might otherwise seem contradictory—a juxtaposition of an ideology of equality and meritocracy with the reality of extreme inequality in our society.

Nicholas Lemann's provocative book, *The Big Test: The Secret History of the American Meritocracy* (1999) documents the twentieth century evolution of "meritocratic" college admissions. He recounts how "mental testers" and college presidents worked to make the SAT and other objective measures of merit the means for securing positions in the best colleges, instead of family wealth and privilege that had traditionally governed admissions. Neither the test developers nor college officials objected to social sorting per se, but both sought a sorting process grounded in innate ability, rather than in inherited privilege. Many believed that objective measures of human ability—such as the SAT—were essential to finding and cultivating the human resources necessary for modern, industrial society. They argued further that equality of opportunity required a "meritocracy"—a social system in which the race for social rewards is fair. Those who reach the finish line first must be faster and thus more meritorious runners than those who come in last. Those not winning educational advantages and elite status must lose because of their own deficiencies (inability to run fast). Such a system constituted an apparently fair and "natural" sorting process for determining who should become society's elites.

Today's meaning of intelligence remains very close to that of the early mental testers. Theirs was one constructed by elite groups who, because of their political, economic, and social power, were able to frame their definitions of intelligence as "common sense." Today, the ways of knowing of white, wealthy, and thus most powerful Americans not only remain more valued, they continue to be acted upon by K–12 schools, universities, and society as if they are a function of innate ability. The logic remains so pervasive and has such explanatory value that we still find tolerable, if unfortunate, the large gaps in college admissions between upper-class, white Americans and lower-income applicants and applicants of color. Cloaked in the aura of science, testing's persistent stratifying effects continue to make deep, unquestioned sense to many in society. The cultural capital of white and wealthy families masquerades as meritorious "natural" ability, rather than as a function of social privilege. Nothing in most outreach approaches promises to change this.

Cultural Politics and College Eligibility

Social constructions such as merit aren't merely shared beliefs. They shape and are themselves reinforced by social structures and individuals' decisions about how to act. As Mehan (1992) has noted, "Culture is not merely a pale reflection of structural forces; it is a system of meaning that mediates social structure and human action" (Mehan, 1992, p. 3). Thus, conceptions of merit actively relate to structural forces in the political and economic life of the larger culture as well as those in school, and the conceptions are salient as educators decide how to organize curriculum and how to respond to students.

University attendance brings credentials with extraordinary exchange value in terms of high status occupations, with middle class income and lifestyle—outcomes that many Americans fear are becoming unattainable without a college degree. So it shouldn't be surprising that many are loath to alter the current construction of eligibility that favors their children.[1] The heightened stakes raise the anxiety levels of powerful parents and educators; they see any effort to democratize access to the high-status curriculum as jeopardizing the chances for their own children, who in earlier years would have had a smoother path toward a place at the top of the social structure. Given increasing competition, families will employ the full range of resources, knowledge, and associations at their disposal to enhance their children's chances of capturing the available slots. The result will be an ever-escalating standard for eligibility. With no planned increases in the proportion of high school graduates in the state (currently 12.5 percent) that will be admitted, the competition for UC admissions is a zero-sum game. Put bluntly, the bonds between differentiated schooling and social stratification may prove too strong for Outreach to break.

For example, families who are resolved to ensure their children's competitiveness for the university provide direct support to their children and use their resources and influence to increase the capacity of their children's schools. So we should not be surprised that as student-centered programs seek to bolster students' academic prowess with tutoring and bridge programs beyond the school day and year, advantaged families increasingly will provide similar help at their own expense. As we extend our academic support programs to middle schoolers, advantaged families will begin even earlier. As we make popular SAT prep programs more widely available, advantaged families will seek more intense and longer-lasting preparation. As we increase our hands-on assistance with preparing college applications, advantaged parents will increasingly turn to private college counseling services. While some might see this competition as helping all students to be smarter, few university officials see such intense pressure as improving young people's preparation for actual college-level work.

At the same time, to the extent that we help our school partners pursue effective college-going cultures and curricula, we can expect that wealthier and more powerful parents will push their schools to better position their children at the top of the new educational hierarchy. While not a firm equation, hard work plus privilege will usually trump hard work alone. Relatively advantaged schools will face far fewer obstacles as they upgrade their programs. As outreach brings a college-preparatory program to a broader, more diverse range of students, the backlash may well bring new, more intense forms of differentiation within the college preparatory track both in outreach and more advantaged schools.

We have already seen how Advanced Placement (AP) classes with their strict entrance requirements and test-driven curricula have become a required part of the upper college-preparatory track, especially in high schools in affluent neighborhoods. Since the mid-1980s, the AP program has grown dramatically. In California in 1988, 39,040 public high school students took 56,668 exams. By 1998, these numbers had grown to 87,683 students taking 145,000 exams. As a consequence, participation in AP (or other weighted honors courses) classes has become essential for students seeking admission at UC's most competitive campuses.

However, the growth in AP opportunities for well-off white and Asian students has outdistanced those for Latinos and African Americans. AP courses are generally limited to those meeting strict entrance requirements, rather than being available to all students. Schools serving poor and minority students typically offer few or no AP classes (especially in critical gate-keeping subjects like science and mathematics), whereas schools in more affluent communities can offer 15, 20, or more. Some schools in low-income neighborhoods claim that they simply do not have students qualified to take these courses. In mixed schools, restrictive admissions usually bring vastly disproportionate enrollments by race and social class, with few low-income students or African Americans and Latinos participating.

Often AP classes are confined to selective magnets or choice programs, essentially separate schools on large urban high school campuses. In overcrowded, multi-track year-round high schools, AP courses are often restricted to one of the school's many tracks, permitting only those students enrolled in the right track to participate. Most telling, in what a *Los Angeles Times* story called an "academic arms race," we see that as "educationally disadvantaged" schools increase their AP offerings, more advantaged schools add even more.

These schools can more easily increase the breadth and rigor of their academic offerings, partly because they are more likely to have teachers prepared to teach advanced courses.

Clearly, as Outreach works to create UC student bodies that reflect California's diversity, it confronts powerful cultural forces bent on preserving the status quo. These responses are not limited to politically conservative parents. Some of the most anxious are highly educated liberals, many who support affirmative action. Unfortunately, in a stratified educational system where children's life chances depend so heavily on their ability to secure places in good colleges, such parents may have little other choice. This is the climate in which Outreach must operate and for which Outreach has no mandate to change.

A Countervailing Case

In what follows, we offer the experiences of high school students, teachers, and UC faculty in an innovative summer course. This course was part of a larger project exploring how UCLA Outreach might simultaneously address the technical, cultural, and political challenges to college access for low-income African American and Latino students. In partnership with a local school district, UCLA offered an introductory summer seminar for high school students, in the field of the sociology of education, ED 001— Special Topics in Sociology of Education.[2] The seminar invited a group of working class Latino and African American youth to read seminal works in sociology of education and participate in a set of mini-research projects around the broad theme of "Race, Class, and Access in American Education." While all of the student participants had recently completed tenth grade at a local high school, they represented a fairly broad range of academic backgrounds. Roughly one-third of the students had high GPAs, one-third mid-range, and one-third low.[3]

The summer seminar stemmed from the premise that high school students' actual engagement in the activities, protocols, and scholarly dispositions required of researchers would be a valuable "readiness" experience for their eventual success as students at a research university. By expanding and elevating the rigor and conceptual content of social studies coursework typically offered to high school students—particularly those students lacking a record of competitive academic success—a research seminar demands college-level work from participating students. Such engagement enables high school students to produce work products that meaningfully demonstrate their preparation for university work.

Over the course of three intensive weeks of study, the high school students worked in five-member teams to produce a piece of original research that they presented to a panel of UCLA faculty members with expertise in the area of educational sociology. For example, one research group studied the impact of Hip-Hop music and culture on high school students in urban America and its implications for how teachers might approach the conventional curriculum. This group read social theorists such as Freire and Bourdieu on the relationship between popular culture and the canonical curriculum. They disseminated a survey to high school students and conducted interviews with teachers, friends and family, and undergraduates at UCLA. Another research group sought to make sense of different manifestations of student resistance at their high school. The group drew upon a conceptual framework on student resistance developed by Daniel Solorzano that distinguishes among different sorts of resistance—from self-defeating to politically transformative. Through surveys, interviews, and conversations with politically active students, this group attempted to locate different models of student resistance that fit into Solorzano's typology.

During the three weeks of the seminar, student participants spent an hour each day with the whole group and two hours in small groups with their research team adviser. All of the advisers had experience working with urban youth as well as conducting research in areas of urban schooling. During the two-hour research team meetings, the students discussed concepts and readings relating to the Sociology of Education, learned the various aspects of the research process, prepared interview protocols and surveys, analyzed transcripts, and prepared presentations of their findings.

On the final day of the seminar, the students presented their work to a panel of university faculty involved in research relating to the Sociology of Education. Each student research group guided the panel through a set of Power Point slides outlining a research question, literature review, methodology, findings, and policy implications. They then fielded questions and comments about their research from the faculty panel and public audience. Several faculty members remarked that the quality of student research compared favorably with research conducted in their undergraduate sociology or sociology of education courses. Speaking after the session, Solorzano offered this assessment:

> I think they were able to grasp this field called the Sociology of Education generally. And then within the field they were able to . . . look at a particular area within the Sociology of Education as a potential area for research and eventually an actual area of research. . . . Once they were able, in a very short period of time, to understand what research meant, they seemed to grasp the epistemology of research, the epistemology of theory, the epistemology of concepts, of method, et cetera. They were able to understand what they meant and pull it all together in a short period of time. . . . That's what really stuns me, . . . I mean, it's not like we have a group of our graduate students and we're talking about them. We're talking about 10th graders.[4]

A New Technology of Learning:
Apprenticeship in a Community of Practice

Like other Outreach projects, the research seminar designed a program aimed at supporting students' development of the knowledge and skills that would prepare them for college-level work. However, rather than accepting the technologies of a teaching and learning curriculum as neutral and apart from the normative and political dimensions of college preparation, the project embraced an understanding of learning that challenged accepted notions of college "readiness." The seminar posed student learning as a form of apprenticeship within the research community of educational sociology. Following Lave and Wenger, we understand a community of practice as a site of learning and action in which novices and experts come together around a shared enterprise, in the process developing a whole repertoire of activities, common stories, and ways of speaking and acting. (Wenger, 1998; Lave, 1996; Lave and Wenger, 1993). Communities of practice—for example, research groups, members of twelve step programs, or artisan communities—constitute reality in a particular manner and encourage specialized ways of acting and thinking. Learning occurs constantly in these communities as people participate in activities that are more and more central to the core practice.

According to Lave and Wenger's theory, the summer seminar sought to place high school students in the role of "legitimate peripheral participants" within the broader community of practice of sociology of education research that was focused on the theme of access and equity. As novice researchers, the high school students forged competence by participating with university faculty and graduate students in authentic and valuable work. "Apprentices," reasons Lave, "learn to think, argue, act, and interact in increasingly knowledgeable ways, with people who do something well, by doing it with them as legitimate, peripheral participants" (Lave, 1997, p. 19). The students' emerging competence thus arose in the process of being inducted into the research university's community of practice. Critically, this view of student development stands in stark contrast to the logic of college admissions that presumes demonstrations of competence must precede induction.

Understanding learning through a community-of-practice lens reshapes the relationship between high school students and college-level work. Most college preparatory programs seek to transmit a body of college-sanctioned knowledge and skills that young people ultimately will need to succeed at the University. Yet, transmission does not necessarily lead students to acquire college-ready skills. This drop-off between what is taught and what is learned is greatest when students feel alienated from the college preparatory curricula or college itself—when they cannot see a clear relationship between the curriculum and who they are or hope to become.

Conversely, a curriculum guided by a community-of-practice lens encourages high school students to acquire college-level skills and knowledge by participating as (novice) members in the work of research universities. Hence, student researchers in the seminar gradually appropriated the tools of the research community. We mean by this that the students increasingly understood and internalized the language, culture, and purpose of research as they synthesized existing literature and ideas with their own experiences and concerns.

The changing relationship between the high school students and college-level work can be seen in a field note from a class session midway through the three-week seminar:

> The entire class of 20 students is assembled in a seminar room on the third floor of UCLA's education building. The long tables are in an L shape and there are students on both sides of the tables with binders (which contain their summer readers) and notebooks. The groups are preparing a small portion of their presentation to share with the rest of the class. The assignment calls for the students to explain, in a one-paragraph statement, why they feel that their project should be funded for further research. The research team advisers sit off to the side and watch the students work. After the groups finish writing, the group studying school-family relations volunteers to read its paragraph, which addresses the group's research problem and question. Teresa reads for her group. She looks down on a yellow legal pad that is filled to about half of a page. As Teresa reads rapidly, Imani can be seen in the background taking notes. When Teresa finishes, Tanya can be heard near the camera saying, "Yeah, that was good," as the students clap. Tanya volunteers to read for the hip-hop group: "The hip-hop group should be funded because it's amazing how young (she makes the sign for quotation marks) "minorities" can find a bunch of information about social reproduction in the school curriculum. We should share with other people so they can learn about how it relates with students and teachers and teachers can become more in touch with their students."

A week and a half into the seminar, Tanya already has developed a different relationship to the research university than most high school students. She demonstrates facility with critical research terminology such as "social reproduction," she recognizes the distinctive ways that researchers communicate, and she sees the work of the research university as a significant player in her own future.

More important, the seminar did not merely acculturate high school students to the prevailing culture and practice of a research university; it also created a context for students to influence the work of the university. A case in point was the research group examining student resistance. By testing Solorzano's resistance rubric against their own experiences in schools, the student researchers developed new ways of understanding student behavior that informed Solorzano's thinking. "They really did help me make sense of this concept of resistance. . . . I guess they brought these new eyes to look at this. And I liked the idea that they looked at that area around the [rubric's] margins. . . . My graduate students [and I] felt that the quadrants were more fluid, but we never talked about, what does it mean at that marginal area?"[5] Solorzano's experience echoes Lave and Wenger's claim that novices can play a critical role in promoting learning within the broader community of practice because "naïve involvement invite[s] reflection" from more expert members of the community" (Lave and Wenger, 1993, p. 117).[6] The student researchers thus demonstrated their "readiness" to shape, as well as participate within, the research university.

The Cultural Task: Constructing and Appropriating a Countervailing Ideology of Merit.

The technology of learning employed in the summer seminar points toward an understanding of merit that is far more in keeping with the ideal of a research university than prevailing markers of college readiness. Students' performance in conventional college-preparatory and advanced high school courses often bears scant resemblance to high-level intellectual work in research universities. That is, rigorous high school classes rarely engage students in the process of creating or discovering new knowledge—the defining characteristics of a research university. As UCLA Chancellor Albert Carnesale reasons: "A great university is a community of scholars in which the frontiers of knowledge are explored and expanded, ideas and issues are debated, problems are formulated and solved, information is exchanged, and minds are opened" (Carnesale, 1998).

By including young people in the work of a research university, the seminar challenged two notions undergirding the logic of college admissions—that students must demonstrate readiness before, rather than through, participation, and that student performance on standardized assessments is the most meaningful indicator of readiness or merit. The seminar allowed us to explore whether participation within authentic tasks enables students to demonstrate preparation for research universities by engaging in research themselves. Instead of using canonical knowledge, mainstream culture, and middle class language habits and skills to screen out students of color, the seminar challenged conventional notions of merit and college preparation by assuming that students' own cultures and experiences could be drawn upon to construct highly valued knowledge.

In this process, students themselves, many of whom began by sharing the generally low estimation and relevance schools placed on their experiences and cultures, began to become convinced that their "backgrounds," instead of being a deficit or barrier to rigorous learning at school, in fact could be an asset. This experience challenges prevailing understandings of student motivation. A new conception of merit transformed these students' engagement with high-status knowledge for the duration of the seminar. Their "merit," rather than being conferred prior to their starting the seminar or judged and awarded at the end, was instead indistinguishable from their successful participation. Hence, the seminar enabled the students to construct—for themselves and the broader research community—an existence proof and a convincing demonstration of a socially just conception of merit.

The Political Task—Converting Countervailing Forms of Merit into Access

We conclude with an additional challenge. As we noted at the outset of the chapter, any new construction of college eligibility will inevitably bring political resistance. Consequently, a penetrating critique and pedagogy grounded in sociocultural theories of learning, while liberating and educationally enriching, can do little to expand college access unless it is tied to a theory of political action. College preparation programs cannot be islands in a sea of inequity; we must work to change the social and cultural dynamics of educational opportunity. Our work with the summer seminar not only highlights the importance of political action, it hints at possible directions for political change. What follows is thus an initial attempt to sketch out a theory of political action based on the lessons of the summer seminar.

A theory of political action around college access needs to inform attempts to instantiate new ideas about merit within college admissions. Such change requires a widespread shift in public understandings of merit and college readiness. For new understandings to emerge, different constituencies must sense that their prevailing "common sense" is problematic, that the existing system conflicts with their values and interests, and that a viable alternative exists. Hence, what is needed is a politics from the "ground up" that engages multiple constituencies in reexamining the meaning of college readiness.

Our summer seminar laid the groundwork for such a politics by creating a site that challenged long-standing beliefs—of high school students, university researchers, and community members—about the knowledge, skills, and dispositions needed to participate meaningfully in college-level research. It encouraged a group of working class Latino and African American high school students to view their lived experience as a potential resource for university work. Further, it enabled a cohort of university faculty to recognize the distinction between traditional markers of college readiness and the skills required to participate in university research.

Needless to say, the limited scope of the seminar's work bounded its political impact; only a relatively small number of students and faculty members directly participated in the seminar. Yet future efforts might play a more expansive political role with wider participation of community members. In addition, the student research products offer a powerful tool for communicating new ideas about merit to members of the broader public. Hence, the knowledge that students construct in demonstrating readiness ultimately becomes a source for the social and political reconstruction of college access.

Notes

1. While "powerful groups" is a necessarily imprecise term, members of such groups are more likely than members of "less powerful" groups to be white, wealthy, have children who attend schools that send students to elite universities, have personal and professional associations with others who are similarly powerful, have themselves attended universities, and so on.

2. Our data about the seminar is drawn from interviews with students and their teachers; student work products from the seminar; and interviews with the UC faculty members who served as panelists for the presentation about the quality and depth of the student understanding and student work. It also draws upon an extensive analysis of digital videotapes from the summer seminar. During the seminar, we managed to capture footage from every aspect of the process. This footage includes large group meetings, discussions of pertinent issues and literature relating to the sociology of education, research planning, students involved in data collection and analysis, and preparation for the concluding presentations. During the succeeding fall semester at the traditional high school, we recorded observations of the students in the project class, which meets each morning at 7:20, in their traditional classes, in outside of class activities, and in informal interviews.

3. For our purposes here, we are defining high GPA as 3.0–4.0; mid-level as 2.0–3.0; and low as below 2.0.

4. Interview with Daniel Solorzano, 28 August 1999.

5. Interview with Daniel Solorzano, 28 August 1999.

6. While it is beyond the scope of this paper, it is worth noting that the summer seminar tapped another important element of learning through legitimate peripheral participation—namely the opportunity for members of the community of practice who are neither novice nor expert to hone their understanding through interactions with novices. Hence, graduate students who also served as research team advisers spoke of how explaining methods clarified terms and pushed forward their own understandings. For example, one reported, "It forced me to be much more explicit and to kind of decide what are the things that I'd learned about interviewing, you know, in classes, and

stuff, meshed or didn't mesh with what my actual experience was and what of that I really wanted to convey to these younger people, as far as beginning the process themselves."

References

Berger, P. L. & Luckman, T. (1966). *The social construction of reality: A treatise in the sociology of knowledge*. New York: Doubleday.

Carnesale, A. (1998, November). *A Strategy for a Great University*. Paper presented to the faculty and administration of the University of California at Los Angeles, Los Angeles.

Gramsci, A. (1971). *Selections from the prison notebooks*. New York: International Publishers.

Jensen, J. (1999, October 23). What the deserving deserve and whether they get it. *The New York Times*, p. A19.

Lave, J. (1996). Teaching, as learning, in practice. *Mind, Culture and Activity, 3* (3) 149–164.

Lave, J. (1997). The culture of acquisition and the practice of understanding. In D. Kirshner & J. Witson (Eds.), *Situated cognition: Social, semiotic, and psychological perspectives* (p. 17–35). Mahwah, NJ: Lawerence Erlbaum Associates, Publishers.

Lave, J. & Wenger, E. (1991). *Situated learning: Legitimate peripheral participation*. New York: Cambridge University Press.

Leman, N. (1999). *The big test: The secret history of the American meritocracy*. New York: Farrar, Straus, and Giroux.

Lewontin, R. C. (1992). *Biology as ideology: The doctrine of DNA*. New York: Harper Perennial.

Mehan, H. (1992). Understanding inequality in schools: The contribution of interpretive studies. *Sociology of Education, 65* (1), 1–20.

Solorzano, D. (1998). Critical race theory, racial and gender microaggresions, and the experiences of Chicana and Chicano scholars. *International Journal of Qualitative Studies in Education 11*, 121–136.

Thompson, J. B. (1990). *Ideology and modern culture*. Stanford, CA: Stanford University Press.

Wenger, E. (1998). *Communities of practice: Learning, meaning, and identity*. New York: Cambridge University Press.

CHAPTER 6

(In)(Di)Visible Identities of Youth

College Preparation Programs from a Feminist Standpoint

MICHELLE G. KNIGHT AND
HEATHER A. OESTERREICH

Maria, a senior who attends Westin High School in Bronx, NY, immigrated to the United States five years ago from the Dominican Republic. Maria is one of five children in her family—she has an older brother who graduated from a local community college and entered a four-year city college in criminal justice this past year, an older sister who is married and attends a community college, and two younger sisters attending public schools in the Bronx. She is, and always has been, eligible for free lunch and has worked regularly in a neighborhood bodega to help subsidize her family's income. Maria wants to attend a four-year city college in her neighborhood and earn a degree to be an elementary schoolteacher.

This year, during the spring of her senior year, she learned that the English as a Second Language (ESL) and mathematics courses she took as a freshman at her high school did not meet the city's graduation requirement for math and English. After a family meeting, her parents agreed that she should quit her after-school job to attend a math course at a high school forty-five minutes away from her home school in order to graduate. During the summer, she will enroll in another high school–level English course to compensate for the ESL English course. In addition, Maria must pass three college entrance exams—one each in mathematics, writing and reading—to attend a four-year city college fifteen minutes from her family's apartment. She has spent the past sixteen consecutive Saturdays from 12:00 p.m. to 3:00 p.m. attending a college preparation program designed to enhance her ability to qualify for admission to a city college by providing supplemental instruction to pass the freshman entrance exams coupled with mentoring and counseling. (FN, 2000, p. 9) [1]

Maria's experiences highlight the complex dynamics of college admission policies, college preparation programs, and the realities of adolescents. These complexities emerge from within the intersections of her socially constructed identities as a Dominican, working-class, female, English language learner who wants to attend a City University of New York (CUNY). CUNY, the nation's largest urban public university, has recently limited access for students such as Maria by ending remediation and increasing admission standards. These changing CUNY policies had an impact on Maria's decision to attend a college-preparation program. Her decision to quit her job and take an after-school math course emerges from within the intersections of her familial economic status and her multiple and shifting identities. As we shall discuss, she challenges the "notion that any [person's] life is merely a conglomeration of isolated components that neatly fit into an indivisible whole" (Etter-Lewis and Foster, 1996, p. 3).

This chapter utilizes two tenets of feminist policy research analyses to examine college preparation policy and programs: (1) an intersectional framework and (2) the significance of local contexts (Marshall, 1997; Collins, 1998). An intersectional framework is a lens to examine how the intersections of multiple social structures are constructed to produce equities or inequities. We utilize this framework to analyze the interactions within, between, and among the following in college preparation: youth's multiple and shifting identities, state-level policy formation and implementation, and youth's daily experiences (Wing, 1997; Stage, 1997; Grillo, 1995). Specifically, we critique the conceptualizations of youth as single, mutually exclusive categories of race, class, or gender. The local contexts refer to the historical and political environment of a New York State-funded college preparation program—The Liberty Partnerships Program.[2] We contend that by attending to the intersectionality of youth's identities within local contexts, services improve and access to a college education increases for those very students constructed as "at-risk" in many state policies.

We interweave analysis with description of the four-stage process of a New York State educational policy: problem identification, policy formation and authorization, implementation, and recommendations for change (Harman, cited in Stromquist, 1997). Initially, we provide an overview of the formation of New York State's Liberty Partnerships Program (LPP), describe two Liberty Partnerships Programs, and explain changing CUNY admissions policies. Then, we analyze the implementation of Liberty Partnerships Program by examining the policies, structures, and practices of two Liberty Partnerships Programs to understand how the policy and its implementation are serving youth. Finally, we conclude with recommendations for college preparation within the Liberty Partnerships Program.

Problem Identification and Policy Formation

The Liberty Partnerships Program (LPP) was created as a response to New York's school dropout rate. In July 1988, the New York State legislature voted to amend its Education Act with Education Law 611 and 612 to establish the Liberty Scholarship Program and the Liberty Partnerships Program. The overall goal of the laws is "to develop and implement systemic and supportive interventions and opportunities for students identified as being at risk of dropping out of school to ensure that these students will graduate from high school and are prepared to enter postsecondary education and the workforce."[3] This state-level initiative had been influenced by a national agenda pushing to document school failure for specific student populations (Oakes, Rogers, Lipton, and Murrell, chapter 5). To this end, the New York State Education Department distributes grants to collaborations among postsecondary institutions, secondary schools, and community agencies and identifies them as Liberty Partnerships Programs.

Currently, 58 of these collaborations, known as Liberty Partnerships Programs, serve 49,912 students in urban, suburban, and rural sites throughout New York State. Each LPP identifies students who are considered at risk for dropping out of school and not going on to college. The programs are designed to provide comprehensive services throughout the school day and/or after school to meet the needs of the "whole child" through four types of services: academic support, personal and social development/counseling, workforce preparation, and parent involvement. Within these four types of services, each LPP provides various activities such as tutoring for core academic subjects (math, English, social studies, and science); college, career, and financial aid counseling; ESL Programs; internships; career development; enrichment activities; and comprehensive, holistic needs assessment. In each of the LPPs a caseworker individualizes each students' program.

Westview and Prescott Liberty Partnerships Programs

We conducted case studies of two urban college preparation programs, Westview and Prescott, within the New York State Liberty Partnerships Program over a two-year period. Data included interviews with a director, assistant directors, program coordinators, the college adviser, school guidance counselor, staff members, parents, and students. We observed academic courses, community performances, and staff-student interactions. We reviewed program documentation including semi and annual reports of Westview and Prescott. In addition, we reviewed the 1996–1997 New York State Annual Report on all 58 Liberty Partnerships' Programs.

Westview LPP, situated in a community center, recruits its participants from a predominantly Puerto Rican neighborhood. The program serves 250 intermediate and high school students in an after-school program from 2:00 p.m. to 7:30 p.m. One hundred and one students are concentrated in three intermediate schools and approximately one hundred forty nine students are scattered throughout thirty-four high schools. Academically, students receive homework help, attend supplementary math and English classes, and partici- pate in SAT preparation and one-on-one tutoring. The program offers a va- riety of social and athletic activities during the week. Students who attend Westview LPP play in youth sports leagues and participate in arts-based performances for the local community. In addition, the Westview LPP part- ners with thirty-nine different agencies to provide services from social work- ers, medical providers, and health educators, and to offer jobs and internships for students. The assistant directors and staff are primarily women of color who grew up in the community.

In contrast, Prescott LPP is situated within a high school in New York City where Asian, African American, and Latino/a students commute from all five boroughs. This program serves 130 high school students and focuses specifically on the academic and logistics of college application, acceptance, and attendance. Students take a college skills course, attend summer enrich- ment classes at a university, visit college campuses, and receive continuous tutoring and advisement throughout the day on the high school site. Life skills, rap groups, and boys' and girls' teen groups take place after school. During the summer session, museum and library visits are integrated into the program. The assistant directors and staff are primarily women and men of color who commute to the high school to work.

CUNY Admissions Policies

Although LPP is a statewide program, almost 75 percent of the students who participate reside in New York's urban centers. According to the Annual Report in 1996, 75.4 percent of the 13,370 student participants were admitted to college. Specifically, 31.3 percent, or 4,145, of LPP participants who were admitted to college planned to go on to a CUNY college (LPP Annual Report, 1996–1997). With this high rate of LPP's youth planning to attend CUNY, it is imperative for policy makers and programmatic staff to understand the changing and shifting political context of CUNY's admissions and remediation policies.

CUNY has held a unique place in the history of opens admission policy since 1970 with its emphasis on access at the baccalaureate level. This "baccalaureate-oriented" emphasis provided opportunities for ethnic minori- ties to gain access to four-year colleges at a much higher rate than other state open admissions policies, which focused on access to community college

(Lavin &Weininger, 1999a, p. 3; see also 1999b). However, recent changes in the open admissions policy of CUNY will jeopardize New Yorkers from working class, lower socioeconomic status, and immigrant backgrounds that have historically comprised the majority of the 350,000 who attend the 20 campuses of CUNY.

In June 1998, the CUNY Board of Trustees resolved, "that all remedial course instruction shall be phased-out" of the CUNY senior colleges. In addition, the resolution explained that following the discontinuation of remediation, any student who had not passed all three Freshman Skills Tests in essay writing, reading comprehension, and mathematics and had not met other admission criteria, including mandated SAT scores, "shall not be allowed to enroll and/or transfer into that college's . . . programs" (Hershenson, 1998, p. 2). Lavin and Weiniger (1999a, p. 4) argue that the new admissions regulations will "shift 30 percent of White [applicants] out of senior CUNY institutions and into community colleges, [and] more than half of Asian, Black, and Hispanic [applicants] will be diverted to the latter." These changes in admissions requirements and the impact they will render on students who have long been missing from the demographics of college accentuates the importance of identifying policies that prepare students for access and entry into postsecondary education.

Policy Implementation: Absences and Ambiguities

Policies that create and drive college preparation programs such as Liberty Partnerships Program are constructed in political arenas where issues of multiple economic and social interests vie for legitimacy as part of the public agenda. Some policy analysis operates on the premise that legislation can ensure implementation according to the specific formulated intentions of a policy. We suggest that policy and implementation can mutually inform each other to improve services within programs toward the intentions of the policy and the needs of youth.

Frequently policy implementation within college preparation programs becomes problematic when policies do not require assessment of the efficacy of the programs (Laible, 1997; Tierney, this volume). LPP's policies, however, directly connected to initial funding and continued funding, call for individual programs to be put on probation for ineffective implementation of programmatic services. After a year on probation, individual LPPs can lose their funding if the necessary changes for program compliance are not made and documented. This sanction is based on the required self-reported interim reports of services provided by each individual program, intending programs to move beyond mere symbolic policy compliance. Each LPP program complies with the state requirement to provide reports listing the race, gender, and grade level of the students enrolled in the program, the utilization of academic year activities, and expenses. We argue that it is imperative to determine the impact of such policies on implemented programs and how implementation can inform such policy.

Race, Class and Gender

Conventional policy analysis of programs "argue for the efficacy of particular approaches [services] for all groups of the students, irrespective of race, class, or gender" thereby making it difficult to ascertain what effect these services have for students of different backgrounds (Foster, 1999, p. 80). In the following two sections, we examine the ambiguities of the absence and presence of race, class, and gender in the New York State Education Laws, interim and annual LPP reports, and implementation of the Westview and Prescott LPP programs. We demonstrate how LPP's policies and reports provide important information about students in regard to race, class, and gender. We further explain how attention to where and how these identities intersect and create strength and struggle for youth and their families can support programs.

Within the formation of the LPP Annual Report are the social and historical constructions of youths' identities. Youths have been constructed as monolithic entities of raced, gendered, or classed individuals. The opening sections of the LPP Annual Report include four charts of the 13, 370 students within the program distributed by ethnicity, gender, grade level, and geographical region. Attention to fixed, single categories provides one picture of

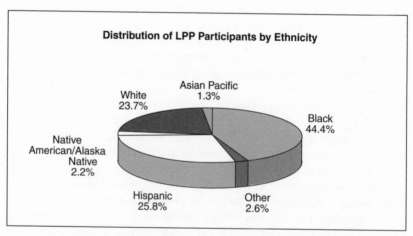

Figure 6.1. Demographics of Liberty Partnerships Program
as Presented in LPP Annual Report 1996–1997

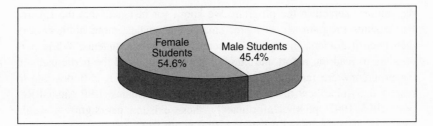

Figure 6.2. Distribution of LLP Participants by Gender

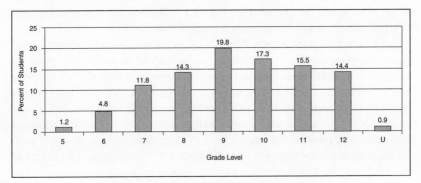

Figure 6.3. Distribution by Grade Level

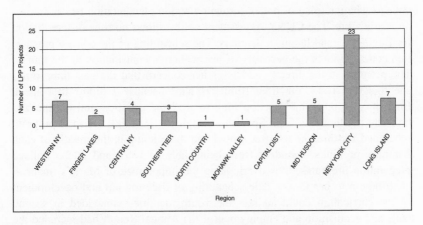

Figure 6.4. Where do LPP Students Come From?

the students served in the program. We know, for instance, that the Liberty Partnerships Program serves more females than males, more ninth graders then twelfth graders, more Black students than Asian students. While it is possible to read the report and know that 54.6 percent of the participants in the program were female and 44.4 percent were Black, it is impossible to readily determine how many students were Black females (LPP Annual Report, 1996–1997, p. 4). Unfortunately, these existing paradigms of single categories have permitted urban and rural youth from low-income neighborhoods to fall between the cracks—"becoming literally and figuratively voiceless and invisible," leaving organizational, programmatic structures and practices in college preparation as things that are grounded solely in mutually exclusive categories (Wing, 1999, p. 16). This construction limits the types of services in college preparation programs to address one group of students without consideration for differences within these groups.

Maria participates in two remediation programs and one college preparation program—both of which treat her as part of a monolithic group of students who must meet graduation requirements and pass CUNY entrance exams in order to attend a four-year college. The LPPs' policies shape current practices in a way that students like Maria are represented as a one-dimensional student without the interacting complexity of her socially, racially, gendered and politically constructed selves. The LPP Annual Report (1996–1997, p. 4) includes Maria in the 54.6 percent of female LPP participants. She is part of the 25.8 percent Hispanic students represented on the ethnicity chart. Her socioeconomic and English language learner status are both invisible in the LPP Annual Report.

The intersections of Maria's socioeconomic status and English second language learner status deserve significant attention in her preparation for college. The interplay of policy formation and implementation has an impact on Maria's life. The CUNY Assessment policy allows no time differentiation for English second language learners. The scheduling of the college preparation course ignores the necessity of her economic contribution to the family. The program never directly addresses her concern that the past three times she took the test, "the time [limit] is hard because I didn't first speak English . . . it takes me just too long to read the question and outline and translate my thoughts from Spanish to English" (II, 2000).[4] Also, a program scheduled for three hours after school and three hours in the middle of each Saturday prohibits a student from being able to work and attend college preparation programs, thus overlooking the importance of Maria's financial contribution to her family. The scheduling of the program and development of the curriculum could address the youth identities embedded in second language acquisition and employment if the Annual Report had included the statistic that 75 percent of the participants in Maria's program were English language learners and worked on weekends and after school. What information could an annual report offer to uncover the multiple types of services needed to sustain participation in school and prepare students for postsecondary education who are working class and English language learners?

When policies require an intersectional analysis, policy makers and educators can better chart and analyze who is being served, at what grade level, and with what outcomes. With this information, staff could determine what services are needed and for whom. For example, in the Westview Program, there is a sharp drop-off in student enrollment from ninth to tenth grade. However, this data does not include which students drop out of the program and what services could be offered to promote continued participation. This information might conceivably provide an opportunity to ask students why they are leaving and what services they need (Heath & McLaughlin, 1993). In a program such as Westview, serving predominantly Puerto Rican students, this information could add to what lies at the root of the absence of some Hispanic groups in postsecondary institutions. Furthermore, specific programmatic components could be implemented in a timely fashion.

An intersectional analysis of student's identities and program services promotes opportunities for students by creating activities to build upon their strengths and their needs. For example, the Westview LPP is aware that many of the students' are Puerto Rican second language learners. Cultural enrichment activities such as drama and newspaper classes emphasize reading and writing in English and Spanish to strengthen students' academic skills. More programmatic structures that meet the needs of students could be offered if the Annual Report reflected these types of intersections for the other 57 LPP programs.

Laws, Policies, and Programmatic Structures

Sleeter (1993, p. 223) states "gender issues can rarely be separate from race and class issues." When these intersections are ignored or "argued that they can and should be dealt with separately," the status quo is maintained. We contend that dealing with the intersections of race, class, and gender disrupts the status quo of who attends college by providing services for students that can and will directly affect their college-going identity. In the following sections, the absence of race, gender, and social economic status in the state legislation is contrasted with the visibility of the student's essentialized identities of race, gender and class in the LPP Annual Report. Intersectional analyses of gender, race, and class in LPP enables educators to understand more fully youth's daily experiences in college preparation.

According to Education Law 611 and 612, proposals for the funding of Liberty Partnerships Programs must explain how the program will identify "students who are at risk of dropping out as measured by academic performance, attendance, discipline problems . . . teenage pregnancy, residence in a homeless shelter, substance abuse, child abuse or neglect, or limited English proficiency" (Education Law, 1988). In addition, the services outlined for students in this policy read as "compensatory and support" such as "skills assessment, tutoring, academic and personal counseling, family counseling and home visits" (Education Law, 1988). In the policy funding and program, "students" are always referred to as a homogeneous group of "students."

While the use of "students" is blind to race, gender, and socioeconomic status in Education Law 611 and 612, all these categories are present in the Annual Report and required in the annual mid-year and end-year self-evaluation by the 58 funded programs. This public annual report is sent to the governor, the senate president, and the speaker of the assembly of New York. The New York State Education Department assesses each program's degree of compliance with the legislation and eligibility for continued funding.

Socioeconomic Status-Race

Although the Annual Report states that "for Black and Hispanics in certain urban centers, and for groups affected by poverty in both urban and rural communities, the dropout rate is increasing" (LPP Annual Report, 1996–1997, p. 1), demographics presenting socioeconomic status in the Annual Report are absent. This absence makes it difficult to ascertain if the program is reaching Black and Hispanic urban youth "affected by poverty" to address how economic status can effect a student's occupational status and attendance in college preparation programs, or influence options in a student's choice of college to attend.

Financial resources are frequently a major barrier to college access for students from low-income neighborhoods. However, few programs can afford to provide substantial financial aid to their participants (Gándara, this volume; Fallon, 1997; King, 1998). In the Prescott LPP, students are encouraged to make choices about colleges through consideration of cultural and financial factors. African American, Latino, and Asian female students expressed how they could not be a burden to their mothers. They explained that if they did not get a scholarship, they would have to go into the military. The college adviser at Prescott believes that financial assistance is crucial for his students, so he consistently assists students in securing financial aid packages that include scholarships and grants. Prescott also actively arranges for students who participate in LPP to participate in other college preparation programs such as Upward Bound in order to secure funding. These elements of the Prescott program are silent in the Annual Report. Similarly, a program such as Westview, which does not offer any assistance or guidance in the realm of financial aid, may benefit from knowing the socioeconomic status of its students and its impact on college attendance.

When Education Law 611 and 612 were passed to create the Liberty Partnerships Program, the latter law explicitly addressed a financial aid component for participants in LPP. It made provisions to adjourn a committee to propose a budget and a plan for providing financial scholarships to twelfth grade participants in LPP who were accepted to universities. In implementation and evaluation, however, the financial scholarship component of the program and students' socioeconomic status have slipped through the cracks, and with them, the inclusion of financial services that have been identified as essential to the success of college preparation programs.

Gender-Race

The Annual Report states that when factoring for gender, differences occurred in the four following areas:

1. Male students were at greater risk of dropping out because of academic performance.
2. Male students were at greater risk of dropping out of school because of behavior.
3. Females were at greater risk because of inconsistent or poor attendance.
4. Females were at greater risk because of pregnancy/parenting responsibilities (LPP Annual Report, 1996–1997, 7).

These gender "differences" slightly extend statements made about males and females earlier in the report. For example, in the opening section of the report entitled "Challenges to Learning: Education and Social Realities," students are discussed in single categories of race/ethnicity, gender, and/or class.

> These students [children in poverty] may feel more pressured to drop out of school because they can't balance their need to earn money with school requirements. Although female students also work to contribute to the financial security of the family, they tend to leave school in greater numbers if they have a caregiver role that becomes overwhelming. (LPP Annual Report, 1996–1997, p. 1)

Information on gender differences is salient in college preparation programs, and learning opportunities in the LPP programs are emerging with the understanding that males and females may require differential provisions for a period of time (Hubbard, 1999). Presently, female students in the Prescott LPP have had access to a rap group for a few years; whereas, a group for males just began in Spring 2000 when the demographics of the program demonstrated the necessity (FN, 2000).

However, the 6,069 young men and 7,300 young women active in LPP do not represent homogeneous monolithic categories of male and female (See Adelman, this volume; Harris, 1997). Lyn Yates (1997) argues that up until the mid 1980s many feminist analyses focused initially on girls or women as a single category. These analyses implicitly took the dominant cultural group as their subject; other cultures and the concerns of other groups within the culture were discussed through an ethnocentric lens. The underlying assumption is that "there is a monolithic 'women's experience' [and men's experience] that can be described independent of other facets of experience like race, class, and sexual orientations," which leaves intact the idea that there is an essential woman or essential male (Harris, 1997, p. 11).

How might services in college preparation programs look if policymakers and educators took into account the intersections of Black, White, Hispanic, Native American, and Asian female and male adolescents' identities? Are all females at greater risk for dropping out because of pregnancy and parenting responsibilities? Do males ever drop out because of pregnancy and parenting responsibilities? Additional questions need to be asked of teens to determine their experiences behind gender-interpreted statistical outcomes. This data needs to be analyzed to determine the ways in which intersections of their gender, class, and racial identities and schooling experiences can affect college preparation.

Intersectionality of Services

The LPP Annual Report's attention directed toward gender and race is noteworthy, as other programs frequently ignore even these demographic markers and evaluate programs with little attention to differences among its participants (Foster, 1999). We are concerned, however, about the policy's failure to conceptualize the intersectionality of the youths' identities with services provided within college preparation programs (Crenshaw, 1993). A framework attuned to the various ways these young peoples' identities intersect enables educators to broaden and strengthen the interplay of services needed for adolescents who participate in college preparation programs. The analyses of the "whole child," the family, and promotion/postsecondary trends that follow are meant to explore the ways in which a structural intersectional framework broadens the way we conceptualize and change services in order to increase youths' postsecondary options.

The "Whole Child"

In seriously taking into consideration the premise that "it takes a whole village to raise a child," LPP provides services through a collaboration of community-based agencies, postsecondary institutions, schools, and govern-ment agencies (LPP Annual Report, 1996–1997, p. 7). The LPP Annual Report charts the services provided through these collaborations such as tutoring, family counseling, and academic counseling, which can address teenagers' multiple identities and lived realities. Unfortunately, the services and the student identities within the program are presented, analyzed, and dissemi-nated for public consumption in a summary of decontextualized percentages (Marshall, 1997).

The summary of services provided for the "whole child" is divided into the following categories: tutoring (64.7 percent), academic counseling (66.1 percent), personal counseling (69.3 percent), enrichment activities (57.6 per-cent), special classes (51.1 percent), college/career/financial aid counseling (48.3 percent), family counseling (32.6 percent), and mentoring (17.4 per-cent). This generalized summary of the services provided is incomplete with-out an understanding of which children in which programs are utilizing which services. What percentage of the 48.3 percent services provided for college/career/financial aid counseling, for example, do Hispanic males receive? At what grade level were the college/career/financial aid counseling services being provided for the 1997 graduating Hispanic males and females which constitute approximately 8.4 percent of the college-going students (Digest of educational statistics, 1999)?

By giving only general statistics of services provided, the report does not disclose how the programmatic services achieved through different collabo-rations have affected different students in different ways. Although the demo-graphics of LPP include White students, we do not find their particular concerns as it relates to college preparation or as it intersects with economic concerns addressed. We have seen in the Westview LPP and Prescott LPP that services are provided to meet the needs of their respective student populations through additional emphasis on reading and writing and financial aid counseling ser-vices, respectively. In the Westview and Prescott LPP a high level of attrition occurs in the ninth and tenth grades. Heath and McLaughlin (1993, p. 220) note: "even the most effective [youth-based] organizations often experience a membership drop-off as youngsters enter their late teens." They no longer want to be a part of organizations that are "just for kids" considering their "elder status" or that have an absence of "programs or activities relevant to their interests." College preparation policies addressing the concept of intersectionality in mid-year, end-year, and annual reports, and within orga-nizational programmatic structures, could be utilized to provide culturally specific programs to understand diverse youth without essentializing them.

We do not know the ways in which the contextualization of the students' lives is taken into account when developing and assigning particular services for college preparation in the interim and annual reports. How is the unique culture of Hispanic females similar to and different from African-American females and White females within the same socioeconomic status, and in what way are the services provided inclusive of their cultures (Reyes & Jason, 1993; Hubbard, 1999; McDonough, 1997)? How do we begin to explain different program effects with different populations without attention to the intersectionalilty of students' lives as determined by race/ethnicity, class, gender, promotion, and college-going rates? How do programs provide services that recognize and incorporate the experiential differences between and among individuals and groups?

Family

If we return to Maria's story at the beginning of the chapter, we uncover another important aspect in attending to structural intersectionality as it relates to cultural integrity and the role parents from diverse backgrounds play in ensuring college attendance (Jun & Coylar, this volume). Families are represented in the Annual Report in the context of "home visits." These home visits are listed as routine, academic, discipline, attendance, family related, health related, and other. They are delineated in terms of the percentage of the whole, not the number of visits made over time.

In addition, these categorical representations do not recognize the types of contributions families make to ensure their student's success. In keeping with LPP's vision and mission statement that "it takes the whole village to raise a child," perhaps the Annual Report should not only acknowledge parents as demographic figures but also create and report ideologies and practices of parental involvement that are culturally situated (Knight, Newton, & Oesterreich, 2000). Much has been written about the importance of parental participation without reframing the notion of family and their participation from the cultural standpoint created in the intersections of parents' multiply identified positions.

Maria's family exemplifies a type of family support that has been frequently overlooked and even misrepresented as uncaring. Maria's income from an after-school job assists her family with meeting their financial obligations. One of the White female instructors in the college preparation program, however, explained that the one thing ". . . we need to get rid of, it is the parents—toss them out because of the way they make them work to make money they don't even get to keep" (II, 1999, p. 4). A Black male tutor in the Prescott LPP explained that students' "parents are unavailable," and if he tries to call them, they never return his calls. He leaves his school number, which is accessible from 8:00 a.m. until 3:00 p.m. each day (II, 1999, p. 3). This type of parental contact and expectation for phone conversation ignored the working reality of several parents.

Immigrant families from low socioeconomic or working class status may have unique needs that must be addressed by instructors, program administrators, policy makers, and counselors (Jun & Coylar, this volume). Within a larger cultural understanding of Dominican immigration, economic, and occupational status in New York City, time and income afforded by certain jobs alters and challenges traditional norms of parental involvement and support (Pessar, 1997). Maria and her parents made a decision to forfeit the supplemental income her after-school job provided in order for her to take the courses she needs and to participate in an enrichment program to enhance her chances of attending a four-year senior level city college. This action translates as strong support for their daughter and her education.

Policies that required programs to represent parents within the frameworks of support from which they are operating might enable administrators and staff to conceptualize parental involvement differently. They could begin to explore deeper levels of parental involvement other than the traditionally constructed financial support, phone calls to check on progress, and involvement in the program itself. Information about the types of support parents from differing socioeconomic and racial backgrounds could provide changes the types of programmatic structures in college preparation programs to build on family strengths rather than subtract from them.

Promotion/Postsecondary Trends

A structural intersectional framework broadens understandings of the interplay of youth's identities and services in college preparation programs to provide insight into how these programs influence and affect youths' positions in occupational and college-going patterns within larger societal opportunity structures. Although we see that 80.3 percent of the students have been promoted to the next grade level and that 75.4 percent of the seniors plan to attend college in 1997, how many actually made it to college? How many stay in college and graduate? If the vision is to ensure that students "enter postsecondary education and the workforce as highly competent young adults," where is the data that show what types of jobs students obtained and how many went on to and completed college (LPP Annual Report, 1996–1997, p. 1)? The trend for LPP graduates' plans to go to college has increased and varied from 59.2 percent in 1990–1991 to an all-time high of 79.6 percent in 1994–1995. How many of these students enter the four-year schools versus community colleges? The Prescott LPP is beginning to address these issues. They are tracking high school graduation rates and college access and retention rates of their LPP students through the Federal Loan Database. We suggest that all LPPs and the Annual Report include retention, access, and graduation rates from high school and college of their participants (Tierney, this volume).

With the new CUNY regulations and the knowledge that ethnic minority students from lower income neighborhoods tend to attend community colleges that lead to lower earnings (Lavin & Weininger, 1999), how will the services provided in this program change students' future economic realities? Given their present economic reality, how is enrollment in CUNY's senior colleges made a viable option? We need to question how the implementation of the 48.7 percent of college/career financial aid counseling services provided intervene on the level of economic support and academic preparation for the Freshmen Skills Tests for the 4,000 who plan to attend CUNY.

For those students who do not go on to college and instead enter the workforce, what type of work are they doing? Did staying in school make any difference for the type of work they are doing, their pay and/or their quality of life? While students who complete high school make a larger presence in the workforce than those who drop out of school, students with only a high school degree and no college face at least a 50% greater chance of being unemployed. Black males and Hispanic females face the most difficulty in securing work. And, even with high school diplomas, Blacks and Hispanics create a larger percentage of manual workforce labor than any other group (United States Department of Labor, 1999).

Bridging the intersections of race and gender and college preparation structures and practices may emphasize the necessity for assisting Black and Hispanic students in understanding the realities of the social and economic stratification that exist within job placement. However, this emphasis must include opportunities to not only critique, but also to fight against current inequitable occupational patterns (Morrell & Rogers, 2000; Gándara, this volume, Oakes et. al, this volume).

Recommendations: Where Do We Go from Here?

Feminist critical analysts seek to provide recommendations that will shape policies, structures, and practices differently to enable adolescents traditionally underserved in schools access to postsecondary institutions. We have argued that policies, structures, and practices in college preparation programs that incorporate an intersectional framework can transform conceptualizations of these youths and shape services to meet their needs. The frame of intersectionality shifts conceptualizations of youth from monolithic descriptive single identifiers of race/ethnicity, class, and gender to the complexities of their multidimensional identities and day-to-day experiences. This shift allows for a broadening of our understandings of their daily lives, policy analyses, and program services that can better meet their needs in college preparation programs and affect postsecondary attendance. We make policy recommendations in programmatic structures and staff development to demonstrate how the utilization of intersectionality can improve programs to increase high school graduation and postsecondary attendance.

Programmatic Structures

Services and activities within LPP embrace the "whole child" and not just a single issue or component such as ethnicity, college preparation, pregnancy, or academic behavior. Thus, although a focus such as college and/or workforce preparation defines the organization, the intersectionality of youth identity at localized levels must direct the structure and the services provided. We offer recommendations for change in five categories: scheduling, localized services/activities, curriculum and pedagogy, retention rates, and staff professional development.

Scheduling

Programs ought to schedule activities around the realities of the daily lives of those whom they serve. For those programs situated in high schools and for students who need to work after school, the scheduling of programmatic meeting times can become part of the systemic structure of the youths' regular schooldays through the implementation of another period during the schoolday. In the case of Prescott's LPP, students met during lunch for tutoring and advisement. For those programs situated in community centers, the scheduling of programmatic meeting times can focus on the ebb and flow of youth in and out of the neighborhood. At Westview's LPP, situated in a local community center, tutoring and support occurred in the late afternoons and evenings after students had returned from their respective schools. Performances were scheduled for Saturday evenings so that parents, relatives, and friends could attend.

Localized Services/Activities

Within the framework of high school graduation, workforce training, and college preparation, all services and activities in each of the LPPs should attend to the intersectionality of the adolescents' identities and needs within a local context (Welch, Hodges & Payne, 1996; Heath & McLaughlin, 1993). As noted in the case of Westview, Hispanic students' academic and social bilingual Spanish/English skills were reinforced in a community performance honoring the Puerto Rican community. Community members and stores provided monetary as well as their own skills in the trades to support the performance that was attended by over 200 members in the Puerto Rican community.

Educators need to further understand the differential achievement of the youths' multiple identities within local contexts. The interplay and intersections of race/ethnicity, gender, class, language, sexual orientation, disability, religion, and other social structures greatly influence the students' experiences and shape how educators and policies construct their needs. Therefore, their college preparation experiences must be seen within the intersections of their identities as indivisible within local contexts. Rather than treating a Hispanic female such as Maria as only a girl or only a Hispanic adolescent, gender-race intersectionality offers the possibility of understanding the uniqueness of culture and needs of a Hispanic female. Including understandings of the intersections of the youths' identities in context necessitates the local and state flexibility and ability to develop programmatic services and recommendations that respond to them and their parent's identities and cultures.

Curriculum and Pedagogy

Curriculum and pedagogical concerns are situated within parity of students' participation as well as the content of the curriculum offerings. Enrollment and achievement within curriculum offerings, academic and electives, need to be monitored for race-gender parity. For example, in the Prescott LPP only African American females were enrolled in the college preparation course. In a program that serves Asian, African American, and Hispanic male and female adolescents, the junior-level college preparation course ought to serve more than African American females. Intersectional analyses will provide support for greater equity in participation and achievement rates of Asian and Hispanic males and females in the program.

In addition to preparing students for the realities of being on college campuses, the curriculum could examine more carefully the relationship between the interplay of youth's multiple identities, work, and postsecondary attendance. In particular, topics could focus on their development of a critical understanding of the dynamics occurring between and among their identities. This critical understanding might include the students' analysis of the division of labor in the workforce and in homes for people with different levels of education. This critical examination provides opportunities for students to construct knowledge linking their present realities and experiences to broader social structures and the possibilities of change.

Retention Rates and Workforce Preparation

Reports from programs must include statistical information that answers to the intent set forth in the policies that created them. LPP was created with the purpose of preparing youth to graduate from high school and enter college or the workforce. LPP might begin to require immediate and tangible evidence of what happens to young people when they leave high school. Many college preparation programs are concerned with the equality of access to postsecondary institutions. These programs keep records on student's intent to enter the workforce or attend a postsecondary institution. Yet, a commitment to equity in college access and attendance within college preparation programs becomes extremely important in a climate of changing admissions policies, retention requirements, and economic realities for youths in urban areas. Records need to be kept on the workforce and postsecondary options chosen and available to these students.

Within each of these levels, records should be kept to examine the inter-sections of multiple and varied social characteristics to determine if the status quo is maintained or challenged by who enters a particular type of college, profession, or trade. For example, Hispanics are the fastest growing popula-tion in the United States, especially among youths ages 18–24. However, many Hispanic males from low-income neighborhoods are continuously con-structed and represented by their absence in postsecondary education. Pro-grams must be able to ascertain from gathered information if the services provided to Hispanic males are challenging these state and national trends in postsecondary education. These types of data enable programs to determine their effectiveness in improving outcomes that their students might not oth-erwise have been expected to obtain.

Professional Staff Development

In order to bridge college preparation in programs and changing col-lege admissions and remediation policies, staff need continuous, in-depth professional development opportunities to align programmatic structures with policies. Staff and students need to be made aware of the differences and similarities between high school graduation, college admissions, and remediation options and other state requirements as soon as possible. Moving beyond one-day workshops, staff can also use existing programs like SEED (Seeking Educational Equity and Diversity) to provide curricu-lar and pedagogical approaches that are culturally responsive and effec-tive with adolescents.

State level reports such as the LPP Annual Report and administrative reports such as each LPP's mid and annual report should be shared with the staff that work with the youths. Sharing the report with staff allows them to identify the students they serve and how to serve them in order to increase their potential for college attendance. Examining the intersections of race, class, and gender give educators a different vision of the experiences and outcomes of the youths and the services needed to promote educational eq-uity and postsecondary attendance.

Opportunities for administrators and staff to visit other LPPs throughout the state provide important staff development. A Westview LPP, whose strengths lie in its ability to involve students in its program and maintain high levels of student and community involvement over six years, could share strat-egies with a Prescott LPP. A Prescott LPP that has strong college admission and attendance rates could provide important curricular and programmatic strategies for a Wescott LPP.

In the midst of concerns about the impact of narrowing college admissions policies, stringent high school graduation policies, and increasing standardized testing requirements, policy makers and educators are working to maintain access and retention for historically underrepresented populations in postsecondary institutions. Increasing the way policy and implementation can work together is crucial to establishing programs to combat these concerns. Students like Maria are caught in the middle of the dynamics of rapidly shifting college admission policies, college preparation programs, and complex daily realities. An intersectional framework provides information for college preparation programs to create concrete policies and programmatic structures to recognize and support the strengths and struggles within the mixture of these realities. Policies that include the intersections of youths' identities with programmatic structures will create opportunities for greater access to postsecondary institutions for students from low-socioeconomic-status neighborhoods. This access undergirds possibilities for youth to reach their potential for the benefit of themselves, their families, and their communities.

Notes

The authors wish to thank Sylvia Celedon-Pattichias, William Tierney, and Betty Lou Whitford for comments on earlier drafts of this paper.

1. FN represents field notes from a two year case study of two New York Liberty Partnerships Programs.

2. Further information on Liberty Partnerships Programs including policies, evaluations, and participating sites is available from the New York State Department of Education.

3. New York State Consolidated Education Law, sec. 612.

4. II represents data from individual interviews with Liberty Partnerships Program participants, administrators, and staff of two LPP programs located in New York City.

References

Berkhout, S. J., & Wielemans, W. (1999). Toward understanding education policy: An integrative approach. *Educational Policy, 13* (3), 402–420.

Collins, P. H. (1998). *Fighting Words: Black Women and the Search for Justice.* Minneapolis, MN: University of Minnesota Press.

Crenshaw, K. W. (1993). Beyond racism and misogyny: Black feminism and 2 Live Crew. In M. J. Matsuda, C. R. Lawrence, & R. Delgado (Eds.), *Words that Wound.* (pp. 111–132). Boulder, CO: Westview Press.

Digest of education statistics. (1999) Washington, DC U.S. Government Printing Office.

Etter-Lewis, G., & Foster, M. (Eds.). (1996). *Unrelated kin: Race and Gender in Women's Personal Narratives.* New York: Routledge.

Fallon, M. V. (1997). The school counselor's role in first generation students' college plans. *The School Counselor, 44,* 384–393.

Foster, M. (1999). Race, class and gender in education research: Surveying the political terrain. *Educational Policy, 13* (1/2), 77–85.

Grillo, T. (1995). Anti-essentialism and intersectionality: Tools to dismantle the master's house. *Berkeley Women's Law Journal, 10,* 16–30.

Harris, A. (1997). Race and essentialism in feminist legal theory. In A. K. Wing (Ed.), *Critical Race Feminism* (pp.11–18). New York: New York University Press.

Heath, S. & McLaughlin, M. (1993). *Identity and Inner City Youth: Beyond Ethnicity and Gender.* New York: Teachers College Press.

Hershenson, J. (1998). *City University of New York trustees approve resolution to end remediation in senior colleges* (pp. 1–3). New York: CUNY, Office of University Relations.

Hubbard, L. (1999). College aspirations among low-income African American high school students: Gendered strategies for success. *Anthropology & Education Quarterly, 30* (3), 363–383.

King, J. (1998). *The Decision to Go to College: Attitudes and Experiences Associated with College Attendance Among Low-Income Students.* Washington DC: College Board.

Knight, M. G., Newton, R., & Oesterreich, H. (2000, April). *It doesn't happen by accident: Creating successful cultures of college preparation for urban youth.* Paper presented at the annual meeting of the American Educational Research Association, New Orleans, LA.

Laible, J. (1997). Feminist analysis of sexual harassment policy: A critique of the ideal of community. In C. Marshall (Ed.), *Feminist critical policy analysis I: Perspective from primary and secondary schooling* (pp. 1–39). Bristol, PA: Falmer Press.

Lavin, D. E., & Weininger, E. (1999a). *The 1999 trustee resolution on access to the City University of New York: Its impact on enrollment in senior colleges.* New York: Ph.D. Program in Sociology, Graduate School and University Center, City University of New York.

Lavin, D. E., & Weininger, E. (1999b). *New admissions policy and changing access to City University of New York's senior and community colleges: What are the stakes?* New York: Ph.D. Program in Sociology,

Graduate School and University Center, City University of New York.

Liberty partnerships program 1996–1997 Annual Report. (1997). Albany, NY: University of the State of New York State Education Department, Bureau of College, School and Community Collaboration.

Marshall, C. (Ed.). (1997). *Feminist critical policy analysis: A perspective from post-secondary education Vol. 2.* Washington DC: Falmer Press.

McDonough, P. (1997). *Choosing Colleges.* Albany, NY: State University of New York Press.

Morrell, E., & Rogers, J. (2000, April). *A case study in reconstructing college "readiness."* Paper presented at the annual meeting of the American Educational Research Association, New Orleans, LA.

Pessar, P. (1997). Dominicans: Forging an ethnic community in New York. In M. Seller & L. Weis (Eds.), *Beyond Black and White: New Faces and Voices in U.S. Schools.* Albany, NY: State University of New York Press.

Reyes, O., & Jason, L. (1993). Pilot study examining factors associated with academic success for Hispanic high school students. *Journal of Youth and Adolescence, 22* (1), 57–71.

Sleeter, C. (1993). Power and privilege in White middle-class feminist discussions of gender and education. In S. K. Biklen & D. Pollard (Eds.), *Gender and education: Ninety-second yearbook of the National Society for the Study of Education* (pp. 221–240). Chicago: University of Chicago Press.

Stage, F. K. (1997). Reframing research, informing policy: Another view of women in the mathematics/science pipeline. In C. Marshall (Ed.), *Feminist critical policy analysis: A perspective from post-secondary education Vol. 2.* (pp. 99–121). Bristol, PA: Falmer Press.

Stromquist, N. (1997). State policies and gender equity: Comparative perspectives. In B. J. Bank & P. M. Hall (Eds.), *Gender, equity, and schooling: Policy and practice* (pp.31–62). New York: Garland Publishing.

United States Department of Labor. (1997). *Labor Force Statistics from the Current Population Survey* (BLS Series ID LFU211762800). Washington, DC: Author.

Welch, M., Hodges, C. R., & Payne, L. T. (1996, April). *Project Excel: Developing scholar identity within a community of respect.* Paper presented at the annual meeting of the American Educational Research Association, New York.

Wing, A. K. (1997). *Critical Race Feminisms.* New York: Westview Press.

Wing, A. K. (1999). Race and gender issues: Critical race feminisms. *The Journal of Intergroup Relations, 26* (3), 14–25.

Yates, L. (1997). Gender, ethnicity and the inclusive curriculum: An episode in the policy framing of Australian education. In C. Marshall (Ed.), *Feminist critical policy analysis I: Perspective from primary and secondary schooling* (pp. 43–53). Bristol, PA: Falmer Press.

CHAPTER 7

Partners for Preparation

Redistributing Social and Cultural Capital

SUSAN YONEZAWA, MAKEBA JONES, AND HUGH MEHAN

To understand an institution, try to change it

—Karl Marx

Introduction

In this chapter, we describe efforts at the University of California, San Diego (UCSD) that engage local elementary and secondary schools in underrepresented communities in collaborative partnerships. The goal of these partnerships is to increase the number of underrepresented students eligible for university admission and, more broadly, to increase the range of opportunities available to underrepresented students after high school. More specifically, we describe the process by which the university, districts, and schools have developed these partnerships. We also report that these partnerships shape and are shaped by the social and political contexts of which they are a part.

The University's Ban on Affirmative Action and the UCSD Response

As with the case study offered by J. Oakes and her colleagues, we consider here the challenges faced by one university to achieve a diverse student body so that this case may have resonance in other institutions of higher

145

education. After the passage of the UC Regents decision in 1995 and the subsequent California state proposition 209 eliminating race- and gender-based affirmative action in admissions, the UC system initiated new outreach efforts to increase campus representation from underrepresented communities (University of California Outreach Task Force Report, 1996). One such effort calls for every UC campus to establish partnerships with local K–12 schools serving educationally disadvantaged populations. New outreach funding of approximately $38 million was earmarked by the state to support these and other outreach efforts annually. Since then, each UC campus has responded to the call for UC–K–12 partnerships in different ways (see Yonezawa & Levine, 2000).

Even before the Regents' ban on affirmative action, the UCSD under-graduate and graduate student body did not reflect the composition of the state of California. In 1997–1998, only 2 percent of the undergraduate student body was African American, whereas African Americans comprised approximately 9 percent of the State's high school graduates. Mexican American and Latino students comprised 10 percent of the undergraduate student body, considerably less than the percentage of Mexican American and Latino students graduating from high school.

Since the University of California eliminated the use of race and ethnicity in admissions, UCSD's population of underrepresented students has dropped significantly. UCSD granted admission to 172 African American students for fall quarter 1999; this is a 15 percent drop from fall 1998 enrollment figures. Compared to affirmative action years, however, UCSD's African American enrollment is down 54 percent. Despite slight increases from 1998 to 1999 in Mexican American admissions, UCSD's enrollment of this group has still not recovered from its initial plunge while simultaneously the Mexican American population in the state continues to grow.

UCSD has responded to the challenge of developing a diverse student body in the absence of affirmative action by establishing the Center for Research in Educational Equity, Assessment, and Teaching Excellence (CREATE). CREATE is charged with coordinating outreach efforts campus-wide and with helping establish and implement the university's K–12 partnerships. Moreover, CREATE encourages many existing UCSD outreach programs to provide services for the university's K–12 partnerships, and helps schools develop new programs for students and teachers. CREATE also monitors UCSD's new on-campus college preparatory, 6–12 secondary school—the Preuss School—which opened in 1999 and enrolls low-income students who show promise and whose parents never completed a four-year degree.

As of this writing, CREATE is partnered with 18 San Diego County schools, 4 high schools and 4 of their "feeder" middle and 10 of their feeder elementary schools. All of the schools meet UC Outreach Task Force requirements in that they are all "low-performing" as defined by their below-40-

percent state standardized test scores, and all serve a majority of low-income students. The 18 schools are "urban," with 8 located in the largest district in San Diego County and the other 10 located across three other districts in the county. Collectively, they enroll a total of 19,762 students K–12.

The partnerships are organized by a comprehensive framework laid out by CREATE to focus the university's interactions with the K–12 schools. The components of this framework are community health, parental involvement, teacher professional development, motivation and information, and academic enrichment. Although the framework was initiated by CREATE, it is deliberately broad enough to include schools' goals and does not proscribe a set plan. Schools work collaboratively with CREATE to decide how best to improve student and family health services, increase parental involvement, enhance teacher development, motivate and inform students and families about post-secondary options, and provide students with additional academic services (e.g., tutoring, Saturday Academies, SAT prep, etc.).

This framework is very useful for presenting a basic understanding of CREATE's initiatives. It appears systematic, comprehensive, and is supported by basic research.[1] The formality of this framework is deceiving. It masks the fluidity and fragility of the work. The partnerships are not solid and static; they constantly change and are in continuous danger of toppling. The presentation of the partnership work as encompassed by such a framework masks the conditions of the local environment and the process by which the schools and university interact to affect change.

UCSD's Recent Efforts in Historical Context

In the eyes of many local educators and community members, UCSD has historically been ambivalent toward K–12 education and particularly distant from the low-income communities in San Diego. Located in an affluent area of San Diego County, UCSD is at least 20 miles from many of the county's low-income and underrepresented communities. In some circles, the university has been perceived as interested in students and schools only as research subjects. Moreover, the teacher education program, although distinguished, is small in size, and not deeply involved in many schools. In addition, the dozens of independent outreach activities on campus have not been well coordinated.

The university's less-than-stellar history of supporting local schools means that CREATE has had to work hard to persuade local educators that UCSD is serious about educational improvement, and that it will sustain the effort. Although the Center has managed to craft some fledging relationships with local educators and institutions, some see CREATE as representing the university, and others view it as an anomalous cadre of individuals interested in

K–12 education but not necessarily representative of the university. A key tenet of CREATE is to establish long-term, trusting relationships with schools and their students, parents, teachers, and administrators.

This notion of partnerships as collaborative and trusting relationships sometimes runs counter to traditional notions of university "outreach" (UCOP Outreach Task Force Report, 1997; UCSD Outreach Task Force, 1997; Yonezawa & Levine, 2000). In the traditional definition, the university brings valued resources such as tutors, mentors, and counselors to grateful schools. At UCSD, CREATE has concluded that it is necessary to go beyond such a one-directional conception and think of school-university partnerships in terms of collaboration, co-construction, and redistribution. We think of the enterprise as working *with* schools to create exciting educational materials and challenging opportunities to learn and, when necessary, to redistribute valuable resources such as high-quality instruction and well-prepared teachers within schools.

Technical, Cultural, and Political Dimensions of School Change

To understand how best to engage in this collaborative process, CREATE considered how theories on educational change and social interaction might inform our practice. From research by Oakes (1992; cf. Oakes et al., 1999) we recognized that school change efforts—particularly those with an equity-minded focus—needed to consider the technical, normative (what we call cultural), and political dimensions of the change process (see Figure 7.1). This meant that while we recognized that schools and students need extra technical resources such as computers, SAT prep, Saturday Academies, and the like, we also saw the value of working with schools and the university to examine the political and cultural dimensions of educational change in a manner akin to what others in this book have called cultural capital. We know that schools and universities as institutions often respond to external and internal political, cultural, and economic pressures that promote inequitable practices and resistance to change. We believe that only by working alongside schools to improve collective cultures of learning for low-income and underrepresented students can our educational institutions become more equitable.

While each dimension of school change is equally important, they are not equally easy to take on. Consequently, we found it necessary and useful to begin with the technical dimension of change. What we have come to realize, however, is that the partnership moves back and forth from the technical dimension of change to the cultural and political dimensions through an iterative process. We also realize that this process influences and is influenced by the surrounding contexts (e.g., districts' reform efforts, or state-mandated testing requirements).

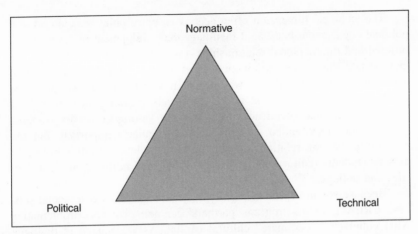

Figure 7.1. Dimensions of Change

Constructing and Redistributing Social and Cultural Capital

Bourdieu's work (Bourdieu & Passeron, 1977, Bourdieu, 1977; 1986, 1991) is particularly useful in helping us conceptualize how we move from and through the technical, political, and cultural dimensions of school change. By contrast to the chapters by Hagedorn and Fogel, and Jun and Colyar, we use Bourdieu's work in an institutional, not individual sense. We see social contexts, that is, various "fields," as flexible and dynamic sites where interaction helps facilitate the accumulation, development, and exchange of many kinds of cultural and social capital. Tangible "goods," like tutoring programs, enrichment activities, professional development opportunities, and college counseling, are technical kinds of capital we make available to schools, to be sure. But we also see these as opportunities within which encounters between teachers, or between students and tutors, for example, provide chances to teach and exchange cultural capital. Cultural capital is those "institutionalized, i.e., widely shared, high-status cultural signals (attitudes, preferences, formal knowledge, behaviors, goods and credentials) used for social and cultural exclusion." (Lareau & Lamont, 1988, p. 156). However, providing students in disadvantaged schools access to institutional and cultural tools can also use cultural capital for inclusion. Thus, we view tutoring and college counseling, for instance, as means to help underserved schools and students acquire the capital necessary for school success, college admission, and university matriculation, all important parts of creating an opportunity-rich future.

The technical dimension often acts as an entry point for cultural and political engagement because it facilitates the development of strong institutional and interpersonal relationships—what Bourdieu (1986) calls "social capital," that is, the participation in networks of affiliation that facilitate access to cultural capital. The way in which we work to redistribute technical resources and tangible goods constructs greater access to valued cultural capital and social networks. It is not getting university students to tutor underrepresented students that is singularly important, but the possibility that the relationship will provide students of color access to college students' cultural beliefs, orientations, and norms about learning, life, and college.

Because social capital is part of a dynamic, interactional social process, CREATE and its program "partners" can help educators problematize what counts as "legitimate" cultural capital. As we engage in dialogue with schools and districts about working together, we exchange ideas about what counts as learning, "high" ability, and "rigorous" curriculum in various social contexts. By building trusting and supportive relationships with schools, and paying attention to the contexts that shape those relationships, CREATE can assist schools in developing and redistributing the social and cultural capital they hold, and facilitate a discourse of political and cultural critique. Because exchanges occur during social interaction among people (Goffman, 1963), arenas that bring people together (even in cyberspace through e-mail or distance learning technology), they always carry the potential for universities, schools, and students to exchange and create cultural and social capital.

It is through examining these relations of exchange in the partnerships we work within that we have found evidence that all exchanges have emergent properties (Mead, 1951). Past events, such as an interaction between a university professional development program and a high school academic department, can influence the meaning or significance of present events, such as an all-day professional development retreat. So, too, the definition of the present is influenced by past memories and inferences about the future, as when a principal anticipates the university's commitment based on a history of past exchanges. And events that transpire in the future help participants reinterpret the meaning and significance of events in the past.

The creation of cultural and social capital is an iterative process. We may lead with technical assistance, but each social encounter has the potential to redefine the relationship between the school, the community, and the university. Thus, we recognize the limitations of economic metaphors such as "exchange" and "capital." We see these as part of a social process, in which partners to our collaboration are part of an iterative process of building relationships of trust, constructing understandings together over time.

The Multiple Dimensions of Capital

The emergent and iterative nature of exchange shapes the ways in which UCSD's partnership coordinators and director work with schools, districts, and the university. Their multidimensional role includes building relationships with individuals across multiple contexts. During various encounters in one dimension, for example, the partnership coordinators engage in dialogue with administrators, teachers, professional development programs, and students about their needs, the school context, and possible support. On the other hand, during encounters with faculty, programs, and academic and student services across UC campuses, CREATE's director and the partnership coordinators can presumably draw on their encounters with local educators and programs as they engage in a broader dialogue within the state. Because the partnership coordinators in particular work with individuals across multiple education contexts, their role is best understood as moving back and forth between being immersed in school contexts, and being distant from that context to reflect how their ground-level interactions might shape education

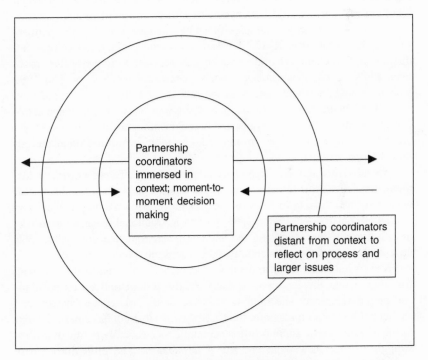

Figure 7.2. Partnership Coordinator Role

in a larger policy-making arena. The partnership coordinators can also learn from their encounters in statewide activities and apply those lessons "on the ground." Figure 7.2 characterizes the partnership coordinators' role.

CREATE's director and partnership coordinators reflect and document their encounters across various contexts in field notes, research memos, and weekly research meetings. We analyzed these data for ways in which CRE-ATE forms relationships with districts and schools, facilitates dialogue with local educators, and moves between the technical, cultural, and political dimensions of school change to accumulate, redistribute, and redefine cultural capital.

The Process of Engaging Schools—and Our University

We now describe how we engage in a collaborative process with faculty, K–12 educators, and students in order to build trusting relationships so that cultural and social capital can be accumulated, redistributed, and redefined. We present examples to illustrate how we engage schools and how this engagement moves from technical considerations to relationships within which more cultural and political dimensions of change are addressed.

Before we describe examples of some exchanges within the partnership, we note that, as in K–12 education across the country, the schools and districts in San Diego are under tremendous pressure to improve their practices and outcomes, particularly state standardized test scores. The 1999 launch of new "academic performance indexes" (APIs) ranking California schools statewide based on standardized test scores has further heightened this frenzy. To this end, the schools and districts have engaged in their own projects—many of them reform-minded—in addition to (and often preceding) the partnerships.

Most notably, the San Diego City Schools (SDCS) began a district-wide, literacy-based reform initiative under new district leadership the same year we approached them to form partnerships. This reform calls on principals and district administrators to adopt new roles as instructional leaders and to take more active roles in supervising and improving classroom teaching. All schools have had to increase substantially their focus on literacy and most have received an on-site, district-trained staff developer to assist in their reform. But in exchange, the district has reduced district administrative staff positions and pulled significant site funding to cover costs. This context has created challenges and opportunities for the UCSD partnerships. It has caused schools to see us as welcome support (often economic, occasionally political) as they struggle to meet new demands. But it has also created difficulties. These include navigating unfamiliar roles and political relationships recently formed in the district and schools, reconvincing educators of the needs beyond literacy instruction (e.g., math, science, history) at their sites, and responding to increasingly disaffected teachers under tremendous pressure to improve their practice and align with the district's vision.

From Economic Exchanges to Trusting Relationships

As the following examples show, CREATE tries to promote a collaborative partnership process. One way CREATE does this is by establishing relationships between high school educators and partnership coordinators. Through these relationships, we work together to assist the school in meeting district mandates, and tackle issues not easily addressed by mandates, namely learning environments and school culture.

Part of the tension between a process-oriented approach to a collaborative partnership and producing specific outcomes is the mistrust with which many schools regard the university. Establishing supportive relationships with schools is key to the success of any school-university partnership. Even more challenging is establishing a supportive relationship with low-performing schools. Schools serving a predominantly under performing and underrepresented student population often face complex problems with uneven guidance or support from their districts.

As CREATE initiates conversations with school principals about a partnership tailored to meet their schools' needs, the partnership coordinators recognize how important it is that principals see our interests as mutual. As the primary partnership coordinator for this high school, Makeba Jones's initial interactions with Mrs. Franco were mostly formal, businesslike, and about funding issues. Mrs. Franco seemed particularly concerned with how CREATE might financially supplement current activities at the high school. The partnering process thus began as an economic exchange. Hoping to shift Mrs. Franco's economic view of the partnership, the partnership coordinator used these encounters with Mrs. Franco to try to build a mutual understanding about the many possibilities available because of the partnership with CREATE and UCSD.

For example, early in the school year, a misunderstanding occurred over the cost and payment of San Diego Area Writing Project (SDAWP) activities with the English department. After a teacher told the partnership coordinator that Mrs. Franco was concerned about who pays for these professional development activities, Makeba made an appointment to discuss the issue with Mrs. Franco. Makeba hoped this was an opportunity to initiate a dialogue about creating support for teachers. As the partnership coordinator and Mrs. Franco sat down in her office to talk, Makeba noticed that Franco appeared slightly annoyed, and Makeba wondered if she already saw the university as unreliable. With this possibility in mind, she apologized to Mrs. Franco for the misunderstanding about paying SDAWP, and said that CREATE does not want to cause schools any unnecessary financial burden. Franco's tense face relaxed a little, and she continued listening. Makeba assured Mrs. Franco that CREATE would cover most of the cost because we recognized how valuable SDAWP's work is to teacher development. Mrs. Franco said she agreed, and that the English department was excited after their first retreat day at UCSD with the Writing Project. Franco seemed more relaxed and less suspicious of CREATE. Through an economic exchange (CREATE pays for professional development, the high school encourages its teachers to attend), the partnership coordinator established some credibility with Mrs. Franco, and therefore, gained capital.

Using an economic exchange to show support for the high school opened a small window of opportunity to talk more deeply about the partnership. Since the partnership coordinator represents CREATE and UCSD at the high school, Makeba thought it was important that Mrs. Franco understand her perspectives about urban schooling. She wanted Mrs. Franco to understand that she personally is dedicated to her students. Makeba talked a little about her educational background, her views concerning public education, and the needs of underrepresented students. Makeba shared her deep concern about the state of California's college-going rates for underrepresented students after the end of affirmative action. She also said that the legislature's efforts to change the tide of equal educational opportunity in California gave her renewed hope that students like those in Franco's high school might have a wide range of options available after they graduate from high school. Mrs. Franco then said she too worried about underrepresented students' achievement and aspirations at the high school. She told Makeba about one Latino student who told Franco on the schoolyard that the best way to raise test scores is to enroll more white students. Such a statement from a student of color told Franco that the high school's culture of college attendance didn't always include high expectations for underrepresented students. During this encounter, the partnership coordinator and Mrs. Franco exchanged perspectives, another form of capital, but more cultural in formation. Their exchange of perspectives, in turn, was a first step in establishing a mutual understanding about the many important issues facing underrepresented students, and the role of professional development in improving the kinds of learning opportunities available to students at her high school. This example shows how shared understandings emerge simultaneously with economic exchanges (Mead, 1951). Exchanging economic capital in this encounter helped the partnership coordinator establish rapport and build cultural capital, important first steps in developing a collaborative partnership.

Exchanging Capital in the Moment

The partnership coordinator also used this encounter with Mrs. Franco as an opportunity to suggest an activity that reflects CREATE's overall philosophy of a collaborative partnership and Mrs. Franco's views about the culture of college attendance. As the encounter seemed to be proceeding well, Makeba hoped her suggestion might help Mrs. Franco see the many possibilities available with CREATE's support. Makeba offered to conduct "Student Inquiry Groups" as a way to help Mrs. Franco learn about her high school from students' perspectives. Makeba explained that student inquiry groups could do more than gain access to students' insights about how the high school might be improved (e. g., curriculum, pedagogy, teacher-student relationships); she said such groups also enable students, particularly students from underrepresented groups, to develop a community. Makeba explained that inquiry groups might help students change how they see their participation in school (a cultural consideration) and how they see their futures, both of which may lead to improving student outcomes (a more technical consideration). Mrs. Franco agreed that such groups could be very valuable. In this instance, Makeba (and CREATE) gained a little more capital by working with Franco to create activities and opportunities that reflected a shared vision of the partnership.

By emphasizing "support," "flexibility," and "collaborating around new ideas," the partnership coordinator and Mrs. Franco shifted the view of the partnership and CREATE from a "funding source" to a "problem-solving collaborator." The suggestion to start student inquiry groups illustrates how school-university partnerships can go beyond addressing the school's technical needs. Partnerships can also generate innovative activities that try to tackle the more deep-seated cultural and structural barriers in schools.

Withdrawing from a "Savings Account": Building on "Old" Capital

Capital does not have to be used or exchanged in the same context in which it is acquired. To be sure, Makeba started to build trust and rapport with Mrs. Franco in the above example. This particular encounter allowed CREATE to set the tone for the partnership. Over time, through a series of similar encounters, Makeba accumulated capital with Franco, in the form of trust, support, and mutual interest. As unexpected challenges arose, the partnership coordinator could draw on her "savings account" of capital to solve problems and generate more capital with Mrs. Franco.

For example, the school's professional development coordinator became concerned about the purpose of the student inquiry groups, particularly how students' perspectives about their teachers might affect the morale of teachers, and the staff developer's professional development plan for the faculty. Student inquiry groups at each of the partnership high schools were organized differently, depending on what the school hoped to learn from the groups and in what department the idea first emerged. At Franco's high school, Makeba had several conversations with a science teacher about the benefit of student inquiry groups. After this teacher offered to work with the science department to organize a diverse cohort of student volunteers, Makeba and Mrs. Franco discussed the idea. Makeba then began working with the science teacher to arrange the groups. Makeba did not formally present the idea to the entire faculty or department chairs, but she shared the idea with individual teachers during informal conversations. Makeba talked with one teacher who, in turn, told the staff developer that CREATE was organizing student groups as one way to learn about teachers' curriculum and pedagogical needs. The staff developer had reservations about listening to students' opinions of teachers, and she felt as though CREATE might be infringing on her "territory" (i.e., supporting the faculty). Soon after, the staff developer arranged a professional development planning meeting with department chairs. She asked the faculty several questions about the student inquiry groups, none of which they could answer, and became even more concerned that CREATE's recent activity might be without the principal's or teachers' support.

The staff developer's reaction seemed to trigger similar reactions from the few faculty and staff at the meeting. Makeba received phone calls and e-mails about the meeting; she needed to clarify the purpose of the groups. Faculty and staff were particularly worried that the partnership coordinator was talking to students without parental permission and Mrs. Franco's approval. As Makeba had already talked with Franco about the groups, she could draw on this and other capital she had accumulated over several months of partnership activities, and feel confident that Franco would support how she addressed their concerns. Makeba responded to an e-mail from a staff person that listed the concerns expressed at the staff developer's meeting. The department chairs and Mrs. Franco were included in the e-mail. They wanted to know the purpose of the groups, how the students were selected, if the selected students represented the school's student population, and if Mrs. Franco approved of the groups.

The partnership coordinator replied to the e-mail and answered the questions, but she copied the e-mail to Mrs. Franco. Makeba wanted Franco to know about the faculty and staff developer's concerns, and that Makeba's response to those concerns was based on her discussion with Franco. Makeba gave a detailed explanation of how the groups were organized. She was careful not to write anything that might inadvertently cause tension or divisiveness. Makeba wrote that Mrs. Franco approved and valued the groups. She talked about the broader purpose of the groups (community building) as though Franco and Makeba jointly agreed that the groups should have such a purpose. She wrote, for instance, "[Franco] supports the idea of learning about students' lives at [the school] from the students' perspectives. We also talked about the overall goal of the groups— to evolve into some kind of community, where students learn to draw on one another for support and information." Because of the conversation between Makeba and Franco about underrepresented students, Makeba wanted to appeal to her concern about supporting students of color, and build capital by strategically portraying Franco as contributing the conceptualization of the groups. In doing so, the partnership coordinator hoped to simultaneously draw on the capital she gained with Franco during previous encounters, and create more capital by telling the faculty that the principal sees students' voices as a powerful tool to learn about the school.

In these examples, dialogue during encounters transformed exchanges of capital from economic considerations (or "goods") within the technical dimension of change to cultural capital (i.e., mutual understanding) within the cultural and, presumably, political dimensions. Moreover, by building and exchanging cultural capital with the principal, the partnership coordinator used that capital to solve unexpected problems, such as the faculty's concerns about the student inquiry groups. Doing so allowed Makeba to continue shaping the partnership according to the vision she and Mrs. Franco discussed in previous encounters. Over time, that vision can be shaped and reshaped as the partnership coordinator has encounters with school faculty.

However, an exchange of capital with a school's leadership doesn't always transfer into an immediate exchange of capital with school faculty. In the example below, the capital exchanged between the principal of Churchill High School and the partnership coordinator provided a starting point for the partnership—to work with the English department. But, as the example shows, the partnership coordinator had to proceed carefully and respectfully so that she could first build rapport and trust before building and exchanging capital with the English teachers.

The Development of Mutual Understanding as a Form of Cultural Capital

Churchill High School and UCSD also moved toward a genuine partnership through a series of exchanges between UCSD and Churchill High School's English department. Susan Yonezawa, CREATE partnership coordinator, several San Diego Area Writing Project teacher consultants, and Churchill educators used capital acquired in multiple encounters to develop shared understandings, interdependence, and transform talk into action.

At the time UCSD begin working with Churchill's English teachers, the department was divided and demoralized. Churchill's principal Elizabeth

Jenkins characterized the department as split between the old- and new-guard teachers. The department was so divided that they often met in two halves—old and new teachers—in separate rooms during department time. One old-guard teacher held a particularly caustic attitude that, according to Elizabeth, "poisoned" the climate within the department and silenced many teachers. Despite her best efforts, Principal Jenkins was at a loss about how best to unite the English department. During one conversation with Susan Yonezawa, Elizabeth Jenkins requested UCSD help her by working intensively with the English department teachers.

Because the request for assistance came from the school administration and not the teachers themselves, Susan felt she had to approach the English department very carefully. She arranged through the English department chair to attend the next department meeting, and at this meeting brought with her members of the San Diego Area Writing Project (SDAWP) to join the conversation. The UCSD group met only with the "old-guard" English teachers only because the partnership coordinator and the Churchill leadership agreed that this group was the larger of the two and the teachers most likely to resist working with UCSD. At the meeting, Susan explained carefully to the English teachers why UCSD was partnering with their school (focus on increasing college eligibility of Churchill students) and how UCSD hoped to work with them. She explained the university's intense focus on collaboration and recognition that the only way this would work was if we took the teachers' opinions and knowledge seriously. The Writing Project consultants listened carefully to what the teachers wanted from this budding relationship. Many of the teachers listened attentively but were skeptical. After some discussion, the group agreed to begin a conversation with UCSD and the Writing project. But they wanted, according to one teacher, "humane professional development." They wanted to hold any professional development sessions off-site, during the week, with paid release time. Susan and the SDAWP consultants proposed a day off-site at UCSD with lunch and parking provided. The teachers agreed.

The partnership coordinator and the Writing Project engaged in an economic exchange with the English teachers of Churchill High. The teachers relented to give UCSD some of their time in exchange for release time, food, and parking. While this exchange of money for time and food, occurred, also taking shape was a beginning rapport between CREATE, SDAWP, and Churchill's English teachers. In a manner similar to Makeba Jones's interactions with Mrs. Franco, Susan's interactions with the Churchill High School English department began as an economic exchange, but moved to rapport building.

The future impact of the exchange was still open-ended, however, because UCSD had not yet used the time with the teachers. Susan and SDAWP facilitators worked with the CHS English department chair and site professional developer to plan the upcoming day's activities. The planning group decided that, given the divided culture of the department, time for structured dialogue about what might be "possible" was critical. Teachers had been trapped in the language of impossibility for so long that the planning team felt that they needed to disrupt that discourse before any other change could occur.

At the off-site meeting, teachers dialogued with SDAWP facilitators and the partnership coordinator on needed changes to improve student achievement in English. Teachers worked in small groups with Susan or one of the Writing Project consultants to clarify their ideas. Most significant, was the English department's self-discovery that although they were divided, they embraced similar goals regarding student achievement and ideas on how to improve it. This development of mutual understanding was important because significant challenges lay ahead that would test the will of the UCSD-SDAWP-Churchill English department collaborative.

By the end of the year, Susan, the Writing Project consultants, and the Churchill English department, held four lengthy meetings. Throughout the series of meetings, all participants engaged in activities and interacted in ways that built trust and informed one another of their mutual interests in supporting Churchill students. For example, the partnership coordinator, the Writing Project consultants, and the teachers did quick-writes about positive classroom experiences they had had recently, or why they had entered teaching in the first place. Susan and the SDAWP consultants worked with the teachers in small groups to help them unpack what they valued most when teaching their students at Churchill. Through these meetings, the team collectively produced two major proposals—a Transition to College Summer Professional Development program and a Writing Center—to submit to CREATE and Churchill High administrators.

Despite their enthusiasm for the process and growing collegiality with Susan and the Writing Project consultants, Churchill teachers remained skeptical that their ideas crafted in collaboration with UCSD would come to fruition. Years of experience in public schooling told them that hidden hurdles would crop up. In particular, they worried that the head counselor would see the Transition to College Summer Professional Development Program as impossible for the ever-problematic "schedule." The key stumbling block was the program structure that had all participating summer school English teachers working together in professional development groups in late morning and consequently, required summer school English classes to be offered in the early hours. It was up to the entire group to try and persuade the counselor to support their proposal.

The partnership coordinator knew that getting at least one of the Churchill teachers' ideas accomplished was essential to furthering the partnership work at Churchill. The teachers had given up several days during the year and much energy to brainstorm with her and the Writing Project consultants and were just becoming energized about future possibilities. If their ideas were quashed, they would return to the language of impossibility.

Susan approached Elizabeth Jenkins, CHS Principal, and asked her for assistance. Susan explained the growth that the department had made (which Elizabeth had seen evidence of on-site already) and the importance of persuading the head counselor to make the schedule work for the upcoming summer program. The partnership coordinator wanted Elizabeth to understand that the English Department was developing momentum, which could be lost without support from the high school administration. Elizabeth was enthusiastic and arranged for the head counselor and her to attend the last UCSD—English department off-site meeting to work out program details. Meanwhile, the Writing Project consultants and the English teachers prepared a brief presentation of the programs they were proposing and why these programs were important. Everyone realized that this interaction between English Department and counseling/administration was important because it was the first test of the collaboration's efforts to move from talk to action, the unity that Freire (1968) calls "praxis."

After the meeting, Elizabeth Jenkins and the head counselor both said that they had been trying to figure out a way to make the program work with the summer school schedule but that they had come to the conclusion that the program was "impossible." The counselor explained that he could not offer all the English courses in the morning because he had more students enrolling in English than sections that could then be offered. The teachers leaned back in their chairs with a discouraged, "see-I knew-that's-what-he-would-say" look.

The partnership coordinator began asking questions to unpack the specific challenges and to brainstorm ways around them. She began raising potential solutions. "What if we brought in UCSD teacher interns to teach the second summer school English block?" "What if we found faculty or graduate students from State College or the university who could teach the summer school courses?" Soon other members of the group began modeling Susan's actions by thinking up ways to add English courses in the late-morning block. Halfway through the impromptu brainstorming session, the counselor began to relinquish his stance that the program was impossible. He began to nod his head when he heard a viable idea and even offered potential solutions. Throughout these exchanges, the counselor, principal, teachers, and UCSD, and SDAWP representatives came to realize that the impossible might be possible after all.

The exchanges described above sound in many ways "complete." But in actuality, they constitute one series of exchanges embedded within many others that happened earlier and later. This is because exchanges always carry with them a promissory quality. When goods or understanding are exchanged there remains a residual of possibility (Mead, 1951). The exchanges described above not only made possible the subsequent summer activities, but they also raised the level of trust and buy-in that the English teachers had in the UCSD-CHS efforts. The teachers believed in the partnership more because through these exchanges they had witnessed a concrete manifestation of our collective work. This would be significant for their participation in future conversations with us and, we hope, eventually for them as a department absent university involvement

Even a series of exchanges that result in a "happy ending," however, can produce unintended consequences. Because exchanges do not happen in a vacuum, activities, products, or understandings that stem from such exchanges can be appropriated by outside actors and used in other settings. Let us provide a concrete example.

The Appropriation of Cultural Capital by Outside Actors

In the fall of 1998, as CREATE began work with Cook and Everett Elementary Schools, Susan and her colleagues from the San Diego Area Writing Project (SDAWP) engaged in conversations similar to those at Churchill High. As at Churchill, CREATE and SDAWP worked with key educators (e.g., administrators, lead teachers, etc.) to create a professional development plan for the two elementary sites. Susan exchanged economic capital (money for release of time and food) again and brought teams of site-selected teachers and administrators from Cook and Everett to UCSD for three consecutive days in early December 1998. The teams worked with Susan and SDAWP to develop a joint plan for literacy professional development. The focus was literacy because of the district's intense focus on reading and writing as part of an intensive new literacy reform effort launched that same year by the district administration.

Similar to the Churchill High English Department, the time at UCSD was important as it gave the partnership coordinator and the Writing Project facilitators' time to develop rapport with the elementary educators. The group eventually developed an extensive proposal. The proposal called for site teachers to work with SDAWP facilitators in professional reading groups, observe in one another's classrooms, send teams to New York to collect data in selected schools regarding effective classroom practices, and participate in intensive summer and Saturday Institutes by the Writing Project.

Yet, again, despite the group's collective effort to craft a thoughtful professional development proposal, Cook and Everett educators remained wary that their new district leadership would approve it. The elementary principals, Mary Martinez and Kathy Woo, were especially nervous given that they had not asked their district supervisors in advance before developing the proposal. Kathy Woo suggested representatives from CREATE, the Writing Project, and the two principals meet with their district supervisors to present the professional development plan. Several CREATE representatives including the partnership coordinator and an SDAWP facilitator, Lisa Miller, attended the generally positive meeting. The principals presented to their supervisors the plan they had developed with Susan and the Writing Project. The district leadership was pleased that the principals had initiated such a comprehensive and thoughtful plan. Everyone left the meeting enthusiastic. Not only had UCSD and the Writing project developed rapport with the schools and had the group turned dialogue to action, but they had also developed credibility with the district instructional leadership.

Susan, however, could not control what would happen next. Frances Kim, one of the district supervisors who attended the meeting, was also the district supervisor over Churchill High School. Ms. Kim had been looking for ways to "encourage" CHS's principal Elizabeth Jenkins to push her faculty harder toward literacy-minded change. After seeing the literacy proposal that Cook and Everett Elementary Schools put together with UCSD, Frances took the Everett-Cook proposal and showed it to Elizabeth as a challenge. Frances used the elementary proposal—used capital developed by UCSD and the schools elsewhere—in the new context of the high school to further the districts ends. Elizabeth interpreted Frances's act as a comparative critique of her high school leadership with a "here's-what-they-are-doing-what-are-you-doing" tone. Elizabeth was taken aback. She hadn't known very much about CREATE and the Writing Project's work with Cook and Everett.

Elizabeth called Susan and conveyed what had happened during her inter-action with Frances. Elizabeth wasn't mad, only anxious that her high school's partnership with the university wasn't earning the same praise as that enjoyed by the elementary schools. Susan was dismayed. She explained how the el-ementary schools proposal was developed and that it had been shared with the district supervisors at the elementary principals' request. She assured Elizabeth that the comparative critique Frances had exercised was unexpected. Susan and Elizabeth discussed whether a similar meeting should be held with the district supervisors. Susan assured Elizabeth that she and the others at CREATE and the Writing Project would be happy to participate in such a meeting.

At the end of their meeting, Susan and Elizabeth had repaired most of the damage caused by Frances Kim's appropriation of capital. They did this by using some of the rapport and trust they had established with each other through prior exchanges. They realized that Frances had used a product Susan and others created through exchanges in the context of the Cook and Everett El-ementary partnerships, to prompt district-desired exchange and action (through a very different style: authoritative versus dialogic) at Churchill High.

Summary

CREATE is engaged in a process of institutional change in schools—and the University. In Bourdieu's (1986) terms, we are broadening notions of cultural and social capital to include the technical, cultural, and political dimensions of change. We are trying to build cultural capital in schools and, when necessary, redistribute it in the direction of students who have been badly served by the social system. We mobilize campus groups and bring resources to the schools. In exchange for those resources, we seek cooperation in enhancing the learning environment in schools and making them more democratic, socially just places.

Our manner of engaging schools does not conform to "technical-rational" models of change (e.g., Smith & Keith, 1971; Pressman & Wildavsky, 1973). In that conception of school reform, the arrow of change travels in one direction—from active, thoughtful designers to passive, pragmatic implementers. Our examples of engagement show that the arrow of change flies in many directions—often simultaneously. It moves back and forth between our partnership schools and the university. This suggests a more dialogical model of change in which educators from all institutions *shape* the partnership effort while at the same time are *shaped by* the political, economic, and cultural conditions within their environments.

Although we often initiate partnerships with an offer of material resources, we view this technical dimension as an entry point for engaging schools in the cultural and political dimensions of change. These three dimensions of our engagement with schools operate in an iterative fashion. We cycle through them across an extended period. Indeed these three may operate all at once—laminated into one encounter with schools.

Our work within the technical, cultural, and political dimensions of change includes acquiring and exchanging valued cultural and social capital within the schools and university (Bourdieu, 1986). Makeba's initial accumulation of capital with Mrs. Franco allowed her to exchange that capital in that encounter when she introduced the idea of student inquiry groups. Here we see a technical move that also has the potential to promote school-wide cultural critique (e.g., teacher expectations and access to information). The encounters that Susan and the Writing Project had with Churchill High School illustrate how the accumulation of capital can also be exchanged to disrupt typical power relations between the counselor, the principal, and English teachers.

We find that relationship building and dialogue are central to developing and using capital in the context of school change. Through these dialogic relationships, educators from all institutions shape the partnership process. But, in order to shape the partnership process in effective ways, school and university folks must also use dialogue to understand the political, economic, and cultural contexts that circumscribe the partnership. Only through dialogue can schools and the university facilitate technical, cultural, and political dimensions of institutional critique and change. Because we see the success of institutional change as relying on collaborative partnerships, we have learned to look very carefully at relations of exchange. We have found:

- There are multiple kinds of exchanges. Economic exchange and the development of mutual understanding are two types of such exchanges.
- Exchanges—both those that exchange resources and those that develop mutual understanding—have instrumental and relational dimensions.
- Exchange as mutual understanding can facilitate dialogue about partnership possibilities and constraints. Such dialogue can allow space for authentic collaborative action.
- The occurrence of more than one kind of exchange (economic or mutual understanding) can happen simultaneously in a single encounter.
- Capital developed in one encounter can be used to develop capital in another encounter—exchange is emergent.
- Capital developed in one encounter can be appropriated by outside actors for either productive or counter productive purposes.

As we continue to work with schools and the university around institutional change, we often worry that those who occupy positions of privilege will perceive our collective efforts as subversive. We realize that power and privilege can pose obstacles or undermine our efforts. Given that the success of school-university partnership is dependent on relationships, we realize we must also engage people who occupy positions of power in constructive dialogue. This is the issue that places our work in a fragile and vulnerable state and forces us to proceed carefully and conscientiously.

Notes

1. For the value of improved health on educational achievement, see Nader et al., 1996 and 1999. For the value of improved professional development on educational achievement, see Darling-Hammond, 1998; Elmore, 1996; Greenwald et al., 1996, Haycock, 1997; and Meier, 1996.

References

Bourdieu, P. (1986). The forms of capital. In J. G. Richardson (Ed.), *Handbook of Theory and Research for the Sociology of Education* (pp. 241–258). New York: Greenwood Press.
Bourdieu, P. (1977). Cultural reproduction and social reproduction. In J. Karabel & A. H. Halsey (Eds.), *Power and Ideology in Education* (pp. 487–511). New York: Oxford University Press.

Bourdieu, P., & Passeron, C. (1977). *Reproduction in Education, Society and Culture.* London, Eng.: Sage.

Cole, M. (1996). *Cultural Psychology: A Once and Future Discipline.* Cambridge, MA: Belknap.

Darling-Hammond, L. (1998). Teachers and teaching: Testing policy hypotheses from a national commission report. *Educational Researcher 27* (1), 5–15.

Drake, P. & Spitzer, N. (1997). *Outreach Task Force Report.* La Jolla: University of California, San Diego.

Elmore, R. E. (1996). Getting to scale with good educational practice. *Harvard Educational Review, 66* (1), 1–26.

Freire, P. (1968). *Pedagogy of the Oppressed.* Boston: Herder & Herder.

Goffman, E. (1963). *Encounters.* Indianapolis, IN: Bobbs-Merrill.

Greenwald, R., Hedges, L. V., & Laine, R. D. (1996). The effect of school resources on student achievement. *Review of Educational Research 66* (3), 361–396.

Haycock, K. (1997). *Achievement in America.* Washington, DC: The Education Trust.

Lareau, A. & Lamont, M. (1988). Cultural capital: Allusions, gaps and glissandos in recent theoretical developments. *Theoretical Sociology, 6* (2), 153–168.

Mead, G. H. (1951). *The Philosophy of the Present.* Chicago, IL: Open Court.

Mehan, H., Villanueva, I., Hubbard, H., & Lintz, A. (1996). *Constructing school success: The consequences of untracking low-achieving students.* Cambridge, UK: Cambridge University Press.

Meier, D. (1996). *The Power of Their Ideas.* Boston: Beacon Press.

Nader, P. R. (1996). The effect of adult participation in a school-based family intervention to improve children's diet and physical activity. *Preventative Medicine, 25* (4), 455–464.

Nader, P. R. (1999). Three-year improved diet and physical activity: The CATCH cohort. *Archives of Pediatric & Adolescent Medicine, 153,* 695–704.

Oakes, J. (1992). Can tracking research inform practice? Technical, normative, and political considerations. *Educational Researcher,* (May) 12–21.

Oakes, J., Quartz, K.H., Ryan, S., & Lipton, M. (1999). *Becoming Good American Schools: The Struggle for Civic Virtue in Educational Reform.* San Francisco: Jossey-Bass.

Oakes, J. (2000). Outreach: Struggling against culture and power. *University of California Outlook.* http:/ www.ucop.edu/ outreach/ outlook/ OL3_voices.html

Pressman, J. L., & Wildavsky, A. (1973). *Implementation.* Berkeley, CA: University of California Press.

Smith, L., & Keith, P. (1971). *Anatomy of an educational Innovation.* New York: John Wiley.

University of California Office of the President. (1997). *Outreach Task Force Report.* Oakland, CA:UCOP.

Yonezawa, S., & Levine, H. (2000). *The institutionalization of K–12 outreach efforts at two University of California campuses: Processes, outcomes, and dilemmas.* Paper submitted to the American Educational Research Association.

P A R T III

Suggestions and Policy for the Future

CHAPTER 8

Making School to College Programs Work

Academics, Goals, and Aspirations

LINDA SERRA HAGEDORN
AND SHEREEN FOGEL

Introduction

As many of the other chapters have indicated, despite the existence of special programs designed to assist urban, rural, and minority youth from low-income areas to attain college degrees and subsequent occupational success, the stark reality remains—only a small number will earn a bachelor's degree or beyond (U.S. Department of Education, 2000; Levine & Nidiffer, 1997; Bureau of the Census, 1997). As Swail and Perna have indicated, the government, private foundations, and others have instituted many programs to counteract obstacles preventing these students from going to college. But despite the proliferation of programs, there remains a lack of research to assess effectiveness. As Patricia Gándara noted, most of the literature regarding special programs does not include empirical data to test for efficacy. Moreover, the existing evaluations tend to be short-term and do not follow students to college graduation and beyond. But most important, the extant literature is not counterfactual; in other words it does not disclose what would have happened to the subjects sans intervention.

The present chapter is divided into three sections. In the first section we present the literature on various key components that have been shown to be significant predictors of college attendance and subsequent college retention. In section two, we fashion a model of evaluation designed to assist policy makers to evaluate school-to-college programs subsequently testing it through the evaluation of three college preparation programs. To conclude the chapter, we present the voices of students included in our analyses. Like the other two chapters in this section of the book, we provide policy suggestions based on our empirical findings.

The three programs of interest were located in California. Chapter 7 (Yonezawa, Jones, and Mehan) aptly described the unique conditions and politics of the state. Although one may argue that California is unique in many ways, the directions that the state has recently taken are also in practice in other states (i.e., bans on affirmative action in admissions and elimination of remedial courses in public universities) and still other states are following California's example. Within this increasingly hostile environment we examine the efficacy of programs through the following specific questions:

- Do students enrolled in school-to-college preparation programs enroll in college in greater proportion than their non-program counterparts?
- Do school-to-college programs affect student cognitions, such as academic self-efficacy, goal orientation, and ego anxiety?
- What are the ingredients for college preparation programmatic success?

The Literature

College admission and subsequent retention are highly related to academics (Gladieux & Swain, 1998; Maeroff, 1999). In chapter 2, Cliff Adelman reminds us that one of the most consistent and dominant variables capable of predicting degree completion is "Academic Resources, a composite index of pre-collegiate preparation that is dominated by the *academic intensity and quality of one's high school curriculum.*" But it is important to link academic achievement with important and key factors such as family characteristics, student self-efficacy, goal orientation, academic support, college information, and the development of study skills.

Based on its strong link with academic performance (U.S. Department of Education, 2000), family involvement has become a salient issue in the popular and academic literature and a focal point of many federally funded programs. However, much of the literature linking families and achievement is correlational rather than causal and focuses on demographic traits such as parent income, education, or occupation (Leslie & Oaxaca 1998; also see Jun and Colyar, chapter 9). While the evidence may indicate a relationship, the demographic conditions of parents may be only a proxy for another construct more directly responsible for student achievement—family social and cultural capital (Clark, 1983; Delgado-Gaitan, 1991; Delpit, 1988; Funkhouser & Gonzales, 1998; Lam, 1997; Lareau, 1987).

As Jun and Colyar will elaborate in the following chapter, the essence of Cultural Capital Theory is that families of each social class transmit the cultural values, knowledge, skills, abilities, manners, style of interaction, pronunciation, and language facility consistent with their social standing. Pierre Bourdieu (1977; 1986) provides a framework of cultural capital, asserting that cultural capital of middle and upper class students provides privilege in terms of educational mobility, economic security, organizational contexts, and personal support systems integral to predicting educational achievement. Many college preparation programs supplement student cultural capital by exposing students to activities and role models that most middle and upper class students would find commonplace but that would be less likely to occur without intervention.

While the range of cultural capital can be quite extensive, equally extensive is the range of academic capital—the level and intensity of experienced academic rigor (Bourdieu & Passeron, 1977; Clark, 1991; Coleman, 1990; Kozol, 1991; McDonough, 1994; Mehan et al., 1996). As Gándara has noted, academic capital is typically higher in wealthy communities. For example, while 86 percent of high school graduates from high-income families are academically qualified for admission to higher education institutions, less than 53 percent of low-income graduates are similarly qualified (U.S. Department of Education, 1998). The situation is compounded by deficits of background knowledge and experiences related to college. In other words, students from lower socioeconomic neighborhoods and family situations may not have taken the appropriate courses or established proper scholastic habits, resulting in grades and test scores that do not meet the admission standards of colleges and universities. Further, the situation is exacerbated when students have language deficits and attend schools with insufficient resources. In addition, college attendance can also be threatened by a lack of familiarity regarding the process and availability of college financial aid (Carger, 1996; Levine & Nidiffer, 1996). The relationship between family socioeconomic status and academic achievement is neither perfect nor linear. Simply stated, parents who are familiar with and understand the importance of higher education are more likely to convey and support the social and academic characteristics leading to college attendance. Overall, many low-income students are not "college familiar"—they are unlikely to have participated in campus visits, spoken with college representatives, leafed through college catalogs, or participated in other activities that create "college readiness" (see Attinasi, 1989). In response to the deficits and conditions aforementioned, school-to-college programs typically seek to expand students' cultural and academic capital and to provide them with the experiences and knowledge consistent with that of their more affluent and privileged peers.

Student Cognitions

Self-efficacy. Involvement in a college preparation program may positively influence students' cognitive beliefs about themselves and their abilities. Bandura (1977) defines self-efficacy as beliefs regarding one's self-capabilities to organize and execute the courses of action required to accomplish specific tasks. Self-efficacy is related to academic performance by affecting the tasks people choose, the amount of effort they expend, and how long they persevere in the face of obstacles (Bandura, 1993; Bandura, 1997; Dweck, 1986; Middleton & Midgley, 1997; Pajares, 1996). A meta-analysis by Zimmerman, Bandura, and Martinez-Pons (1992) indicated that academic self-efficacy has an impact on academic achievement directly as well as indirectly by influencing self-regulatory practices and goals.

Within a socio-cognitive framework, self-efficacy encompasses the cognitive beliefs of one's ability and the expectations of the environment's support of success. While many studies focus on self-efficacy in terms of beliefs about ability (Anderman & Young, 1994; Schunk, 1996; Skaalvik, 1997), less attention has been given to the impact of these beliefs on the student's ability to navigate the environment. For high self-efficacy, it is important that students believe both that they are able to accomplish a given task, and if successful, fair and appropriate gains will be achieved. Without a high sense of self-efficacy, task engagement is unlikely (Clark, 1998), as people do not choose to engage in tasks in which they are likely to fail or not be appropriately recognized or rewarded. College preparation programs frequently work with students to increase their feelings of self-worth and to encourage them to adopt an "I can do it" attitude.

Goal Orientation. Goal theory is a prominent perspective in explaining aspects of motivation (Wiener, 1990; Dweck & Leggett, 1988; Skaalvik, 1997). In addition to goals, orientation is also important when explaining why people engage in specific tasks. There are two main types of goal orientation, mastery and performance (Dweck & Leggett, 1988; Nicholls, 1984).

Individuals with a mastery orientation engage in learning tasks primarily for the enjoyment derived from learning new information, and/or to increase competency in a given area. In comparison, individuals with a performance orientation engage in learning tasks primarily to gain or maintain favorable judgments of their ability (Pintrich & Schunk, 1996). Simply put, a person with a mastery orientation learns for the love of learning, while one with a performance orientation learns in order to be perceived in a positive way.

Adopting either a mastery or performance orientation is associated with subsequent patterns of behavior, cognition, affect, and performance (Ames, 1992; Dweck, 1986; Dweck & Leggett, 1988). Mastery goals are generally associated with more positive patterns of educational behavior, affect, and cognition (Ames & Archer, 1988). For example, mastery-oriented students are believed to be more persistent when faced with challenging tasks, to choose appropriate level tasks, and to partake in active task engagement (Dweck & Leggett, 1988).

Performance goals are generally associated with less adaptive patterns of behavior, affect, and cognition (Ames & Archer, 1988). Performance-oriented students often attribute their performance to fixed, uncontrollable causes such as unfair grading practices or bad luck; while mastery-oriented students more often attribute their performance to changeable, controllable causes such as the amount of effort expended when attempting to accomplish a task (Roedel, Schraw, & Plake, 1994). In addition, performance-oriented students are more likely to assess their ability through feedback from past performances. After failing a task such as a test, performance-oriented students are inclined to believe that their performance reflects low ability (Reisetter & Schraw, 1998; Dweck & Leggett, 1988). Because performance-oriented students are more likely to believe their ability is a fixed entity, they may be less likely to expend significant effort to try to improve their performance in the future. As a result, performance-oriented students often prefer less challenging tasks that maximize success and minimize failure.

Mastery-oriented students are more likely to use feedback effectively after poor performance to determine how they may improve in the future. Since mastery-oriented students often view intelligence as incremental and alterable, they may expend more effort even after a poor performance (Reisetter & Schraw, 1998). Furthermore, mastery-oriented students frequently prefer challenging tasks that offer the greatest opportunity for growth (Ames & Archer, 1988; Nicholls et al., 1989). Mastery-oriented students generally use more self-regulatory strategies, persist longer on tasks, expend more overall effort, and achieve more than performance-oriented students (Bandura, 1996; Pintrich & Schrauben, 1992; Pajares, 1996). Within this framework, the type of goal orientation with which a student approaches school has impact on their successive academic performance, which in turn affects their choice to enroll in college. Thus many college preparation programs take steps to instill within the students the "love of learning."

Goal Orientation and Achievement Behavior. Historically, mastery and performance goal orientations were believed to be two ends of the same spectrum. Current research, however, indicates that goal orientation is actually multidimensional. That is, individuals hold varying amounts of performance and mastery goal orientations simultaneously. Accordingly, having a high level of one orientation does not necessarily mean a low level of the other. Rather, one can be high mastery- and high performance-oriented simultaneously. It is the various combinations of mastery and performance goal orientations (goal configurations) that are associated with cognition and behavior in a variety of areas. Table 8.1 illustrates four goal configurations and related cognition and behavior.

While performance orientation is generally cast as producing less advantageous patterns of achievement behavior, recent research has indicated that

TABLE 8.1
Cognition and Behavior by Goal Orientation Configuration

	High mastery/low performance	High mastery/high performance	Low mastery/high performance	Low mastery/low performance
Value of learning	Self fulfillment and social affiliation	Self fulfillment, social affiliation, and status	Status, social affiliation, and self-protection	Utility, status
Ability and effort	Emphasis on effort	Innate ability enhanced by effort	Ability, with effort in areas of innate ability	Ability with selective effort
Locus of Control	Internal emphasis	Internal and external	External	External with selective internal
Social responsibility	To self	To self, family, and others	To family and others	To self
Role of interest in learning	Important but controllable	Important but controllable with outside help	Critical, controlled by ability perceptions	Critical, controlled relevance perceptions
Role of the teacher in the learning process	Not critical	Important as an ally and support	Critical as gatekeeper of success or failure	Important as pertains to interest and relevance, otherwise, not
Influences of goal orientation	Parents, supportive family, and culture	Parents, family culture with high performance	Performance-oriented family, sibling competition	Detachment, neutrality, utility
Affective dimension	Enthusiasm, hopeful, high expectations for success in all areas	Enthusiastic, hopeful, high expectations, but more anxious	Hurt, hostile, fearful, anxious, resigned endurance, sense of betrayal	Resignation indifference, detachment, passivity, independent choices

performance-orientation does not necessarily lead to negative behavior patterns. Rather, it is those performance-oriented students who also can be classified as "high ego anxiety" that are more likely to exhibit the negative achievement behavior patterns often associated with performance orientation. The combination of high performance orientation and high ego anxiety is termed performance-avoid approach.

In contrast, students who are performance oriented but do not have high-ego anxiety exhibit advantageous behavior patterns similar to mastery-oriented students. This orientation is known as performance-approach. Therefore, it is not whether one is performance oriented, but rather if one has high ego anxiety along with a performance orientation that determines achievement behavior patterns.

Since student cognitions substantially affect achievement behavior, the relationship between college preparation program and student cognition may be an important evaluation consideration.

The Evaluation Model

The School to College Programs Included in the Analyses

This study focused on three programs that served low socioeconomic urban areas, emphasized college preparation, targeted low-achieving to marginal achieving students, and were longitudinal—spanning multiple grades including twelfth.

Program 1. Grand Outreach[1]. The Grand Outreach program targets historically underrepresented minority students with demonstrated potential but marginal grades. Grand Outreach operates throughout California in more than 100 school districts and public higher education sectors. Its mission is to ensure that all students, especially the disadvantaged and underachieving with academic potential, will: succeed in a rigorous curriculum, participate in mainstream school activities, enroll in baccalaureate-granting institutions, and subsequently become responsible citizens and leaders. Direct student services include preparation for college admissions and placement testing, academic support for rigorous curriculums, advisement and career preparation, parent education, and instruction on writing. Most Grand Outreach programs provide an informational class, often meeting before school or during a regularly scheduled class period.

Program 2. Partial Support. The Partial Support Program assists promising students from disadvantaged backgrounds to graduate from high school, pursue postsecondary education, and become contributing members of the community. Accordingly, the Partial Support Program aims to expose at-risk students to college preparatory curriculum, and to provide appropriate mentors for student support. Students who complete high school and are accepted to a post-secondary institution receive a partial college scholarship, renewable for up to five years.

Program 3. Total Immersion. The Total Immersion program operates on a college campus providing multiple levels of academic and nonacademic services. Total Immersion targets middle-achieving (C average), low-income students from underrepresented minority groups. Program students meet daily at the college in before-school sessions that target reading, writing, and mathematics, as well as mandatory sessions on skill development encompassing note taking, extent of time spent on various activities, problem solving, and critical thinking. The program also provides mandatory parent sessions as well as individual, group, and family counseling to assist students in dealing with emotional and psychological issues.

Students Included in the Analyses

The analyses presented in this chapter involve 203 students (112 girls, 95 boys) from low socioeconomic, urban areas in Southern California that were seniors in high school during the 1998–1999 school year. While 144 of the students were enrolled in one of the three college-preparation programs previously described, 63 were not enrolled in a special program but were enrolled in the college prep track of the same high schools attended by the program participants and fit the ethnic and socioeconomic demographics profile. Students enrolled in college preparation programs will hereafter be called the treatment group while those not enrolled in special programs served as an effective control group.

Data Collection and Instrumentation

Initial data collection occurred between September and December 1998. Control group students and those enrolled in Programs 1 and 2 completed survey forms at their high school. Program 3 students were surveyed at the location of their program. All students heard the same introductory comments and were assured of the confidentiality of their responses. All students completed a seven-page survey of questions targeting demographic information, family background and expectations, friends, courses, achievement and college enrollment tests, academic plans, goal orientation, academic self-efficacy, ego anxiety, extent of time spent on various activities, college preparation program participation, grades, and assessment of college preparation program support. Students' cognitive beliefs, such as academic self-efficacy, goal orientation, and ego anxiety, were measured by three separate inventories included within the survey. These inventories were adapted from the Self-efficacy scale of the Expectancy Component of the Motivated Strategies for Learning Questionnaire Manual (NCRIPTAL, 1991); the Roedel, Schraw, & Plake Goal Orientation Inventory (1994); and the Shorkey, Whiteman Ego Anxiety Scale (1977). In addition, two items measuring agency component of self-efficacy were also included on the survey.

Follow-up surveys were sent to both treatment and control students at two points following the initial contact. The first follow-up was mailed approximately six months after students completed the initial survey and was intended to coincide with participant's receipt of college admission notification. The second follow-up was sent one year after the initial contact and was intended to verify that students were actually enrolled and had matriculated at their chosen college.

Analysis

The preliminary analysis consisted of (1) coding variables; (2) developing valid and reliable scales; (3) exploring demographics such as age, ethnicity, and course-taking patterns, and (4), performing preliminary comparisons between the treatment and no-treatment groups. College attendance was coded in two ways. First, we created a dichotomous variable to indicate if students were attending college (1) or not (0). Second, we created a separate variable in which college attendance was coded by the type of institution attended (0 = no college, 1 = community college, 2 = four-year college or university). We performed two analyses of variance tests to see if in general, students enrolled in college preparation programs (treatment) were more likely to attend college and/or were more likely to attend a four-year institution (rather than a two-year) as compared to those not enrolled in a special program (no treatment).

Conceptual framework of model. The hypothesized model begins with measures of the type and degree of participation in college preparation programs that are hypothesized to influence students' cognitions, achievement behavior, actual achievement, and subsequent enrollment in higher education. The model was analyzed with EQS structural equations program for Windows v5.7b. The analyses were conducted in two stages: the measurement model followed by the structural model. The model was derived from the two-stage Commitment and Necessary Effort (CANE) model of motivation (Bandura, 1997; Ford, 1992; Pintrich & Schunk, 1996). The first stage, "goal commitment," was defined as the active pursuit of a goal over time (Clark, 1999). The model hypothesized that commitment results from the self-assessment of three key factors: personal agency (self-efficacy), value (goal orientation), and affect

TABLE 8.2
Structural Model Constructs

College enrollment	*From follow-up, coded as "1" for yes and "0" for no.*
GPA	1 low (mostly Cs and Ds and mostly Ds or below) 2 middle (mostly Bs, mostly Bs and Cs, and mostly Cs), 3 high (mostly As and mostly As and Bs),
Courses	Summation of basic math, alegbra, geometry, general science, biology, chemistry, physics, foreign language, advance placement, and honors courses. Weighted according to importance in college admissions.
Time spent studying	Self-reported number of daily hours spent studying or doing homework as reported on the initial survey.
Mastery goal orientation	Based on Roedel, Schraw, & Plake's (1994) Learning and Performance Orientation scale
Ego Anxiety	Based on Shorkey-Whiteman (1977) Ego-Anxiety Scale
Academic Self-efficacy	Based on the Motivated Strategies Learning Questionnaire (MSLQ) (NCRIPTAL, 1991)
College preparation program involvement	Measures of involvement and participation regarding academic support, infomation sessions, enrichment activities, and study skills development

(mood). According to the CANE model, goal commitment increases with increases in value, mood, and personal agency.

The hypothesized model consists of four domains of variables operationalized using four measured variables and five latent variables described in Table 8.2. A fifth domain, family characteristics, was originally proposed but due to lack of variance, was excluded from the final model.

Test of the Model

Once the measurement model was determined to measure all latent constructs adequately, the structural model was tested. The structural model tested the factors to determine the extent of causation as related to college attendance. The final model (presented in Figure 8.3) proposes that greater involvement in a college preparation programs (as determined by academic, informational, study skills building, and enrichment activities) affects student cognitions by increasing student's academic self-efficacy, decreasing ego anxiety, which in turn increases mastery goal orientation, and performance goal-approach orientation while minimizing performance goal-avoid orientation. Student cognitive beliefs are then manifested in an increase in enrollment in college readiness courses and time spent in study, which in turn increases GPA. Finally, the model proposes that the increase in college readiness courses and higher grades lead to an increase in college enrollment.

Findings

Overall, the families of the students in all four groups (three college preparation programs and the control group) were quite similar. An analysis of variance revealed no statistically significant differences among program and control group students regarding parent/s educational attainment or expectations regarding their child's academic success.

According to student responses, approximately 66 percent of mothers and 55 percent of fathers did *not* finish high school, yet *all* students reported that their parents would be disappointed if *they* did not finish high school. In addition, no significant differences were found in the number of parents in the treatment as compared to the control group who expected that their child would attend college.

Courses

Although there were no significant differences between treatment and control group student enrollment in basic courses such as basic math, analysis of variance equations indicated distinct differences between treatment and control group with respect to advanced courses. Students in the treatment group were significantly more likely to have taken or be enrolled in algebra, geometry, biology, chemistry, foreign language, advanced placement (AP)

TABLE 8.3
ANOVA Results by Course Type

Course	F Statistic	Treatment group (school-to-college program) Mean (E)	SD (E)	Control (no-treatment) No special program Mean (C)	SD (C)
Algebra	5.94*	.99	.08	.93	.25
Geometry	5.69*	.95	.22	.85	.36
Science	23.73†	.97	.16	.74	.44
Chemistry	33.05†	.89	.31	.53	.50
Physics	0.17ns	.42	.50	.46	.50
AP Courses	13.45†	.80	.40	.52	.50
Honors	57.32†	.83	.38	.29	.46

*$p < .05$; † $p < .01$

courses, and honors courses than control group students. Table 8.3 provides the statistical significance of the course-taking tests.

College Enrollment

Figures 8.1a and 8.1b provide graphic representations of student aspirations with respect to the type of college they attend. In the year following high school graduation, only 9 percent of the treatment group students were not enrolled in college as compared to 24 percent of the control group students. Although 6 percent of the treatment students were attending one of the campuses of the University of California,[2] none of the control group students were similarly enrolled. Further, of the 23 percent of the treatment students who reported attending a four-year college other than one in the public California system, many were at prestigious private institutions such as the University of Southern California. One student was at Stanford University. Significantly more students in the control group were attending community college than students enrolled in any of the three treatment groups ($F = 31.52$, $p < .05$).

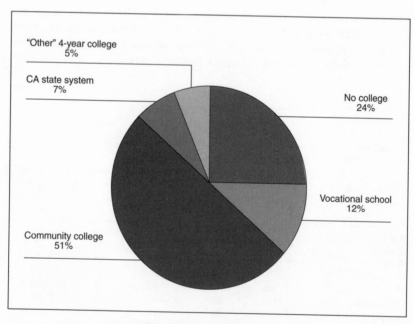

Figure 8.1a. College Choice (Control)

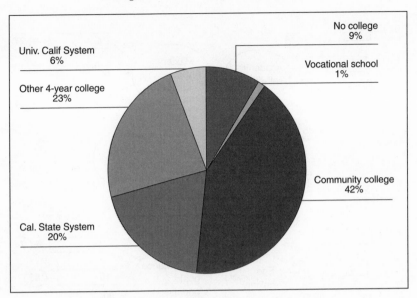

Figure 8.1b. College Choice (Treatment)

Testing the Model

We proposed and tested the measurement model via confirmatory factory analysis (CFA) to determine if measured variables appropriately loaded on latent factors (see Kline, 1998). We further checked to be sure that no indicators were associated with more than one latent variable (crossloading). Both the Lagrange Multiplier modification index, and the Wald (W) statistic were consulted to assure a good fit (Bentler, 1980; Bentler & Bonnet, 1980; Newcomb, 1990). In addition, the fit of the measurement model was examined by the chi-square to degrees of freedom ratio (x^2/df = 155.94/94 = 1.66), (Carmines, & McIver, 1981), the Comparative Fit Index (CFI = .96), and the Non-Normed Fit Index (NNFI = .95).

The standardized measurement model including factor loadings and residual variances is provided as Figure 8.2. Factor loadings may be interpreted as regression coefficients (i.e., factor loadings estimate the direct effects of the factors), while residuals are squared to indicate the variance unexplained.

Structural Model

The hypothesized model, presented in Figure 8.3, and the data for this study fit well. As seen in Table 8.4, the examined indicators of fit all supported adequate model fit.

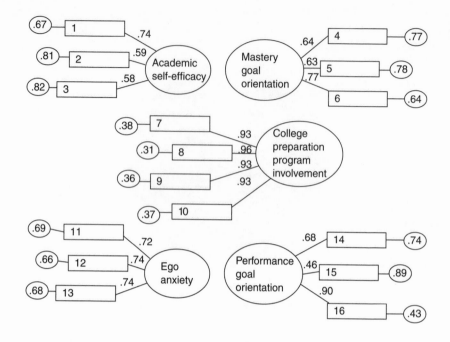

Item Number	Item
1	I believe I will receive an excellent grade in this school.
2	I'm sure I can do a great job in my classes at school.
3	I expect to do well in school.
4	I enjoy challenging school assignments.
5	I keep trying even when I am frustrated by a task.
6	I try even harder after I fail at something.
7	Level of participation in academic assistance.
8	Level of participation in college information sessions.
9	Level of participation in cultural or other enrichment activities.
10	Level of participation in study skills instruction.
11	What other people think of me is very important.
12	I feel I must have the approval of other people.
13	I feel upset when people dislike my looks or the way I dress.
14	It is important for me to get better grades than my classmates.
15	I like others to think I know a lot.
16	It is important for me to always doi better than others.

Note: Rectangles are measured variables, large circles are latent constructs, and small circles are residual variances. Factor loadings are standardized and *all* are significant (*p* < .05).

Figure 8.2. Confirmatory Factor Analysis (CFA) model

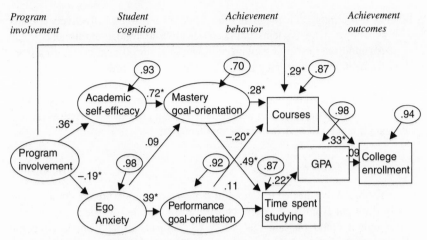

Note: Large circles are latent constructs, rectangles area measured variables, single-headed arrows are paths, and small circles are residual or disturbance terms (variances). All parameter estimates are standardized.
*p < .05.

Figure 8.3. Structural Model predicting College Enrollment

TABLE 8.4
Indicators of Fit for the Structural Model

Fit Index	Definition or Measure	Statistic
Chi-square/degrees of freedom (χ^2/df)	A ratio of 3 or less indicates adequate fit.	243.13/161 = 1.51
Comparative Fit Index (CFI)	Overall proportion of variance explained.	CFI = .92
Non-Normed Fit Index (NNFI)	Adjusted proportion of variance explained.	NNFI = .91

While the model confirms a significant and direct connection between college preparation program involvement and course enrollment, several other indirect paths were also found to influence course enrollment. Our model shows that involvement in a college preparation program influences students' academic self-efficacy, or beliefs regarding ability to succeed academically. Increases in academic self-efficacy then significantly increase students' mastery goal orientation, which in turn leads to significant increases in enrollment in college readiness courses. By increasing students' beliefs in their ability to master the content in a challenging course along with igniting a student's interest in learning, college preparation programs are able to effectively encourage as well as place students in courses leading to college enrollment.

An additional indirect path promoting course enrollment originating from involvement in college preparation program begins with ego anxiety (i.e., student's concern about negative judgments from others.). Lower ego anxiety, operationalized as a decrease in the concern of negative judgments by others, directly leads to decreases in performance orientation or the drive to engage in tasks for an external reward or confirmation.

Conclusions from the Model

The students enrolled in school-to-college programs were not demographically different from their peers who were not enrolled in special programs. Although it could be said that all of the subjects came from low-income homes, both they and their parents had universally high expectations and aspirations.

Clearly, students enrolled in the college preparation programs were more likely to have taken high-school classes that ultimately lead to college admission. The differences were most marked for chemistry, advanced placement, and honors course. Because the direct path from college-level courses to college enrollment in the tested model was highly significant, the policy implications for college preparation programs are evident. Courses likely work in several ways to produce college enrollment. First, the appropriate coursework prepares students to score in the acceptable ranges in college admission tests. Further, college admission committees examine high school transcripts for the enrollment of courses that will allow the student to enroll in true college-level courses.

College Enrollment

Figures 8.1a and 8.1b clearly displayed the different college enrollment patterns of the treatment and no-treatment groups. Specifically, students enrolled in southern California school-to-college programs do enroll in college in greater numbers than their no-treatment counterparts. In addition, treatment group students are less likely to enroll in a community college. Although in some circumstances the choice to attend a community college may be wise, attendance at a four-year institution is more likely to yield a bachelor's degree in a timely fashion (Cohen & Brawer, 1996).

One of the most important contributions of this model is the redefinition of the role of high school courses and grades in college enrollment. While both popular knowledge and college admissions policies often emphasize the importance of high school grades, the model indicates that courses taken in high school may actually be a better predictor of college enrollment than grade point average.

This finding supports the recent emphasis on the role of appropriate courses in college preparation. Current research studies such as Cliff Adelman's "Answers in the Tool Box" study emphasize that despite the concern for high school GPA, grades are not the best predictors of college success (Adelman, 1999). Adelman again emphasized the role of taking the "right" courses *before* college to increase the chances of graduating from college in chapter 2 of this book. Although this connection may almost seem intuitive, many high school students are not taking the most rigorous courses because (a) they fear that harder courses may yield lower grades and lower grades may affect their college admission eligibility; (b) the rigorous courses are not offered at their school; or (c) they are hesitant to take courses requiring high levels of study if they are unaware or unadvised of the significant advantages.

While courses appear to be the best predictor of college enrollment, our model indicates higher levels of mastery performance orientation were not only associated with increased enrollment in college readiness courses, but also increased the amount of time students spent studying. Further, increased study time led to better grades. While this model does not suggest that higher grades increase one's chances of attending college, there may be other benefits of high grades such as scholarship opportunities, awards, and admission to more prestigious institutions.

Cognitions. School-to-college programs may positively affect student cognitions such as academic self-efficacy, goal orientation, and ego anxiety. Involvement in a college preparation program both increases academic self- efficacy and decreases ego anxiety. Thus, students may come to believe in their abilities to obtain a postsecondary education. As academic self-efficacy increases, so does mastery goal orientation. Thus, students may be transformed into life-long learners who appreciate education for its own sake. The combination of these student cognitions may naturally lead to less fear in enrolling in courses in the hard sciences or those designated as "AP" or "honors." As the model clearly indicated, the importance of taking the right high school courses cannot be over-emphasized.

Finally, in answer to our third query, the ingredients for southern California college preparation programmatic success appear to be actions that promote enrollment and success in pre-college courses. Students can be motivated to enroll in courses expected to be challenging by assisting them academically and providing "out of class" enrichment. Practice and exposure to academic content may show students they can do and thus increase academic self-efficacy. Further, programs should strive to enhance students' mastery goal orientation to develop a love and hunger for learning.

Student Voices

In this final section of the chapter, we present the voices of four students whose views were especially poignant, compelling, and useful in understanding how college preparation programs work. Two of the students, Juan and Sandra, were enrolled in a special enrichment program, while the other two, Alma and Trevor, were control group students. Together, they weave a story of the interplay of public education, private enrichment programs, and life's circumstances.

Juan (Partial Support Program—not enrolled in college)

Juan started the Partial Support enrichment program in the tenth grade and attended sponsored functions sporadically throughout high school. Juan confessed that he wanted to go to college and still does, but "things just didn't work out right now." While in his senior year in high school, Juan applied to three institutions, The University of California at Los Angeles, California State at Dominguez Hills, and Loyola Marymount.

> Even when I was filling out the applications I like knew it wasn't going to happen. . . . not yet. I was like doing it because it was what I was supposed to do but I knew it wasn't going to happen.

Juan was accepted at Dominguez Hills and told everyone that he was planning to attend there in the fall. But as the time came closer, he began to feel differently. By summer, Juan was working with his uncle in a family-owned business and knew that the time wasn't right for him to leave home.

> I was working, making money, and being my own self and just didn't feel like going back to school again. A lot of people, especially my parents, told me I should go to college, but I just didn't want to go back to homework and studying and all of that stuff. I needed a change.

In answer to "is there something that the program could have done that would have resulted in his enrollment in college?" he thought a minute and said, "maybe give me more money for college and living. It is hard to see that it makes sense to go to school and spend all kinds of money and take out loans when I can work and make money."

Will Juan ever go to college? He insists he will but he needs to do it in his own time frame and not at the urging of school counselors or program officers.

Sandra (Total Immersion Program—Enrolled in a Private Research University)

Sandra's story boasts of success. She represents the student that a college preparation program could use as their spokesperson. Although Sandra was raised in a very rough part of Los Angeles and attended schools in high crime areas, both Sandra and her parents always had high aspirations for her. When coming into the Total Immersion program in the seventh grade, Sandra and her family knew that she would be attending a private university someday and that her life would be transformed through the experience. Sandra participated in everything the program offered. Her parents[3] attended meetings every week.

Sandra is now enrolled at an elite private university and lives near the campus. She is happy to be at the institution but confesses that the work is a lot harder than what she expected.

> I took all of the hard college-bound courses in high school. I took physics, chemistry, geometry, and foreign language. The work here is really hard, but I know that I am doing ok only because I took all of the hard courses in high school and I had extra help in the program. I had to work hard in high school and that was good because now I know how to work hard and I have to keep on doing that. Being a scholar in the "Total Immersion" program, I couldn't hang out like a lot of kids do. I am glad about that now because I go out with friends and all, but I also know how to work hard and say no to some parties.

In answer to the question would she be in college today if it were not for the Total Immersion Program, Sandra said she doubted it. Her high school friends who were not in the program were not in college and she guessed she wouldn't be either. Sandra is an example of success and will likely continue to be a great spokesperson for the Total Immersion Program.

Alma (Control—Not enrolled in college)

Initially, Alma was very hesitant to speak to us. She even accused us of "looking down on her" because she wasn't in college. Early in the interview she said "just because you guys are in a college you think everyone should go; but I know lots of people who never went to college and they are doing good and are even rich and stuff, so not everyone needs to go to college." As our conversation progressed, however, we fell into a more relaxed conversation in which Alma seemed to be more comfortable.

Alma was in the college track in high school. She thought she would go to college but never really knew what she wanted to become. She is interested in the entertainment field and expressed a desire to be an actress, a model, or even work behind the scenes such as a hairdresser or costumer. Part of the reason Alma didn't go to college was because she just didn't know the type of courses to take to work in the entertainment field. While in her senior year in high school Alma's counselor helped her to request applications from several colleges and universities including UCLA, California State University at Northridge and the University of Texas at Austin. But, Alma confessed that she never completed any of them because she just didn't have the time or the inclination.

Today, Alma's time is filled with her part-time job and her fiancé. She has no immediate plans for college but has not totally dismissed the idea of "someday." We finally asked Alma if she had more support such as assistance in filling out applications or had been taken on campus visits if she might be attending college today. Her response after a long pause was "who knows, I'm happy now and that's all that's important."

Trevor (Control Group, Presently Attending a Community College)

Trevor told us that he never considered college an option—he always planned on attending. He maintained good grades in high school and managed to stay out of trouble despite enrollment in a high school with a large gang population. He reported that he considered four-year universities and even thought about going away from home and joining a fraternity, but deep in his heart he knew that the Ivy League wasn't for him. Trevor reported that his decision was influenced by most of his friends who were going to college and were planning on attending the community college. He also confessed to low SAT scores that would likely have been a problem at prestigious universities. Today, Trevor is enrolled in three courses (10 units) at the community college and holds down a part-time job. He is taking U. S. history plus a mathematics and English course that are both below college level.

We asked about "getting ready experiences" such as campus visits and financial aid forms. Trevor said that he had been on the UCLA campus once, but had not visited any other four-year schools. He had filled out the federal financial aid forms with the help of the high school counselor. With the full support of his family, Trevor had not applied to any four-year colleges because his mind was made up that he would attend the community college.

Trevor aspires to be a lawyer. At this time he does not know where he would like to transfer—"I have time to worry about that. . . . maybe I will go to New York or someplace."

We asked Trevor why he never considered a four-year university and his response was typical of many of the community college students we interviewed. Simply put, nobody ever looked beyond the community college as a postsecondary possibility.

> Four year university? You mean UCLA or something? Whenever I talked about college it was always community college. My counselor, my teachers, and everyone only talked about community college. Maybe it's because UCLA is for rich kids.

During the interview we tried to give Trevor advice about courses and credits, and he seemed to be hearing the information for the first time.

Conclusion

As other authors of the chapters in this book have attested, college preparation programs hold important keys to increasing the college-enrollment levels of low-income and other students. Thus, it appears appropriate to continue to focus efforts on enabling students to believe in themselves, to learn how to learn, and to face academic challenge without fears. We emphasize the importance of offering and encouraging students to enroll in those high school courses that will produce college enrollment. An important way that preparation programs can promote college success is to counsel students to enroll in those courses that will assist them to stay on the college track. However, enrolling the students may not be enough. The programs can further assist students to succeed in rigorous courses through academic assistance, tutoring, and instruction in note taking and study skills. Academics are important!

While the model provided the skeletal structure of how programs can assist students, the voices added the flesh. Through Juan we see that enrollment in a special program may not be enough. Students like Juan needed more guidance to become mastery oriented and immersed in learning. From Alma we learned that without special assistance, students may not realize the lifetime implications of education. Trevor demonstrated that good grades and ambition may not be enough. Finally we see Sandra who enrolled in the "right" courses, partook of the "getting ready" activities, and believed in her abilities—she appears to be the picture of success.

Our evaluation covered only one year's time. To revisit the sample in five years, ten years, or even twenty years may change the picture and the conclusions. For now, however, we close with the positive tone that college preparation programs appear to assist some students to go to college. The United States is frequently called "the land of opportunity"—a country where it is presumed that the trio of ability, determination, and hard work can overcome deficits in wealth or family standing. College preparation programs may be one appropriate medium to develop the ability, encourage determination, and promote hard work among students lacking great wealth or influential family standing.

Notes

1. All program names are pseudonyms.

2. The public postsecondary system is composed of three tiers of institutions. The top tier is the University of California system that admits only the top 12.5 percent of the state's high school graduates. The California State system, middle tier, has less stringent admission policies (generally admits the students in the top 50 percent of their graduating class). The California Community Colleges have an open door policy and hence are considered the third tier.

3. Sandra's mother always attended. Her father attended when his work and/or other schedules allowed. Sandra indicated that her mother rearranged her schedule so that she could be present for everything.

References

Adelman, C. (1999). *Answers in the Tool Box: Academic Intensity, Attendance Patterns, and Bachelor's Degree Attainment.* Washington DC: Office of Educational Research and Improvement.

Ames, C. (1992). Achievement goals and the classroom motivational climate. In D. H. Schunk, & J. L. Meece (Eds.), *Student Perceptions in the Classroom* (pp. 327–343). Hillsdale, NJ: Erlbaum.

Ames, C., & Archer, J. (1988). Achievement goals in the classroom: Student's learning strategies and motivation processes. *Journal of Educational Psychology, 80* (3), 260–267.

Anderman, E. M., & Young, A. J. (1994). Motivation and strategy use in science: Individual differences and classroom effects. *Journal of Research in Science Teaching, 31* (8), 811–831.

Attinasi, L. F. (1989). Getting in: Mexican Americans' perceptions of university attendance and the implications for freshman year persistence. *Journal of Higher Education, 60,* (3), 247–277.

Bandura, A. (1977). Self-efficacy: Toward a unifying theory of behavioral change. *Psychological Review, 84* (2), 191–215.

Bandura, A. (1993). Perceived self-efficacy in cognitive development and functioning. *Educational Psychologist, 28* (2), 117–148.

Bandura, A. (1996). Multifaceted impact of self-efficacy beliefs on academic functioning. *Child Development, 67,* (3), 1206–1222.

Bandura, A. (1997). *Self-Efficacy: The Exercise of Control.* New York: W.H. Freeman and Company.

Bentler, P. M. (1980). Multivariate analysis with latent variables: Causal modeling. *Annual Review of Psychology, 31,* 419–456.

Bentler, P. M., & Bonnet, D. G. (1980). Significance tests and goodness of fit in the analysis of covariance structures. *Psychological Bulletin, 88,* 588–606.

Bourdieu, P. (1977). Cultural Reproduction and Social Reproduction. In J. Karabel & A. H. Halsey (Eds.), *Power and Ideology in Education.* New York: Oxford University Press.

Bourdieu, P. (1986). The Forms of Capital. In J. G. Richardson (Ed.), *Handbook of theory and research for the sociology of education* (pp. 241–258). New York: Greenwood Press.

Bourdieu, P., & Passeron, J. (1977). Reproduction in education, society, and culture. *SAGE studies in social and educational change, 5.* Beverly Hills: CA.

Carger. C. L. (1996). *Of Boarders and Dreams: A Mexican-American Experience of Urban Education.* New York: Teachers College Press.

Carmines, E., & McIver, J. (1981). Analysis models with unobserved variables: Analysis of covariance structures. In G. Bohrnsedt & E. F. Borgatta (Eds.), *Social measurement: Current issues* (pp. 65–115). Beverly Hills, CA: Sage.

Clark, M. L. (1991). Social identity, peer relations, and academic competence of black adolescents. *Education and Urban Society 24,* 41–52.

Clark, R. (1983). *Family Life and School Achievement: Why Poor Black Children Succeed or Fail.* Chicago: University of Chicago Press.

Clark, R. E. (1998). The CANE model of motivation to learn and to work: A two-stage process of goal commitment and effort. In J. Lowyck (Ed.), *Trends in Corporate Training.* Leuven, Belgium: University of Belgium Press

Cohen, A. M., & Brawer, F. B. (1996). *The American Community College.* San Francisco: Jossey-Bass.

Coleman, J. S. (1990). *Foundations of social theory.* Cambridge: Harvard University Press.

U. S. Department of Education, National Center for Education Statistics (1998). *The Condition of Education 1998,* NCES 98-103. Washington, DC, U.S. Government Printing Office.

Delgado-Gaitan, C. (1991). Involving parents in schools: A process of empowerment. *American Journal of Education, 100* (1), 20–46.

Delpit, L. D. (1988). The silenced dialogue: Power and pedagogy in educating other people's children. *Harvard Educational Review, 58* (3), 280–298.

Dweck, C. S. (1986). Motivational processes affecting learning. *American Psychologist, 41,* 1040–1048.

Dweck, C. S., & Leggett, E. L. (1988). A social-cognitive approach to motivation and personality. *Psychological Review, 95* (2), 256–273.

Funkhouser, J. E. & Gonzales, M. R. (1998). *Family Involvement Children's Education: Successful Local Approaches.* Washington DC: U.S. Department of Education, Office of Research and Education.

Gladieux, L. E., & Swain, W. S. (1998). Financial aid is not enough. *The College Board Review* (185).

Kline, R. B. (1998). *Principles and practice of structural equation modeling.* New York: The Guilford Press.

Kozol, J. (1991). Seasons of darkness. *Teacher Magazine, 3,* (2), 35–45.

Lam, S. F. (1997). *How the family influences children's academic achievement.* (ERIC Document Reproduction Service No. ED 411 095).

Lareau, A. (1987). Social class differences in family-school relationships: The importance of cultural capital. *Sociology in Education, 60* (2), 73–85.

Leslie, L. L., & Oaxaca, R. L. (1998). Women and minorities in higher education. In J. C. Smart (Ed.), *Higher education: Handbook of Theory and Research Vol. 8,* (pp. 304–352). New York: Agathon Press.

Levine, A., & Nidiffer, J. (1996). *Beating the Odds: How the Poor Get to College.* San Francisco: Jossey-Bass.

McDonough, P. (1994). Buying and selling higher education: The social construction of the college applicant. *Journal of Higher Education 4,* 383–402.

Maeroff, G. I. (1999). *Altered destinies: Making Life Better for Schoolchildren in Need.* New York: St. Martin's Press-Griffin.

Mehan, H., Hubbard, L., Lintz, A. & Villanueva, I. (1996). *Constructing School Success: The Consequences of Untracking Low-Achieving Students.* New York: Cambridge University Press.

Middleton, M. J. & Midgley, C. (1997). Avoiding the demonstration of lack of ability: An underexplored aspect of goal theory. *Journal of Educational Psychology, 89* (4), 710–718.

National Center for Research to Improve Postsecondary Teaching and Learning (NCRIPTAL). (1991). *A manual for the use of motivated strategies for learning questionnaire (MSLQ)* (Technical Report 91-B-004). Ann Arbor, MI: The Regents of the University of Michigan.

Newcomb, M. D. (1990). What structural modeling techniques can tell us about social support. In I. G. Sarason, B. R. Sarason & G. R. Pierce (Eds.), *Social Support: An Interactional View* (pp. 26–63). New York: Wiley and Sons.

Nicholls, J. (1984). Achievement motivation: Conceptions of ability, subjective experience, task choice, and performance. *Psychological Review, 91,* 328–346.

Nicholls, J., Cheung, P., Lauer, J., & Pataschnick, M. (1989). Individual differences in academic motivation: Perceived ability, goals, beliefs, and values. *Learning and Individual Differences, 1,* 63–84.

Pajares, F. (1996). Self-efficacy beliefs in academic settings. *Review of Educational Research, 66* (4), 543–578.

Phipps, R. (1998). College remediation: What it is, what it costs, what's at stake. Washington, DC; The Institute for Higher Education Policy.

Pintrich, P. R. & Schrauben, B. (1992). A social cognitive model of student motivation. In D. H. Schunk & J. L.Meece (Eds.), *Students' Perceptions in the Classroom* (pp. 149–159). Hillsdale, NJ: Erlbaum.

Pintrich, P. R. & Schunk, D. H. (1996). *Motivation in Education: Theory, Research, and Applications.* Englewood Cliffs, NJ: Prentice-Hall.

Reisetter, M., & Schraw, G. (1998). *The Multi-Dimensionality of Goal Orientations: A Qualitative Study.* Paper presented at AERA annual conference, San Diego, CA.

Roedel, T. D., Schraw, G., & Plake, B. S. (1994). Validation of a measure of learning and performance goal orientations. *Educational and Psychological Measurement, 54* (4), 1013–1021.

Schunk, D. H. (1996). *Self-evaluation and self-regulated learning.* Paper presented at the Graduate School and University Center, CUNY, New York.

Shorkey, C. T., & Saski, J. (1983). A low reading-level version of the Rational Behavior Inventory. *Measurement and Evaluation in Guidance, 46,* 95–98.

Shorkey, C. T., & Whiteman, V. L. (1977). Development of the rational behavior inventory: Initial validity and reliability. *Educational and Psychological Measurement, 37,* 527–533.

Skaalvik, E. M. (1997). Self-enhancing and self-defeating ego orientation: Relations with task and avoidance orientation, achievement, self-perceptions, and anxiety. *Journal of Educational Psychology, 89* (1), 71–81.

U.S. Bureau of the Census (1997). *Educational attainment, by race, and Hispanic origin.* [http://www.census.gov/population/www/socdemo/education.html].

U.S. Department of Education, National Center for Education Statistics (2000), *The Condition of Education 2000,* (NCES 2000–062), Washington, DC: U.S. Government Printing Office.

Weiner, B. (1990). History of motivational research in education. *Journal of Educational Psychology, 82* (4), 616–622.

Zimmerman, B. J. & Martinez-Pons, M. (1990). Student differences in self-regulated learning: Relating grade, sex, and giftedness to self-efficacy and strategy use. *Journal of Educational Psychology, 82* 51–59.

Zimmerman, B. J, Bandura, A., Martinez-Pons, M. (1992). Self-motivation for academic attainment: The role of self-efficacy beliefs and personal goal setting. *American Educational Research Journal, 29* (3), 663–676.

CHAPTER 9

Parental Guidance Suggested

Family Involvement in College Preparation Programs

ALEXANDER JUN AND JULIA COLYAR

Many popular magazines and periodicals offer advice to parents about their children's education: Success, they suggest, depends upon parent involvement at all educational levels. These popular sentiments are echoed in the research journals and other academic literature, and in some instances, are underscored in federally funded programs. While few dispute the notion that children are influenced by their families, different opinions exist on *exactly* how family interaction affects children. This topic has been examined extensively covering children of all ages. While some studies have focused on the affects of family status (Clark, 1983; Delgado-Gaitan, 1988; 1991; 1992; Lam, 1997; Funkhouser and Gonzales, 1998), others have emphasized the importance of family processes (Lam, 1997; Delpit, 1988; Ford, 1993). A majority of the research indicated that students performed better and had higher levels of motivation when they were raised in homes characterized by supportive and demanding parents who were involved in schools and encouraged and expected academic success (Steinberg et al., 1988; Epstein, 1990; 1995). In this chapter we develop a greater understanding of family involvement in the context of college preparation programs, with particular emphasis on low-income urban homes.

A college education can be a life-changing investment offering numerous returns. In general, an undergraduate degree yields better job opportunities, a higher salary, and important skills and knowledge. Enrichment programs have traditionally been based on the premise that every student should have the opportunity to attend college and gain access to these economic and personal gains. Over the years, however, college preparation programs have recognized that students are not the only actors in this process; families and communities of different ethnic and cultural orientations must also be included. Whereas many of the chapters in this book have included references to family involvement, this chapter scrutinizes the relationship in greater detail. Specific to our interest are the following questions:

- How has the literature framed family involvement?
- What social and economic factors should program administrators consider before implementing programs and services for low-income urban youth?
- How do theories of social reproduction, cultural capital, and social networks inform our understanding of family involvement and the overall socialization process for children?
- How can assumptions of family involvement be broadened and challenged to create a more inclusive approach to college preparation and access?

To address these questions, we have organized the chapter into four distinct sections. Initially we provide an outline of previous studies that have identified the definitions, roles, and purposes of family involvement. In the second section we specifically address differences in family involvement with regard to ethnicity and the preservation of individual identities and cultures of low-income, minority families. In section three we outline how the basic tenets of social network theory, social reproduction, and cultural capital affect the overall postsecondary socialization process by preventing low-income families from full participation in their children's education. The final section is devoted to developing an understanding of cultural representation that might help educators apply theory to practice. However, we acknowledge that while we place special attention on family involvement to encourage academic success, this emphasis is merely one aspect of intervention that administrators might consider.

Previous Research on Family Involvement

Family involvement is really nothing more than an umbrella term frequently applied to a wide variety of activities. Broader terms for components of family involvement such as "parent training," "parenting classes," and "family support" have historically been used interchangeably. The overall goal of programs with components of family involvement is to strengthen parents' informal support systems and assist them as they prepare their children for college success. Donald Moore (1992) identified seven varieties of parent and community involvement:

1. parent and school contact via conferences and other communication
2. parental assistance at home through proper nutrition, tutoring, and establishing regular times for homework and rest

3. parent volunteerism at school
4. structural educational and social services provided through community agencies
5. parent service on boards of education or other decision-making roles
6. parental and community advocacy groups
7. use of vouchers for parent choice in the schools their children attend

These forms of parent involvement, Moore asserted, tend to be mutually supportive, and may be most effective when used in combination. While many families might understand and appreciate these efforts, they may be initiated late in their child's academic career (for example during a student's junior or senior year of high school). It is generally accepted that to be effective, efforts must be well planned, consistent, and follow the student from the early childhood years.

There has been a recent surge of interest in parent involvement's role in the educational success of children. Implicit in this interest is the assumption of the traditional family structure. However, as William Julius Wilson (1996) pointed out, the patterns of family formation in urban settings has changed dramatically in the last 20 years; married-parent families have declined while the number of single-parent homes have increased. Further, extended families or community members may at times fulfill parental roles and responsibilities.

Previous studies suggest a link between academic achievement in elementary and high school and parents' regular attendance at meetings and school-related activities (Peterson, 1989; Stevenson & Baker, 1987). In looking at the literature of at-risk students, Donmoyer and Kos added the importance of connecting community, home, and schools, suggesting that normal development is dependent on involving parents and community members in academic life (1993). Other studies supported the notion that families of higher socioeconomic background and levels of education had higher and more effective levels of parental involvement (Lareau, 1987; 1989; Useem, 1991; 1992). Lisbeth Schorr (1988) argued that parental educational attainment was not necessarily a barrier to providing effective support, and that schools that take deliberate action to recognize the importance of the family as educator can establish measurable outcomes.

Utilizing data from the National Educational Longitudinal Study of 1988 (NELS:88), Lee (1995) discovered that family involvement declined as students moved from the middle grades to the early years of high school. However, parents who were highly involved in the middle grades tended to continue their involvement through high school. In fact, the effects of social background characteristics (such as SES, race/ethnicity, and gender) on levels of parental involvement in the tenth grade were minimal compared to the effects of prior parental involvement. Epstein and Lee (1995) found that few middle schools had comprehensive programs for parental involvement and that few parents volunteered their services. They called for middle schools to create programs that encourage school-family contacts and parents' interactions.

Sophia Catsambis and Janet Garland (1997) extended the work of Lee to compare information about parental involvement from middle school to the senior year in high school. They found that for some families, parental involvement dramatically declined as students entered the middle grades and declined further as they entered high school. Their findings also revealed that although most parents were trying to supervise and guide their children during the middle grades, they were doing so with limited assistance from the schools. Families were more likely to supervise and set rules regarding those activities that they traditionally control (such as household chores) than about activities for which they lacked information (such as improving report card grades). Parents reported a lack of communication and infrequent contacts from school personnel. Understandably, Catsambis and Garland found that a large proportion of middle grade students and their families felt isolated or disconnected from their schools and were uninformed about students' progress and school programs.

Involvement Differences by Ethnicity and Culture

According to the extant research, families from different social classes or racial/ethnic backgrounds engage in different types of parental involvement. These differences are found to have varying effects on student achievement and well-being (Schneider & Coleman, 1993). Differential involvement by race could have serious repercussions as it may lead to unequal representation of scout troops, athletic teams, staffed recreation centers, and tutoring activities. Further, adolescents might then have less direct involvement with adults who can act as role models for developing the self, future choices, and goals.

Family Involvement and African Americans

It is important to reiterate that African American and Latino families are no less involved in their children's education than their Anglo and Asian American counterparts; they may differ, however, in the types and levels of involvement. A comparative analysis of family involvement by race may be one useful way to consider African American participation and how it differs from other groups. In one study African American parents were more likely to conduct family discussions, attend school meetings and contact teachers than Caucasian, Asian American, or Latino parents (Lee, 1984). In a later study, however, Heath and McLaughlin (1993) noted at all of their research sites, African Americans experienced lower levels of adult (not necessarily parental) involvement and advocacy than did their peers.

Epstein and Lee (1995) extrapolated differences in expectations and communication finding that while most ethnic groups encouraged their teens to do well academically, few parents established specific rules with regard to homework. Moreover, strict adherence to rules decreased as students transitioned from middle school to high school, particularly among Asian American and Caucasian parents. This finding supports the idea that academic success is not wholly contingent upon an enforcement of rules. Furthermore, they found that all parents reported reducing the frequency of talking to their children about school between eighth and twelfth grade.

When race/ethnic differences were examined among families that maintained rules and communications with their teens, Epstein and Lee found that more African American and Latino parents reported maintaining rules for their high school students in the areas of grade point averages and homework. African American and Latino parents also had higher levels of supervision of their teen's daily activities in both the middle grades and high school, while Caucasian and Asian American parents most often reduced their daily supervision as their children grew older.

An increasing number of articles have emerged challenging previous presuppositional notions of African American school successes (Brody et al., 1995; Clark, 1991; Gándara, 1995; Gonzales et al., 1996; Hrabowski, Maton & Greif, 1998). For example, Reginald Clark's (1983) study on urban families indicated that support for independence, high expectations, close supervision, and respect for the child's intellectual achievement characterized low-income African American parents of high scholastic achievers. Maxine Clark (1991) found that homes with high-achieving students were also highly organized with clearly defined status characteristics. These homes had parents who encouraged academic pursuits, were warm and nurturing toward their children, and engaged in frequent parent-child communication and support. Clark's findings were consistent with White (1982), who found that intervention measures in the home atmosphere (such as parents helping children with homework) correlated with higher academic achievement. Epstein and Lee (1995) found that African American parents' expectations from junior high school to high school (typically between the eighth and twelfth grades) doubled as their children advanced through high school with greater academic success. In general, as children persisted into high school, parental involvement and educational expectations increased with each class advancement.

Family Involvement and Mexican Americans

The term Latino may often be used to encompass a variety of different ethnicities and geographic locations (e.g., El Salvadorans in Los Angeles, Puerto Ricans in New York City, Cubans in Miami). In this section, we do not suggest a universal definition for all Latinos or of Latino family involvement. Indeed, rather than focus broadly or generalize upon multiple perspectives that surround the idea of Latino family involvement, we focus on the perspectives of one particular group, Mexican American families, to understand how their experiences differ from Caucasian families.

Comparative studies of communication patterns between middle class Caucasian and Mexican American families revealed that behavior required for success in school do not differ by race. Mexican American students who were not exposed to certain acculturating experiences more prevalent in Caucasian homes, however, were at risk for school failure (Erickson, 1987). Laosa (1978) demonstrated that Mexican American mothers employed different behavior than Caucasian mothers when teaching specific tasks to their children, and that this behavior sometimes conflicted with demands at school. For example, where White middle class mothers used an inquiry approach to teaching tasks, Hispanic mothers were more likely to provide the solutions for their children.

Steinberg, Dornbusch, and Brown (1992) conducted a study on ethnic differences in academic achievement and found that Hispanic parents were more authoritarian (warm and strict, yet undemocratic) as opposed to authoritative (strict yet democratic) in comparison to their Caucasian counterparts. They suggested that this difference may in part contribute to lower levels of scholastic achievement for Latino students. Other researchers familiar with Mexican American culture have attributed differences in academic achievement to Mexican parents' lack of familiarity with the American school system, a fear of not being able to communicate with school personnel, and competing family and work demands on time (Gándara, 1995).

Although previous literature suggests that working class Mexican American families may exhibit lower rates of participation in school activities, a study of Mexican Americans living in a small town in rural central California found that Hispanic families were not only participating, but were also empowered to effect change in their children's schools (Delgado-Gaitan, 1991). As anticipated, family involvement resulted in increased academic achievement. The roles of authority in parent-teacher organizations were distributed among both Spanish and English speakers, and parents in this community conducted bilingual meetings for PTA and other school-related events. Armed with information about their rights and responsibilities, parents organized themselves into a powerful lobbying force on behalf of their children, showing their deep care for their children's education.

Social Networks, Social Reproduction, and Cultural Capital

Socioeconomic status (SES), often defined as a combination of the educational and occupational status of parents, has often been accepted as the single most powerful predictor of educational outcomes (Gándara, 1995; Jencks et al., 1972; Sigel & Laosa, 1983). Much less consensus exists, however, on the question of *why* socioeconomic status has such powerful effects. Social reproduction theorists have suggested that the social reproduction of status differences between groups leads to the perpetuation of inequities in society—that is, advantages are maintained by upper-income families while opportunities for equity for lower-income families are continually denied (Bowles & Gintis, 1976). As Brofenbrenner (1979) first posited over two decades ago, most parents are genuinely concerned about their children's academic success regardless of family income levels. Although both working and middle class parents desire scholastic success for their children, social positions may force them to employ different strategies to achieve that goal. Thus, social positions and class barriers have inhibited working class families from obtaining social networks, connections, and greater amounts of cultural capital.

Social Network Theory

The social network paradigm highlights the importance of "significant others" within each person's social system for providing support and resources such as information or financial assistance (Blau, 1964; Barnes, 1972; Leinhart, 1977). Although several definitions of social networks exist, the most common reference is to linkages between individuals, groups, and institutions. D'Abbs (1982) suggested that one of the primary functions of an individual's social network is to provide a buffer against negative stresses, thereby promoting greater psychological and personal well-being. Simply stated, children with well-developed social networks will have more positive educational outcomes (Coates, 1987).

Families may play an important role in reproducing the structure of inequality from generation to generation. Social network theorists studying student achievement found that high and middle income families have higher overall resources leading to salient advantages with respect to educational retention, promotion, and placement decisions (Granovetter, 1973; 1983; Yonezawa, 1998). In a qualitative study on family and school relationships, Annette Lareau (1987) found that social class yielded unequal resources for parents when complying with teachers' requests for parental participation. As a result, middle class parents were more likely to participate in school activities. She further found that working class parents promoted educational success differently from their upper class counterparts. Working class parents typically deferred to classroom teachers—in effect surrendering the responsibility of educating their children—while upper class parents did not. In a later study (1989), Lareau found that white, upper middle class parents acquired greater autonomy by learning how to navigate through the school system on their children's behalf. Through social networks, parents also learned how to develop stronger relationships with their children's teachers via greater involvement and volunteerism.

In his study of the effects of social class on parental values, Melvin Kohn (1977) found that the higher a parent's social class position, the more likely he or she valued characteristics of self-direction over conformity to external authority. Kohn suggested that this pattern was related to the different conditions of life faced by parents in different socioeconomic positions. Parents with high SES were more typically independent, freer from close supervision, and more likely worked at nonroutine tasks. Hence, they were more likely to value characteristics such as independence and self-direction in their children.

Another example is provided by Useem (1991, 1992) who found that highly educated wealthy white mothers who were well integrated into a web of school activities and informal parent networks were more likely to influence their children's math placement. Conversely, less educated white mothers with fewer contacts deferred decision making and entrusted school officials with their children's placement.

Coleman (1987) referred to social networks as an integral component of social capital, which he defined as the informational, attitudinal, and behavioral norms and skills that individuals spend or invest to improve their chances for success in societal institutions (such as schools). Individuals obtain capital through their social networks. Coleman, Hoffer, and Kilgore (1982) reported that students in Catholic and other private schools achieved at a higher level in math and verbal skills than students in public schools largely because of the transmission of common messages, expectations, and norms from the family, church, and school.

According to Maxine Clark, social networks provide social support: ". . . the availability of people on whom we can rely, people who let us know that they care about, value, and love us" (1991, p. 45). Clark contended that the greater an adolescent's social support system, the greater the likelihood of success in school. She suggested schools strengthen support systems for youth, especially poor and/or minority youth, by developing mentoring, tutoring, and coaching programs led by responsible and responsive adults.

Epstein's (1987) work on overlapping spheres of influence integrated educational, sociological, and psychological perspectives in social organizations to emphasize the importance of schools, families, and communities working together to meet the needs of children. A central principle of his theory was that certain goals, such as student academic success, were of mutual interest to people in each institution, and were best achieved through cooperative action and support. The attitudes and practices of individuals within each context determined the relationship between different institutions. These findings point to the need to understand notions of social reproduction and relations of power—what the French sociologist Pierre Bourdieu (1974; 1977; 1986) referred to as cultural capital.

Social Reproduction and Cultural Capital

Another compelling argument with regard to inequality is that of reproduction theory, and specifically, cultural capital. Social reproduction theorists have suggested that inequality is a consequence of capitalist structures and forces that constrain the mobility of lower class youth (Bourdieu & Passerson, 1977; Bowles & Gintis, 1976). A central aspect to reproduction theory is Bourdieu's notion of cultural capital. Bourdieu developed his ideas from Weber's theory of status groups (1920), which were considered to be collectives that generated or appropriated distinctive cultural traits and styles as a means to monopolize scarce social and economic resources.

Bourdieu's framework of cultural capital has been highly instructive to studies of class status and educational achievement. He claimed that the cultural capital of middle and upper class students privileges them in terms of economic security, organizational contexts, and personal support systems. In the preceding chapter, Hagedorn and Fogel provided definitions and examples of Bourdieu's framework. According to Bourdieu, the families of each social class transmit distinctive cultural knowledge thus creating a divide between the children of upper and lower class families (Bourdieu, 1977). Cultural capital includes linguistic and cultural competencies that are inherited and learned.

Different scholars have defined Bourdieu's cultural capital in different ways. Lamont and Lareau (1988) defined cultural capital as commonly shared, high status cultural "signals" used for social and cultural exclusion. Signals included attitudes, preferences, knowledge, behavior, possessions, and credentials that may function as informal academic standards as well as characteristics of the dominant class. The notion of social or cultural exclusion includes denial of access to certain jobs or other resources available to some but not others, or the segregation of low status groups from those with high status. Individuals without the required cultural capital may have lower educational aspirations, self-select themselves out of particular situations (e.g., not enroll in higher education), or "overperform" in order to compensate for their less valued cultural resources (Lamont & Lareau, 1988).

Defined another way, cultural capital may be considered "the knowledge that social elites value yet schools do not teach" (McDonough, 1997, p. 9). This implies that parental influence is an important factor to consider. McDonough (1994) documented that parents with high socioeconomic status were quite often strategic in maximizing the likelihood that their children will gain acceptance to top postsecondary institutions. Conversely, this type of support for higher education was found to be missing in families of lower socioeconomic status or from non–college attending families (Mehan et al., 1996). Cultural capital is transmitted from one generation to the next by parents who inform their children about the value, importance, and process of securing a college education. According to McDonough:

> Cultural capital is that property that middle and upper class families transmit to their offspring which substitutes for or supplements the transmission of economic capital as a means of maintaining class status and privilege across generations. Middle- and upper-class families highly value a college education and advanced degrees as a means of ensuring continued economic security, in addition to whatever monetary assets can be passed along to their offspring. (1994, p. 8)

Finally, Dimaggio (1982) suggested that cultural capital not only mediates the relationship between family background and school outcomes, but has its greatest impact on educational attainment through the quality of colleges attended. He surmised that cultural capital plays different roles in the mobility strategies of different classes and genders. Cultural capital, measured as the composite of cultural activities, attitudes, and knowledge, was found to increase the frequency of interactions about postsecondary plans between high school students and "high status" individuals, including teachers, school counselors, and peers (DiMaggio & Mohr, 1985).

Researchers have recently applied Pierre Bourdieu's concepts of cultural capital to enrollment behaviors (Jun & Tierney, 1999; Maeroff, 1998; McDonough, 1997; Mehan et al., 1996; Tierney & Jun, 2001). The traditional rhetoric has been that children could attend college if they worked hard, enrolled in challenging courses, and had the desire to further their education. Parents have been encouraged to demand the highest academic standards and to plan ahead to ensure that their children enrolled in "college prep" courses such as algebra and geometry in the eighth and ninth grade. For low-income urban youth whose parents may not have attended college, this task may seem insurmountable without the assistance of significant others—classroom teachers, mentors, and individuals who work in college preparation programs. These players prove to be keys to success in assisting families with their educational aspirations.

Gaining and Distributing Capital Through Families

The notion of social reproduction and the idea that power is utilized to dominate disadvantaged groups (what Bourdieu referred to as symbolic power), as well as the exercise of this power (symbolic violence) occurs through three distinct educational mechanisms: peer groups, family education, and institutionalized education. Because students are capable of developing agency simply by being inculcated through a particular group, it is important to understand

and address relationships of power. Families that are in tune with and have benefited from a particular educational or institutional system possess greater influence and power than families that have neither participated in nor have an understanding of the educational system. How should educators proceed when some family members may actually hinder rather than help first generation urban students as they work toward their educational aspirations?

Given the evidence it is essential to reiterate that counselors and program administrators should understand the importance of working with parents. Time and income afforded by certain jobs may affect parental attitudes and definitions of teacher and parent roles, while the absence of these resources will alter and challenge traditional notions of parental involvement in schooling. For example, by asking low-income parents to attend school events (PTA meetings, open house night), help in the classroom, or participate in Saturday programs, teachers make demands on the time and disposable income of parents. Attending afternoon parent-teacher conferences might require transportation, childcare arrangements, and job flexibility. This type of time and disposable income may be more readily available to middle and upper income parents than working class parents. Defining education as a cooperative responsibility between parent and teacher may lead to increased participation by parents. However, alternative understandings of some urban parents and their strategy of entrusting the teacher to educate their children may lead to deflated participation by parents that does not promote success (Delgado-Gaitan, 1991).

Mehan and his colleagues asserted that while parents of low income and minority children had high aspirations for their children, they frequently had insufficient knowledge and resources to assist them with higher education goals.

> Although parents support their children's college goals, they don't know the details about required courses and tests, application forms and deadlines, scholarship possibilities and procedures. Although they understand that their children need to go to college to be successful, they express some ambivalence about them leaving home. (1996, p. 158)

While the strategy employed by middle-income parents—actively participating in supervising, monitoring, and overseeing their children's schooling—promotes success, differences in definition and strategy have created a significant impact on low-income families and their children. In order to better serve and incorporate family involvement into the curriculum, counselors, policy makers, and administrators should recognize and address differences in the expectations of families from a wide variety of backgrounds.

Many believe that successful college preparation programs should require families to plan for the future and make important decisions early in a student's life. But how can this be achieved, and what tools are available to parents? To answer these questions, it is necessary to acknowledge the theories of social networks, social reproduction, and cultural capital in relation to parental involvement. In the final section, we review the basic tenets of these theories before providing more particular focus on how social networks and cultural capital might be employed by disenfranchised youth and their families.

Cultural Representation: The Nexus of Ethnicity, Culture, and Integrity

Racial and ethnic diversity is an aspect than has not been historically emphasized in early family intervention efforts (Lee, 1984; Cheng Gorman & Balter, 1997). A decade ago, program designers knew little of the cultural and ecological contexts of the families being served. Programs such as A Better Chance took inner city students away from their families and homes and transplanted them into suburban dwellings, ostensibly removing their families and communities (perhaps seen as a detriment to success) from the education equation.

Recent research on the role of individual culture and local identities suggests a trend toward addressing and involving families more directly. This ushers in a new approach to *cultural representation*. Researchers have found that programs have begun to move beyond merely paying increased attention to family culture in college enrichment programs. Rather, they have turned to a notion of cultural representation based on the tenets of cultural integrity. Cultural integrity is a framework that calls upon students' racial and ethnic backgrounds in the development of pedagogies and learning activities (Deyhle, 1995; Tierney & Jun, 2001). Donna Deyhle (1995) defined cultural integrity as academic success with strong cultural traditions remaining intact. In her own work with Navajo youth, Deyhle found that students who were more secure in their traditional culture were more academically successful in school. According to Tierney and Jun (2001), the notion of cultural integrity for urban minority youth engaged in college preparation programs requires affirmation of local identities in local contexts. Cultural integrity removes the problem from the child, and looks on the child's background neither as a neutral nor a negative factor for learning. Instead, the adolescent's cultural background is viewed as a critical ingredient for achieving success. The framework of cultural integrity extends Jim Cummins's notion that power is "not a fixed, predetermined quantity but rather can be generated in interpersonal and intergroup relations . . . participants are empowered through their collaboration such that each is more affirmed in his or her identity" (1997, p. 424). From this perspective, academic success hinges on the ability of a program to meet students' localized needs by affirming their culture and identity rather than ignoring or rejecting it. Thus the framework operates from the belief that educators' notions of student identities, the roles that teachers assume, and the structures in which teaching and learning exist are important in enabling or disabling the college intentions of low-income urban minority youth.

In the unique ethnic and economic makeup of the neighborhood in the Tierney and Jun study (2001), culture and community were viewed as inseparable. For these students, learning was an activity that occurs on at least three different levels—academic, cultural, and personal—and the students in this study continually labored to develop and improve in all areas. Similar efforts at fusing culture and involvement have been evident in previous research. In developing a typology of parent education programs, Jean Cheng Gorman (1996) identified three categories of programs: *translated, culturally adapted,* and *culturally specific.* A *translated* program was typically identified as a traditional parent education program that was presented in the native language of a particular population. While a translated program was essentially unchanged aside from linguistic modifications, the *culturally adapted* program was the result of cultural fusion. In essence, the design of a culturally adapted program incorporated the values and traditions of the target population. The third type, the *culturally specific* program, was intended to facilitate successful parenting within a specific group's culture. These programs were not merely derivations of traditional programs, but were specifically formatted to be relevant to a particular ethnic group. For African American and Latino families in urban cities, it is crucial for college preparation programs to be responsive to their specific cultural needs, local resources, and neighborhood associations. In some instances, this local knowledge can be essential even for personal safety (McLaughlin, 1993). Statewide programs such as the *Puente Project* in California, a high school–based approach like *Frederick Douglass Academy* in New York City, or a university-based program like the *Neighborhood Academic Initiative* in Los Angeles, are examples of programs and strategies that have framed their services through the lens of the specific ethnicities and cultures of the surrounding community. Program ties are both informational and structural; they "provide the networks of personal knowledge that support personalization and individual responsiveness" (McLaughlin, p. 58), and they allow young people to be understood in the contexts of the challenges they face in their own neighborhoods.

As stated earlier, the development of successful strategies for college preparation requires a redefinition of services to students that encourages academic achievement while affirming the cultural backgrounds of those taught and served. To be sure, students need to learn skills, but in order for learning to take place for those most on the margins, we suggest that one must work from the idea of cultural representation. Program administrators should remember that parents are generally concerned with environments that have strong social characteristics, and may often make schooling decisions based largely on their expectations of the peers their children will encounter.

In light of the above, and as administrators apply theory to practice, we submit the following three components of *cultural representation* that will help reshape and reframe our understanding of how family involvement should be achieved: (a) associate academics with culture, (b) frame academic success within local and cultural contexts, and (c) consider alternative factors for success.

Associate Academics with Culture

The theoretical framework of cultural representation holds two central ideas about education. The first pertains to the concept of culture. Education in culture is not a simple process of teaching neutral facts and figures to a nameless and faceless group. It should be an interactive process of individual identity development along with the creation of community. Educators who merely seek to teach facts and figures to a group of disenfranchised youth might be successful at conveying mastery of specific tasks, but may ignore the cultural processes that advantage some and disadvantage others.

Several models of college preparation and student retention have been widely accepted as useful theoretical frameworks to inform policy. What the majority of models do not take into consideration is how the background and culture of the child enters into college preparation. Our criticisms earlier of Bourdieu's theories are similar to many notions of culture currently employed today—the culture of an individual often becomes irrelevant in programs that emphasize test taking or counseling, and the student is often viewed as the "problem" that needs to be fixed. In fact, however, it is frequently the system, and not the child that is in need of reform. For some enrichment programs geared to serve students from this framework, such an approach may appear to work. However, it does not work for all youth in all circumstances. Further, such a deficit model maintains a form of hierarchy, distinguishing between those that have the "right" culture and those that must acquire it.

Frame Academic Success Within Local and Cultural Contexts

If culture is a central organizing framework, then the second idea pertains to the manner in which all agents of the education community—students, teachers, families, and administrators—work together to meet the varied needs of the student. Programs should be considered successful if they are able to tie academic success to the student's ability to relate to his or her local neighborhood contexts. In an area where social problems such as drug use, crime, and unemployment are significant, a well-intentioned gesture might be to remove adolescents from local communities with the assumption that it was an impediment to learning. Parents or guardians without knowledge of college life might also be viewed as harmful to the learning process. The label of "at-risk" for such students, however benign or sincere, may actually affirm that the social and familial environments where these children live are dangerous and harmful for their social and intellectual health. Furthermore, program administrators should assume that learning cannot occur effectively if educators consciously ignore or neglect aspects of family and environment. Schooling should be linked, not separate from, the out-of-school experiences in which children live, and parents and guardians should be a central component of that learning experience.

In general, students who attend low-income schools either believe that research universities are unattainable because of financial, academic, and social barriers, or they never even consider higher education as an option. As several scholars have documented, students from low-income schools have historically received different curricula, different pedagogical methods, and different assumptions about learning from their counterparts in upper class schools (Oakes, 1985; Lucas, 1999). The results have been that some students learned intellectually and implicitly that they were good enough to be in a trade school but not a university. They learned how to be plumbers, mechanics, or draftspersons rather than architects, engineers, or lawyers. While accepting the reality that an institutional hierarchy exists, administrators should seek to redefine perspectives for adolescents in order that they see all types of postsecondary institutions as viable and reasonable options. Thus, with an equal and ongoing balance of challenge and support, educators can create a climate throughout a scholar's career that is geared toward academic and cultural success at the highest level. To be sure, if a student is able to achieve the grades necessary for admission to an elite institution and decides to travel long distances to a particular college, that individual should be able to maintain a sense of cultural identity, even as his or her neighborhood and campus climate are increasingly disparate. In this respect, the academic universe for students in college preparation programs should always be expansive rather than restrictive.

Consider Alternative Factors for Success

Much of the research reviewed in this study has implications for education reform measures. We believe, for example, that parents who are involved in their children's schools and who attend parent-teacher conferences are more likely to have children who do well. However, older siblings may also provide important emotional or educational support. For example, in Patricia Gándara's (1995) work on Latino families, she challenged the notion that parental involvement in their children's schools led to more academically successful children. Her study of 50 low-income Chicanos who received terminal degrees at elite research universities in the United States revealed that many of the parents never attended a single parent-teacher conference.

In addition, a recent qualitative study on the mobility of first-generation Latino youths in college revealed that siblings, and not parents, had a greater influence on their motivation to succeed (Jun, Forthcoming). These examples of research-based knowledge support a need for greater investigation into the significance of alternative factors in the overall discussion of academic achievement and success for urban youth.

Cultural representation implies not only an understanding of a group's unique values, beliefs, and customs, but also an appreciation of difference and an affirmation of local identities. Rather than judging a group by a particular standard, the idea of cultural representation acknowledges different ways of being, learning, and acting. Therefore, differences should no longer be seen as deficits, and families should no longer be considered part of the problem, but rather a crucial aspect of the solution; successful cultural capital should not be instilled, but rather expanded to include broader definitions of knowledge and merit. Programs based on the notion of cultural representation might be evident by goals, curricular content, and implementation, as well as by administrators' attitudes and beliefs.

Conclusion

Though many program administrators work diligently with families to ensure academic success for their children, and despite excellent teachers, tutors, and volunteers, success cannot be achieved without a clear and cogent theoretical understanding of family involvement. Foundations, government agencies, and other funding groups who support successful programs should also have a systematic understanding of a theoretical framework that drives policy.

In this chapter we have reviewed aspects of family involvement in college preparation programs for low-income urban youth through a variety of measures. Because family involvement may differ by race and ethnicity, administrators who develop programs to engage families should consider local identities and cultures when implementing services to families. Growing residential segregation of families by social class increases the likelihood of unequal access to economic opportunities through the educational system. Further, local funding of public schooling has added to this bias by enabling wealthy parents to "buy" higher quality education by purchasing an expensive home. While upper and middle class families can navigate through the educational system with relative ease, those without easy access to cultural capital and social networks are forced to use other means to accomplish the same goals. Often, they must exchange part of their own culture for a more useful form of capital. It is evident in the literature that both formal and informal networks play a crucial role in student access and outcomes, and significant disparities exist in terms of access to information available to families from different socioeconomic backgrounds.

As administrators of college preparation programs apply theory to practice, they should be cognizant that while many believe that parents are generally concerned with environments that have strong social and network characteristics, little empirical data exists to support additional funding or implementation of programs and services. In the final analysis, more empirical research should be conducted on enrichment programs that approach college attendance from a comprehensive perspective and engage many different agents in the educational system.

References

Barnes, J. A. (1972). *Social networks*. Reading, MA: Addison-Wesley.

Blau, P. M. (1964). *Exchange and power in social life*. New York: Wiley and Sons.

Bowles, S. & Gintis, H. I. (1976). *Schooling in capitalist America*. New York: Basic Books.

Bourdieu, P. (1974). The school as a conservative force: Scholastic and cultural inequalities. In J. Eggleston (Ed.), *Contemporary Research in the Sociology of Education*. London: Metheun.

Bourdieu, P. (1977). Cultural reproduction and social reproduction. In J. Karabel & E. H. Halsey (Eds.), *Power and Ideology in Education* (pp.487–511). Oxford: Oxford University Press.

Bourdieu, P. (1986). The forms of capital. In J. G. Richardson (Ed.), *Handbook of Theory and Research for the Sociology of Education* (pp. 241–258). New York: Greenwood Press.

Brody, G.H., Stoneman, Z. & Flor, D. (1995). Linking family processes and academic competence among rural black youths. *Journal of Marriage and the Family, 57,* 567–79.

Brofenbrenner, U. (1979). *The Ecology of Human Development*. Cambridge, MA: Harvard University.

Catsambis, S. & Garland, J. E. (1997). *Parental involvement in students' education during middle school and high school*. CRESPAR Report #18. Retrieved via World Wide Web [http://www.csos.jhu.edu/crespar/Reports/report/report18.htm] on 7 December 1999.

Cheng Gorman, J. (1996). *Culturally-sensitive parent education programs for ethnic minorities* (PC Reports 7-96-26). New York: New York University, Psychoeducational Center.

Cheng Gorman, J. & Balter, L. (1997). Culturally sensitive parent education: A critical review of quantitative research. *Review of Educational Research, 67* (3), 339–369.

Clark, R. (1983). *Family Life and School Achievement: Why Poor Black Children Succeed or Fail*. Chicago: University of Chicago Press.

Clark, M. L. (1991). Social identity, peer relations, and academic competence of Black adolescents. *Education and Urban Society, 24*, 41–52.

Coates, D. L. (1987). Gender differences in the structure and support characteristics of Black adolescents' social networks. *Sex Roles, 17* (11/12), 667–687.

Coleman, J. S. (1987). Families and schools. *Educational Researcher, 16*, 32–38.

Coleman, J. S., Hoffer, T., & Kilgore, S. (1982). *High School Achievement*. New York: Basic Books.

Cummins, J. (1997). Minority status and schooling in Canada. *Anthropology & Education Quarterly, 28* (3), 411–430.

D'Abbs, P. (1982). *Social support networks: A critical review of models and findings*. Melbourne: Institute of Family Studies. (ERIC Document Reproduction Service No. ED 232 111).

Delgado-Gaitan, C. (1988). Socio-cultural adjustment to school and academic achievement. *Journal of Early Adolescence, 8* (1), 63–68.

Delgado-Gaitan, C. (1991). Involving parents in the schools: A process of empowerment. (1991). *American Journal of Education, 100*, (1), 20–46.

Delgado-Gaitan, C. (1992). *Literacy for empowerment: The role of parents in children's education*. New York: Falmer Press.

Delpit, L. (1988). *Other people's children: Cultural conflict in the classroom*. New York: The New Press.

Deyhle, D. (1995). Navajo youth and Anglo racism: Cultural integrity and resistance. *Harvard Educational Review, 65* (3), 403–444.

DiMaggio, P. & Mohr, J. (1985). Cultural capital, educational attainment, and marital selection. *American Journal of Sociology, 90* (6), 1231–1261.

DiMaggio, P. (1982). Cultural capital and school success: The impact of status culture participation on the grades of U.S. high school students. *American Sociological Review, 47*, 189–201.

Donmoyer, R. & Kos, R. (1993). At-risk students: Insights from/about research. In R. Donmoyer and R. Kos (Eds.), *At-Risk Students: Portraits, Policies, Programs and Practices* (pp. 7–36). Albany, NY: State University of New York Press.

Epstein, J. L. (1995). School/family/community partnerships: Caring for the children we share, *Phi Delta Kappan, 76* (9), 701–712.

Epstein, J. L. (1987). Toward a theory of family-school connections: Teacher practices and parent involvement. In K. Hurrelmann, F. Kaufmann, & F. Losel (Eds.), *Social Intervention: Potential and constraints* (pp. 121–136). New York: DeGruyter.

Epstein, J. L. (1990). School and family connections: Theory, research school, and implication for integrating sociologies of education and family. In

D. G. Unger and M. B. Sussman (Eds.), *Families in Community Settings: Interdisciplinary Perspectives.* New York: Haworth Press.

Epstein J. L., and Lee, S. (1995). National patterns of school and family connections in the middle grades. In B. A Ryan, G. R. Adams, T. P. Gullotta, R. P. Weissberg, and R. L. Hampton (Eds.), *The Family-School Connection: Theory, Research and Practice* (pp. 108–154). Thousand Oaks, CA: Sage Publications.

Erickson, F. (1987). Transformation and school success: The politics and culture of educational achievement. *Anthropology and Education Quarterly, 18,* 335–356.

Ford, D.Y. (1993). Black students' achievement orientation as a function of perceived family achievement orientation and demographic variables. *Journal of Negro Education, 62,* 47–63.

Funkhouser, J. E. & Gonzales, M. R. (1998). *Family involvement in children's education: successful local approaches.* Washington DC: U.S. Department of Education, Office of Research and Education.

Gándara, P. (1995). *Over the ivy walls: The educational mobility of low-income Chicanos.* Albany, NY: State University of New York Press.

Gonzales, N. A., Cauce, A., Friedman, R. J. & Mason, C. A. (1996). Family, peers, and neighborhood influences on academic achievement among black adolescents: One–year prospective effects. *American Journal of Community Psychology, 24,* 365–87.

Granovetter, M. (1983). The strength of weak ties: A network theory revisited. In R. Collins (Ed.), *Sociological Theory Volume I.* San Francisco, CA: Jossey-Bass.

Granovetter, M. (1973). The strength of weak ties. *American Journal of Sociology, 78,* 1360–1380.

Hrabowski, F. A., Maton, K. I. & Greif, G. (1998). *Beating the odds: Raising academically successful African American males.* New York: Oxford University Press.

Jencks, C., Bartlett, S., Corcan, M., Crouse, J., Eaglesfield, D., Jackson, G., McClelland, K., Mueser, P., Olneck, M., Schwartz, J., Ward, S., & Williams, J. (1972). *Inequality: A reassessment of the effect of family and schooling in America.* New York: Basic Books.

Jun, A. (Forthcoming). The price of admission: A qualitative examination of access, mobility and resilience of historically underrepresented minorities in education.

Jun, A. & Tierney, W. G. (1999). At-risk students and college success: A framework for effective preparation. *Metropolitan Universities, 9* (4), 49–60.

Kohn, M. L. (1977). *Class and conformity: A study in values.* Chicago: University of Chicago Press.

Lam, S. F. (1997). *How the family influences children's academic achievement*. New York: Garland Publishing.

Lamont, M. & Lareau, A. (1988). Cultural capital: Allusions, gaps, and glissandos in recent theoretical developments. *Sociological Theory, 6* (3),153–168.

Laosa, L. (1978). Maternal teaching strategies in Chicano families of varied educational and socioeconomic levels. *Child Development, 49,* 1129–1135.

Lareau, A. (1987). Social class differences in family-school relationships: The importance of cultural capital. *Sociology of education, 60,* 73–78

Lareau, A. (1989). *Home advantage*. London: The Falmer Press

Lee, C. C. (1984). An Investigation of psychosocial variables related to academic success for rural Black adolescents. *Journal of Negro Education, 53* (4), 424–434.

Lee, S. (1995). *Family-school connections and student's education: continuity and change of family involvement from the middle grades to high school.* Unpublished doctoral dissertation, Johns Hopkins University, Baltimore.

Leinhart, S. (1977). Social networks: A developing paradigm. In S. Leinhart, (Ed.), *Social networks: A developing paradigm.* New York: Academic Press.

Lucas, S. R. (1999). *Tracking inequality: Stratification and mobility in American high schools.* New York: Teachers College Press.

Maeroff, G. I. (1998). *Altered destinies: Making life better for schoolchildren in need.* New York: St. Martin's Press.

McDonough, P. (1994). Buying and selling higher education: The social construction of the college applicant. *Journal of Higher Education, 4,* 383–402.

McDonough, P. (1997). *Choosing colleges: How social class and schools structure opportunity.* Albany, NY: State University of New York Press.

McLaughlin, M. W. (1993). Embedded identities: Enabling balance in urban contexts. In S. B. Heath & M. W. McLaughlin (Eds.), *Identity and inner-city youth* (pp. 36–68). New York: Teacher's College Press.

Mehan, H., Hubbard, L., Lintz, A., & Villanueva, I. (1996). *Constructing school success: The consequences of untracking low-achieving students.* New York: Cambridge University Press.

Moore, Donald (1992). The case for parent and community involvement. In G. A. Hess, Jr. (Ed.), *Empowering teachers and parents: School restructuring through the eyes of anthropologists* (pp.131–156). Westport, CT: Bergin and Garvey.

Oakes, J. (1985). *Keeping track: How schools structure inequality.* New Haven: Yale University Press.

Peterson, D. (1989). *Parent involvement in the educational process.* Urbana: ERIC Clearinghouse on Educational Management.

Schneider, B. & Coleman, J. S. (Eds.). (1993). *Parents, their children, and schools.* Boulder, CO: Westview Press.

Schorr, L. & Schorr, D. (1988). *Within our reach: Breaking the cycle of disadvantage.* New York: Doubleday.

Sigel, I. E., & Laosa, L. M. (Eds.). (1983). *Changing families.* New York: Plenum Press.

Steinberg, L., Brown, B., Cider, M., Kaczmarek, N., & Lazzaro, C. (1988). *Noninstructional influences on high school student achievement: The contributions of parents, peers, extracurricular activities, and part-time work.* Madison, WI: National Center on Effective Secondary Schools.

Steinberg, L., Dornbusch, S., & Brown, B. (1992). Ethnic differences in adolescent achievement: An ecological perspective. *American Psychologist, 47,* 723–729.

Stevenson, D., & Baker, D. (1987). The family-school relation and the child's school performance. *Child Development, 58,* 1348–1357.

Tierney, W. G., & Jun, A. (2001). Tracking school success: Preparing low-income urban youth for college. *Journal of Higher Education, 2,* 205–225.

Useem, E. L. (1991). Student selection into course sequences in mathematics: The impact of parental involvement and school policies. *Journal of Research on Adolescence, 1,* 231–250.

Useem, E. L. (1992). Middle schools and math groups: Parents' involvement in children's placement. *Sociology of Education, 65,* 263–79.

Weber, M. (1920). *Economy and society.* Berkeley, CA: University of California Press.

White, D. R. (1982). The relation between socioeconomic status and academic achievement. *Psychological Bulletin, 9* (3), 461–481.

Wilson, W. J. (1996). *When work disappears: The world of the new urban poor.* New York: Vintage Books.

Yonezawa, S. S. (1998). *The relational nature of tracking: Using feminist standpoint theory and network theory to examine the course placement process of nineteen secondary school students.* Paper presented at the annual meeting of the American Educational Research Association, San Diego, CA.

C H A P T E R   10

Reflective Evaluation

Improving Practice in College Preparation Programs

WILLIAM G. TIERNEY

Throughout this book we have argued that college preparation programs, otherwise known as "enhancement programs," have taken on increased national importance for a variety of reasons. As Yonezawa and her colleagues pointed out, in California, the elimination of affirmative action led to a precipitous drop in minority student enrollment to the University of California system; policy makers wondered what other actions they might take to enable access to college and their chapter offered one such remedy. Oakes and her colleagues discussed a second possible remedy.

The problem, of course, is not simply limited to California. As Knight and Oesterreich discussed, in New York City well over 50 percent of public school students have been unable to pass the statewide Regents exam, which has led to a similar concern about the drop in minority student enrollment to City University (CUNY, 1999). One response to the dilemma of college access has been the proliferation of college preparation programs. As urban public schools in general continue to grapple with a myriad of what seem to be long-term structural problems, educators and policy makers have turned to discrete solutions that offer a chance for success. In the first part of this book we outlined the conceptual terrain, and subsequently discussed the problems and dynamics of particular programs.

A brief glance at the abundance of programs and multitude of goals that we outlined in Part I highlight a basic inherent tension: How does one decide which programs are most appropriate for particular kinds of students? We have limited the focus of our attention in this book to programs that cater to urban students who attend schools where students are unlikely to attend college. Previous studies using national data sets developed a set of characteristics associated with an increased probability of not making the transition to

217

college (Kaufman and Bradley, 1992). Researchers have pointed out, for example, that lack of college attendance highly correlates with students' demographic characteristics, especially ethnicity, gender, and socioeconomic status. As I discuss below, the following factors also increase the likelihood that the student will not go on to college:

- Grade point averages of C or lower from sixth to eighth grade
- Family socio-economic status in the lowest quartile
- Reading at or below grade level
- Recent immigration to the United States
- Having siblings who did not graduate from high school
- A member of a single-parent family (Horn and Chen, 1998).

Because students who match these conditions are in general those who are most likely not to attend college, they may benefit from the kind of college preparation programs that have been discussed elsewhere in this book. College preparation programs are suited to particular schools that have low transition rates to college and where the students exhibit many of these characteristics. Surely, by outlining these characteristics none of us have posited a deficit model of individuals. Indeed, Hagedorn and Fogel, as well as Jun and Colyar and others throughout the book, have offered analyses of the cultural capital necessary for success.

The college preparation programs we have discussed here seem to come in all shapes and sizes. A rapid increase in college preparation programs has occurred at many funding levels—federal, state, and through private foundations. The congressional GEAR UP (Gaining Early Awareness and Readiness for Undergraduate Programs) initiative is an example of a significant commitment of federal funds for transition programs. As has been discussed earlier, states such as Florida and California have increased state monies for programs such as CROP (College Reach Out Program) and MESA (Mathematics, Engineering, Science, Achievement). Foundations continue to provide significant funds for direct services of college preparation programs.

However, there has been very little analysis of the worth of these programs; therefore, my purpose in this chapter is to offer a preliminary scaffolding for how we might think about evaluating college preparation programs. As I will elaborate, I am not interested in evaluation simply for evaluation's sake. The point of evaluation ought not be merely a theoretical argument or a bureaucratic requirement that does not lead to change. Instead, I propose a reflective schema whereby those involved in operating college preparation programs might undertake specific activities that will lead to direct program improvement.

Background

The vast majority of literature about college preparation programs is no more than a decade old, and most simply tries to make sense of the multiple kinds of programs that exist. One of this book's authors, Laura Perna (1999), for example, has offered an analysis of the various goals of these programs, and Ann Coles (1999) has outlined the kind of information and activities needing to take place in such programs. Daniel Mayer (1999) has offered a preliminary analysis of the success of college preparation programs in getting students ready for college; another chapter author, Hugh Mehan and his colleagues (1996), have analyzed one program and its effectiveness, and Gene Maeroff (1998) has offered a journalistic account of the goals of enhancement programs.

National programs such as Upward Bound have been studied (Myers and Schirm, 1999) and national data sets have provided a bit of evidence about other programs (Gándara, 1999; Horn and Chen, 1998). However, as Robert Fenske, Gil Irwin, and Jonathan Keller point out: "Early intervention programs have proliferated in kaleidoscopic variety" (1999, p. 119), and simply making sense of all of these programs has proven to be a challenge for researchers. Indeed, one of our goals for this book has been to delineate a conceptual framework pertaining to college preparation programs. An overall evaluation schema, however, of what to look for, what to evaluate, and how to evaluate has proven elusive (Coles, 1993; College Board, 1999).

Over the last decade I have been involved in a national study of college preparation programs and I have found no program that states it is anything other than highly successful. However, the evaluations of these programs have usually been simple reports of what took place. For example a program that may have contracted to teach 60 students in the summer will state that, indeed, 60 students were in attendance. Of course, simply stating that 60 students showed up for a learning exercise does not indicate if any learning took place, much less if that attendance led to college admittance.

In many respects, college preparation programs mirror colleges and universities where faculty and administrators claim that the evaluation of their educational programming is difficult, if not impossible; hence, no evaluation has been performed. Further, since most college preparation programs are seriously underfunded, internal evaluations are a luxury that is viewed as possible only if direct services were reduced. Evaluations are often seen as esoteric academic undertakings with little real-world consequences. Perhaps arguing about the impact of variable X on variable Y is important to academics, but many involved in programs feel that such discussions do nothing to help students get into college.

The authors of this book take issue with the above assertion for two reasons. First, the continuing increase in college preparation programs suggests that eventually some programs will prove to be more successful than others. It behooves those who are involved with college preparation programs to have clear indicators of success in order to make their case as persuasively as possible that their program is worthy of continued support. Second, a clearer evaluation design will enable program staff and fiscal agents to gain a better sense of what kinds of activities need increased funding, and which activities do not.

At the same time, I am well aware that academic texts often provide little, if any, concrete suggestions to practitioners who need "real world" solutions to "real world" problems. I am also cognizant that longitudinal evaluations are not easy. However, my goal is to offer a preliminary schema that can be implemented. If such an evaluation framework is workable, then services to students will be improved. Thus, evaluation is not something done as a meaningless task to meet the demands of funding agencies or academics. Instead, we engage in evaluation as a reflective practice to ensure that continuous improvement occurs in programs aimed to help children gain access to a postsecondary education.

Accordingly, in what follows I first outline the problems that exist in many programs I have studied, and I then suggest a five-step framework that might be employed to think about college preparation programs. My point here is neither to disparage any program nor to suggest that the largely overworked and underpaid personnel are ineffective in what they do. To the contrary. Many programs have the elements of success embedded in their services, but because formal evaluations have not been done, no one can say with confidence that a particular aspect of an enhancement program is more important than another. My goal is to provide a reflective framework that will enable college preparation programs to highlight their successes if they exist, or work toward implementing them if they do not.

Evaluation Problems

When one evaluates a college preparation program, what might be an indicator of success? True, as with any project, there are always minimal criteria. For example, if an individual contracts to offer three classes to 30 students over the course of a six-week summer period, then the first evaluative point is to ensure that three classes of 30 students participated in a six-week program. Of course, such information tells nothing about whether the program was effective, or what might be improved. Similarly, if a foundation gives a program $250,000 to conduct those summer courses and the program adheres to the budget that they initially submitted, then another minimal piece of information might be used as an evaluative point. Again, such information is little more than reporting that what was proposed was done. Three questions arise that form the basis for building an evaluative framework to determine success.

1. *Whom does the program serve?* One indicator of success pertains, obviously, to the students who are served and what happens to them. However, whom one serves and what happens to them is not always clear. For example, I have observed some programs that begin to educate students in the seventh grade and continue until high school graduation. Assume that the size of the cohort is 30. As might be expected, students drop out of the program for any number of reasons. Some students find the program too hard and others have social problems; some students move away and others find that they have priorities other than scholastics. The program maintains a constant 30 students by taking in additional students from year to year. Thus, the seventh and twelfth grade classes each have 30 students.

The program then claims that 100 percent of its students graduated from high school if 30 students graduate. If the program begins in the seventh grade, however, and of that original cohort only 10 students remain, then the actual number of students who graduated from the program was 33 percent, not 100. If the concern is about the effects of the program's activities on the students, and the claim is that funding is necessary from the seventh grade, then of necessity one must judge success not by the number of twelfth grade students who graduate from the program but instead by the number of seventh grade students who began the program and ultimately graduated.

A related problem that confronts program administrators is how students are admitted to the program. Most of these programs seek students who otherwise would not go to college. By and large, then, these programs are not designed for the superior student who is likely to go to college regardless of whether he or she is involved in a college preparation program.

However, if an indicator of success is the number of students who graduate from high school and go on to college, then program administrators face the temptation to choose students who are more likely to succeed than fail. That is, if a funding agent wants to see high graduation rates—and who would not?—then the program is more likely to try to pick students who are likely to succeed rather than those who are actually in need of the program's services.

I have been to many inner-city schools that have a multitude of shortcomings. Nevertheless, a certain cadre of students is still able to excel and remain on track to college. These are not the students, however, for whom most college preparation programs are designed. Superior students and their families may try to take such classes because they recognize that academically rigorous and additional classes are helpful. Program directors, like teachers, want good students. Model students show a desire to learn, are highly motivated, and are likely to meet the goals of the program. However, we do a disservice to the concept of taking children with average or below average

222 WILLIAM G. TIERNEY

test scores and equipping them with the necessary skills to go to college if the students who are actually chosen begin with above average test scores. We also place college preparation programs in a double bind when we demand high graduation rates, but then overlook that choosing students with average or below average test scores may mean that those graduation rates will not be as high as desired. Such a problem returns us to the essential question: How might a program determine success?

2. *What are indicators of programmatic success?* In general, programs such as those that have been discussed elsewhere in this book have used three indicators, albeit flawed, when they have discussed their specific student populations. Some programs will say that their studies have raised test scores on examinations such as the SAT, and other programs will point out that a certain percentage of their students have gone on to college. Still other programs will speak of the percentage of students who graduated from high school. If one leaves aside for the moment how the number of students is configured, there are a variety of problems with raised test scores or the movement into college as a summative indicator of success.

If high school graduation is the goal then the simple statement about a percentage of students graduating from high school might be sufficient. However, the vast majority of these programs have broader goals. One program, for example, seeks graduation from college and another emphasizes placement in college. Often, programs that take place on college campuses and a high school or school district have a relationship with the postsecondary institution. Thus, some indicator that involves postsecondary education is usually necessary. I am concerned that graduation from high school or acceptance to college is seen as the final comment on whether a program is successful. Although the measurement of how a student does over time and the import of the initial learning experience is complicated by additional variables when we take a college education into account, the ultimate indicator of effectiveness ought to be not admittance to the college, but graduation from it. As Clifford Adelman has so succinctly pointed out, "degree completion is the true bottom line for college administrators, state legislators, parents, and most importantly, students—not retention to the second year, not persistence without a degree, but completion" (1999, p. v).

Further, one needs to investigate multiple aspects about college-going rates. That is, is a program successful if 80 percent of its students attend college but only 10 percent graduate from college? Which is a more successful program: where 80 percent of its students attended college and 10 percent graduated, or a program where 50 percent of its students attended college and everyone graduated?

An additional issue to take into account is the kind of postsecondary institution where students attend. I surely do not intend to suggest that in all cases a bachelor's degree should be desired over an associate's degree or a diploma from a professional school. Some students will opt to attend a community college and others desire a four-year institution. However, if two programs educate similar students and one program sends the majority of its students to premier research universities while the other program has its students attending a local community college, then one needs to take such information into account as an indicator of success. The point here is not whether some students should attend a community college; of course they should. However, all students should have equal opportunities to choose the kind of institution that best meets their academic and social needs.

A final point about determining the success of a program pertains to the ability to create comparison and benchmark data. Numbers that are provided in absence of any other data is helpful, but incomplete. "Eighty percent of our students go on to college," at least tells individuals a basic statement of fact, although the statement is incomplete based on what I have discussed above. What is also needed is comparative information. If the students come from a high school where 20 percent of the student body go on to college, one interpretation might be made; and if the high school graduates 75 percent college-goers, then an alternative interpretation is possible.

Similarly, many programs overlap in urban schools. It has not been uncommon to find that a high school may have three or four college-preparation programs. If one program sends 50 percent of its students on to college whereas another program only sends 20 percent, then one interpretation exists. An alternative one might be developed if the comparison program graduates 80 percent. Some students also enroll in more than one program, further complicating the process.

3. *What are indicators of organizational effectiveness?* The simple point here is that graduation rates—whether from high school or college—do not provide enough information about program effectiveness. Two programs that graduate a similar number of equivalent students, for example, cannot be considered equally effective if one costs twice as much as the other. In an arena such as education where funding is finite, cost effectiveness needs to be taken into account.

Optimally, discrete information about programmatic aspects is also helpful. A summer bridge program, for example, may have a relatively low-cost tutoring center that is run by college students, and an expensive counseling program that depends upon paying consultant fees to psychologists. A different program may shift its program from a high school to a college with the assumption that it is important for low-income students to get a sense of belonging on a college campus. The instruction on the college campus necessitates that the students be bused to and from their high school, which in turn demands that the program pay for insurance for the students while they are en route. The assumptions that are made with such decisions are that if a particular aspect of the program were eliminated, graduation rates would suffer. Of course, without empirically testing the assumption, costs are not determined by which is more effective than another.

Thus, a potentially expensive component of a program is retained when individuals have no idea about its pedagogical worth. One might be able to gain a sense, for example, about the importance of having students take courses on a college campus rather than in their school by comparing similar programs with similar goals where one program takes place in a high school and the other on a campus. One also might investigate what specifically takes place on campus that makes attendance there presumably important. That is, if students are simply bused to a college campus and walk from the bus to a classroom and then return to the bus, one might wonder about the worth of the college experience in a world with finite resources. On the other hand, if the experiences on the campus are so unique that they are not otherwise available, and if they play a role in student learning, then one might try to maintain that particular program component even if it is expensive.

The final observation about organizational effectiveness has to do with long-term issues. Insofar as most programs rely on soft funding and exist embedded within multiple layers of educational organizations—a program within a school within a school district—programs need to communicate effectively with various constituencies and create sustained, ongoing relationships with different organizations. The more that an organization develops products about itself and communicates an image about what it is attempting to do, the better able program administrators are to create an understanding of what they do, how they do it, and how successful they are. Further, since funding is always tight, to the extent that relationships with postsecondary institutions and community-based organizations are developed, then better coordination will occur.

I am well aware that many of the problems that I have detailed in this section exist because there is not enough staff to accomplish everything that needs to be done. Evaluation designs developed by academics are all too often ignorant of the barriers that exist in the real world, and too, the kinds of answers that academics seek are often different from those of individuals who work on a daily basis in college preparation programs. And still, the purpose of reflective evaluation is to enable program improvement. Without a usable framework for evaluating the strength of a program, we will have no criteria on which to judge what to change and what to keep, which is successful and which is not. I turn now to a discussion about the kind of framework that might be developed to overcome the obstacles I have outlined here.

A Scaffolding for the Reflective Evaluation of College Preparation Programs

1. *Maintain a database of a constant entering cohort of underachieving students.* One piece of advice is to define the parameters of the entering cohort, stick to those points, and publicize them in every evaluation report.

What might those parameters be? Some of the more common admissions points are those that I raised earlier in the chapter:

- Students with families in the lowest SES quartile
- Students from single-parent families
- Students with older siblings who dropped out of high school
- Students with average grades of *C*s or lower from sixth to eighth grade
- Students who are recent immigrants to the United States
- Students reading at or below grade level.

To be sure, each program will also have its own in-house variables that it wishes to use—students from a particular school or those who exhibit a particular desire to learn and the like. By all means such choices are fine, but the goal here is to highlight that a program's participants are chosen according to commonly accepted variables of students who are unlikely to attend college without some kind of help.

In an age of electronic databases and software, the maintenance of information of this kind is not difficult. Indeed, if anything, the collection of such data will lead to formative tasks that will help improve the project immediately. For example, exit interviews with students who have left a project are helpful not only to track where they have gone, but why they have left. Some reasons will provide insight into how to improve a project and others will simply highlight personal reasons for leaving (i.e., the family moved). The success of maintaining information of this kind is that it is systematically done and accurate records are maintained. A periodic snapshot of student cohorts often creates more confusion than clarity. I have heard individuals forget, for example, if two years ago the incoming class had 30 or 40 students, or how many students in a particular cohort were admitted midstream because of departures the previous year.

2. Develop a longitudinal comparative database across organizations Two additional issues raised by the current problems that exist is an inadequate sense of reliable benchmark data, and a limited view of what constitutes success. If an initial database is developed as suggested above, then the program also needs to have on hand a finite number of comparative and longitudinal facts. Presumably, students are chosen from a specific pool rather than simply because they happen to live in a city. Thus, if the program is able to claim that a certain percentage of its students graduate from high school and go on to college, it will be helpful to have on hand a comparison with the schools and/or neighborhoods from which those students are chosen so that a control group exists.

Two pieces of information are necessary: how many students from the comparison group graduate from high school, and how many went on to college? Institutional type is important when defining if the student went on to college. The program and the local schools may have similar graduation rates, but the program may have been able to send students to more academically rigorous institutions, which would be one indicator of program effectiveness.

Some institutions, obviously, have open admissions and other institutions have more rigorous entry requirements. One goal of college preparation programs might be to enable as wide a choice as possible with regard to selection of postsecondary institutions. All too often students get tracked into nonelite institutions. In part, as Oakes and her colleagues have pointed out in chapter 5, enhancement programs are aimed at de-tracking (Mehan, Villanueva, Hubbard and Lintz, 1996; Jun and Tierney, 1999).

The longitudinal data that will be necessary is perhaps the most complicated piece of data to gather. I stated earlier that the indicator of success ought not be whether a student graduates from high school or goes to college, but whether he or she graduates from college. If a college preparation program is able to create relationships with college personnel, such data will be relatively easy to maintain. Indeed, an additional benefit of such relationships is the ability of program and college personnel to maintain contact with one another about immediate suggestions for improvement. An additional way to obtain the data is through the graduates themselves. As colleges keep track of their alumni through a periodic letter, so might a college preparation program. Again, I am not suggesting an onerous tracking system that would consume the hours of a full-time staff member. Instead, I envision two letters a year with a follow-up to every graduate, asking them to respond to a simple survey that the program developed. In an age when virtually every college student has access to electronic mail, such correspondence might be done simply through a listserv or e-mail correspondence.

The goal is to be able to say that four to five years after graduation from high school these particular students have graduated from college. Such data is the clearest information about programmatic success. At a minimum, a program ought to be able to follow a student through to the end of the first term in college. The most preventable dropout rates for students are between graduation and before the start of college, and during the first term of college. The probability that a student will graduate from college rises dramatically if the student makes it to second term. Thus, although the best information to have would be graduation from college, even information about how an individual did during the first term of college would be extremely helpful and provide more insight into a program's success than is currently available.

3. *Use multiple measures of effectiveness.* A comprehensive evaluation schema needs to take multiple objectives into account in order to determine program effectiveness. Those who are closest to the program design are usually the best able to determine which objectives to evaluate. Although there may be an overall goal of graduation from college, for example, there will be related objectives that are open for investigation and analysis. Some programs wish to instill a love of learning in their students, others focus on

enabling students to deal more effectively with adolescent problems. Some programs emphasize drug prevention, and others try to work on improved social interaction with one's peers.

Horsch (1998) has defined such activities as "outcomes" that enable one to obtain a sense of the various components of a program. The point is simply that if a program undertakes various activities, it ought to ensure that the activities are worthwhile and have an impact. The assumption that drug counseling will lead to fewer drug-related problems, which in turn will enable more students to concentrate on their studies and graduate from high school, needs to be investigated. Clearly, one ought not invest time and resources on drug counseling if the services are provided elsewhere, or if the activities are ineffective.

The basic challenge I am putting forth is that common assumptions should be questioned in order to improve program services. Drug counseling might be unnecessary, but some other kind of objective might be helpful. Or drug counseling is necessary, but the program is ineffective and needs to be improved. One needs to break programs down into manageable components and analyze in a standard way what works and what does not.

4. *Conduct one discrete evaluation project per year.* Programs are multifaceted and composed of many different undertakings. Any program can improve. The goal of organizational life ought to be toward "high performance" (Tierney, 1999), and the objective of reflective evaluation is continuous improvement. Thus, if college preparation program administrators borrowed a concept from the "high performance" literature, what they might do is choose one particular aspect of their program per year for investigation, analysis, and improvement. I suggest one topic a year for a reason. Major program evaluations are time-consuming, often threatening to program staff, and frequently lead to insignificant changes. Often the program personnel's only decision is not to go through such an undertaking again since it consumed so much time and produced such paltry results. Such an evaluation is the antithesis of the kind of reflective evaluation I am suggesting here.

As with virtually every suggestion I have made, however, if administrators choose one discrete topic a year, they have the advantage of attempting an evaluation that is manageable and systematic. Rather than a stopgap or emergency measure to investigate an immediate problem, an annual evaluation of one part of a program takes place so that parts of a program might be evaluated and improved. As with any learning organization, the goal is to consider how to improve the organizational aspects of the program in order to enhance primary learning activities. All too often, organizational aspects get in the way of learning. Students want to learn. Teachers want to teach. Counselors want to counsel. The organizational structure and climate, however, are not functioning at an optimal level. In order to enhance the effectiveness of the organization, I am suggesting that college preparation programs ought to reflect on one aspect of their program a year and consider ways to improve it.

4. *Create an ongoing schema for evaluating cost and communicating effectiveness.* Some will argue that a concern for cost is virtually impossible with budgets that are more often than not built on shoestrings. Others will point out that worrying about communication seems like a public relations gimmick. However, at a time when the United States has become staunchly capitalist and results oriented, I cannot emphasize enough the importance of being able to impress upon potential funders that a particular program is effectively organized and costs are contained. I by no means wish to suggest that there are fiscal improprieties in any of the programs that we have studied; indeed, more often than not, individual salaries are lower than they should be; programs would likely benefit if salaries were increased to a level so that administrative positions would be attractive to a wider array of individuals.

However, I have seen a remarkable variation in the manner in which programs organize their fiscal operations. Obviously, everyone has an individual who balances the books and makes payments. Some of the most aggressive and well-funded programs also have individuals who might be thought of as development officers and grants people. A program that focuses on direct services and has a staff member who is not involved with schoolchildren might trouble some individuals. And yet, in an arena where private giving and grants submission is key to being able to carry out those direct services, it is foolhardy to assume that an individual can make time in an already overly busy schedule to court donors and write proposals. The vast majority of college preparation programs exist on soft funding. I have argued elsewhere that school districts and the state should turn such soft funding into hard dollars. At the same time, I do not think it wise policy to wish that soft money becomes hard funding if it is clear that it will not.

Instead, a more consistent, systematic effort needs to be taken to attract external funding. As Horsch has commented, "School-linked services often begin as experimental programs, and the issue of their duration beyond their funding and their possible replication and scale-up are important evaluation considerations" (1998, p. 10). Simply stated, those programs that focus on cost effectiveness are generally better funded and more sustainable than those that have not.

Similarly, one may have an excellent program, but if no one knows about it, then it will be harder to attract funding. At a time where web sites, listservs, and a potpourri of other electronic and technological advances have made communication and information rapid and constant, college preparation programs ought not be well-kept secrets that do not broadcast their accomplishments to the outside world.

Again, I have seen programs that have created quite professional documents and web sites that are much better able to attract interest in their activities as individuals learn about the program. Other programs may not have any printed material or electronic outlets. Those that are better organized for communicating their message to the broad public are also those that generate the income necessary to do their work.

Conclusion

I have outlined problems that appear endemic to well-intentioned programs that are frequently underfunded and understaffed. Although I have cautioned that the problems are capable of eventually undermining a program, I have also pointed out ways to improve program effectiveness by way of a five-point evaluation framework based on reflection by those directly involved in the program. I am quite cognizant that the framework is not one that reaches into the academic arenas of program evaluation and design. However, the points touch on the essential issues that will enable worthy programs to increase their standards, improve program effectiveness, and better serve a crucial population in this country.

Notes

The author wishes to thank Julia Colyar, Linda S. Hagedorn, Alexander Jun, Michelle Knight, Laura Perna, Scott Swail, and Carolyn Webb de Macias for their comments on an earlier draft of the paper, and Bob Shireman for coming up with the phrase, "Reflective Evaluation."

References

Adelman, C. (1999). *Answers in the toolbox: Academic intensity, attendance patterns and bachelor's degree attainment.* Washington, DC: U.S. Department of Education.

Coles, A. S. (1993). *School to college transition programs for low-income minority youth.* Washington, DC: The Education Resources Institute.

Coles, A. S. (1999). Early education awareness activities. *Advances in Educational Research, 4* (winter), 117–133. Washington, DC: National Library of Education.

College Board. (1999). *Reaching the top: A report of the National task force on minority high achievement.* New York: College Board Publications.

Fenske, R., Keller, J., & Irwin, G. (1999). Toward a typology of early intervention programs. *Advances in Educational Research, 4* (winter), 117–133.

Gándara, P. (1999). *Priming the pump: Strategies for increasing the achievement of underrepresented minority undergraduates.* New York: The College Board.

Horn, L. J., & Chen, X. (1998). *Toward resiliency: At-risk students who make it to college.* Washington, DC: U.S. Department of Education, Office of Educational Research and Improvement.

Horsch, K. (1998). *Evaluating school-linked services: Considerations and best practices.* Cambridge, MA: Harvard Family Research Project.

Jun, A., & Tierney, W. G. (1999). At-risk students and college success: A framework for effective preparation. *Metropolitan Universities, 9* (4), 49–60.

Kaufman, P., & Bradby, D. (1992). *Characteristics of at-risk students in NELS: 88 NCES 92-042.* Washington, DC: U.S. Department of Education, National Center for Education Statistics.

Maeroff, G. (1998). *Altered destinies: Making life better for school children in need.* New York: St. Martin's Press.

Mayer, D. (1999). Do early educational awareness programs increase the chances of eighth graders reaching higher education? *Advances in Educational Research, 4,* (winter), 59–73.

Mayor's Advisory Task Force on The City University of New York. (1999). *The City University of New York: An institution adrift.*

Mehan, H., Villanueva, I., Hubbard, L., & Lintz, A. (1996). *Constructing school success: The consequences of low-achieving students.* New York, Cambridge University Press.

Myers, D., & Schirm, A. (1999). *The impacts of Upward Bound: Final report for phase I of the national evaluation.* Washington, DC: Department of Education.

Perna, L. (1999). Early intervention programs: A new approach to increasing college access. *Advances in Educational Research, 4,* (winter), 7–19. Washington, DC: National Library of Education.

Tierney, W. G. (1999). *Building the responsive campus: Creating high performance colleges and universities.* Thousand Oaks, CA: Sage Publications, Inc.

About the Contributors

Clifford Adelman taught at Roosevelt University, the City College of the City University of New York, and Yale University, and served five years as Associate Dean and Assistant Academic Vice President at the William Patterson College of New Jersey before coming to the U.S. Department of Education in 1979. He writes frequently for the general and trade press, most recently on graduation rates, the remedial conundrum, affirmative action, and the empirical core curriculum. Some of his recent publications include: *Answers in the Tool Box: Academic Intensity, Attendance Patterns, and Bachelor's Degree Attainment* (1999), and recently issued, *A Parallel Postsecondary Universe: the Certification System in Engineering Technology* (2000).

Julia Colyar is a research assistant in the Center for Higher Education Policy Analysis at the USC Rossier School of Education. Her research interests include college preparation programs and their impact on student transitions to college, retention of underrepresented students, and undergraduate learning communities.

Shereen Fogel is a researcher in the Rossier School of Education at the University of Southern California. Her research is focused on the role of motivation in learning, especially in terms of the impact that innovative technology can have on learning processes. She is currently developing a book to help instructional designers better understand and respond to the unique advantages and constraints of e-learning.

Patricia Gándara is professor of education at UC Davis and associate director of the University of California Linguistic Minority Research Institute. Her research focuses on educational equity and access to higher education as well as issues surrounding teaching and learning of English Learners. Her latest book, *Where Are All the Latino College Students?* is forthcoming this year from Westview Press.

Dr. Linda Serra Hagedorn is an associate professor, senior research associate, and chair of the Community College Leadership Program at the Rossier School of Education at the University of Southern California. She is also the

231

principal investigator of a federal grant to study the transfer and retention of urban community college students. Recent publications include "Correlates of retention for African American males in community colleges" (*Journal of College Student Retention Research, Theory, and Practice*); "Peer and student-faculty relations of women and of men in a community college" (*Community College Journal of Research and Practice*), and "Building study and work skills in a college mathematics classroom" (*The Journal of General Education*).

Makeba Jones, Ph.D., is a partnership coordinator for the Center for Research in Educational Equity and Teaching Excellence (CREATE) at the University of California, San Diego. Her research interests include urban school reform, and the ways in which race, class, and gender shape reform implementation, and particularly classroom dynamics. She is interested in linking students' everyday schooling experiences with policy making around urban school reform. Her current work is school reform through action research in UCSD's K–12 partnership schools. The goal of UCSD's school partnerships is to increase the numbers of educationally disadvantaged students who are eligible to attend a four-year university by the time they graduate from high school.

Alexander Jun is currently the associate director of undergraduate programs in the Office of the Provost at the University of Southern California. His research interests pertain to issues of access and retention for historically underrepresented students in higher education. He has published several journal articles that deal with the educational, cultural, and social parameters that influence postsecondary access and college preparation for urban youth, and has a forthcoming book on the mobility of five first-generation Latino students in college. Dr. Jun holds a Ph.D. in education policy and planning from USC.

Michelle G. Knight is an assistant professor in the Department of Curriculum and Teaching at Teachers College, Columbia University. Her research and teaching interests center on urban education, qualitative research methodologies, feminist pedagogies, and youth studies. Recent publications include "Ethics in qualitative research: Multicultural feminist activist research in the journal," *Theory into Practice* and "Finding our way: Challenging oppressive educational and societal practices forthcoming," in Sabrina H. King (Ed.), *Building Hope: The divergent thought and practice of anti-racist teaching*. Her current research project is an exploratory study of Black and Latino/a college-bound urban youth's multiple worlds, and is funded by the Spencer Foundation.

Martin Lipton is Communications Analyst for the Institute for Democracy, Education, and Access (IDEA). He is co-author of *Teaching to Change the World* and *Becoming Good American Schools*.

Hugh Mehan is professor of sociology and director of CREATE at UCSD, appointments that link his commitments to research and practice. CREATE coordinates efforts at UCSD to improve the academic preparation of underrepresented students in the community through partnerships with K–12 schools and the Preuss School, an on-campus model charter school at UCSD. Mehan's research interests include classroom organization, educational testing, tracking and untracking, computer use in schools, and the construction of identities such as "the competent student," "the learning-disabled student," "the mentally ill patient," and "the genius." His most recent book, *Constructing School Success* (with Irene Villanueva, Lea Hubbard, and Angela Lintz), published by Cambridge University Press, discusses the educational and social consequences of "untracking" low-achieving students. He was recently elected to the National Academy of Education.

Ernest Morrell is a research associate at the Institute for Democracy, Education, and Access at UCLA. His work examines new literacy, critical, and cultural theories, and their implications for urban schooling and urban teacher education.

Dr. Amaury Nora is professor of higher education and associate dean for research and faculty development in the College of Education at the University of Houston, Houston, TX. His research focuses on college persistence, the role of college on diverse student populations across different types of institutions, the development of financial aid models that integrate economic theories and college persistence theories, graduate education, and theory building and testing. He has served on the editorial boards of *Research in Higher Education, The Review of Higher Education, The Journal of Higher Education,* and *The Journal of College Student Retention: Research, Theory, and Practice,* and he served as program chair for the 1999 annual meeting of the Association of the Study of Higher Education (ASHE).

Jeannie Oakes is Presidental professor of education and director of the Institute for Democracy, Education, and Access (IDEA) at UCLA. Her research examines inequalities in U.S. schools, and follows the progress of equity-minded reform. She has focused attention on how tracking and ability grouping limit the school experiences of low-income students and students of color, most of whom are identified as "low" ability or as "slow" learners. This work is the subject of *Keeping Track: How Schools Structure Inequality* (Yale

University Press, 1985), which was recently named one of the top 60 books of the century by the Museum of Education at the University of South Carolina in Columbia.

Oakes's recent research follows the progress of educators who are attempting to eliminate schooling inequalities and build more democratic school communities. This work is reported in *Beyond the Technicalities of School Reform: Lessons from Detracking Schools* (with Amy Stuart Wells, 1996), in *Creating New Educational Communities*, the 94th Yearbook of the National Society for the Study of Education (University of Chicago Press, 1995) (with Karen Hunter Quartz), in journal articles, and in her latest book, *Becoming Good American Schools: The Struggle for Civic Virtue in Education Reform* (Jossey-Bass, 2000) (with Karen Hunter Quartz, Steve Ryan, and Martin Lipton).

Heather A. Oesterreich is a doctoral candidate in the Department of Curriculum and Teaching at Teachers College, Columbia University. Her emphasis is in urban education, and she is particularly interested in feminist critical youth studies as a method for exploring the complexity of social structures and youth agency in the negotiation of educational policies and practices in order to expand what and whose knowledge counts. She supports her graduate endeavors with a variety of adventures, primarily extensive work in equity, access, and integration of technology in secondary schools.

Dr. Laura W. Perna is an assistant professor in the Department of Education Policy and Leadership in the College of Education at the University of Maryland. Prior to joining the faculty at Maryland, Dr. Perna served as research scientist and then acting director of the United Negro College Fund's Frederick D. Patterson Research Institute. Dr. Perna has also served as the director of institutional research and planning at the University of Dallas and director of Business Operations at the American Institute for Paralegal Studies, Inc. Her research focuses on such topics as racial/ethnic group differences in college access and choice, the effects of financial aid on college choice and persistence, and sex and racial/ethnic group differences in faculty reward systems.

John Rogers is associate director of IDEA and director of Center X Research in UCLA's Graduate School of Education and Information Studies. Dr. Rogers is the principal investigator of UCLA's Futures Project, which seeks to create alternative trajectories that lead underrepresented students through high school and into colleges and universities. His recent work addresses topics ranging from the preparation of urban teachers to the history of the community schools movement. Dr. Rogers received his Ph.D. in education from Stanford University.

Watson Scott Swail is vice president of planning and research for The Council for Opportunity in Education in Washington, DC. His responsibilities include providing leadership and direction for the council's research efforts and for the expansion of council programs, activities, and partnerships. Dr. Swail has held senior research positions with SRI International and The College Board, and his research focus predominantly falls on access to higher education for low-income and other traditionally underrepresented students.

William G. Tierney is director of the Center for Higher Education Policy Analysis and immediate past president of the Academic Senate of the University of Southern California. His research interests pertain to organizational performance, equity, and faculty roles and rewards. Dr. Tierney teaches courses on the administration and governance of higher education and on qualitative methods. His recent publications include *Faculty Work in Schools of Education: Rethinking Roles and Rewards for the Twenty-first Century* (2001), *Building the Responsive Campus: Creating High Performance Colleges and Universities* (1999), and *The Responsive University: Restructuring for High Performance* (1998). He is currently involved in a research project to study the effectiveness of college preparation programs for low-income urban youth, funded by the Ford Foundation.

Susan Yonezawa, Ph.D., is a partnership coordinator at the Center for Research in Educational Equity and Teaching Excellence (CREATE) at the UCSD. Her research interests include race-based policy issues that affect educational equity such as tracking, de-tracking, and affirmative action. She is particularly interested in how students, particularly minority and low-income students, navigate secondary school structures and cultures and how educators and policy makers help shape students' experiences. Currently she is engaged in a long-term action research project with UCSD K–12 partnership schools, the focus of which is to increase the numbers of low-income, educationally disadvantaged students who graduate high school eligible for a four-year university.

Index

SUNY series, Frontiers in Education
Philip G. Altbach, Editor

List of Titles

Excellence and Equality: A Qualitatively Different Perspective on Gifted and Talented Education—David M. Fetterman

Class, Race, and Gender in American Education—Lois Weis (ed.)

Change and Effectiveness in Schools: A Cultural Perspective—Gretchen B. Rossman, H. Dickson Corbett, and William A. Firestone (eds.)

The Curriculum: Problems, Politics, and Possibilities—Landon E. Beyer and Michael W. Apple (eds.)

Crisis in Teaching: Perspectives on Current Reforms—Lois Weis, Philip G. Altbach, Gail P. Kelly, Hugh G. Petrie, and Sheila Slaughter (eds.)

The Character of American Higher Education and Intercollegiate Sport—Donald Chu

Dropouts from Schools: Issues, Dilemmas, and Solutions—Lois Weis, Eleanor Farrar, and Hugh G. Petrie (eds.)

The Higher Learning and High Technology: Dynamics of Higher Education Policy Formation—Sheila Slaughter

Religious Fundamentalism and American Education: The Battle for the Public Schools—Eugene F. Provenzo Jr.

The High Status Track: Studies of Elite Schools and Stratification—Paul W. Kingston and Lionel S. Lewis (eds.)

The Economics of American Universities: Management, Operations, and Fiscal Environment—Stephen A. Hoenack and Eileen L. Collins (eds.)

Going to School: The African American Experience—Kofi Lomotey (ed.)

Curriculum Differentiation: Interpretive Studies in U.S. Secondary Schools—Reba Page and Linda Valli (eds.)

The Racial Crisis in American Higher Education—Philip G. Altbach and Kofi Lomotey (eds.)

The Great Transformation in Higher Education, 1960–1980—Clark Kerr

College in Black and White: African American Students in Predominantly White and in Historically Black Public Universities—Walter R. Allen, Edgar G. Epps, and Nesha Z. Haniff (eds.)

Critical Perspectives on Early Childhood Education—Lois Weis, Philip G. Altbach, Gail P. Kelly, and Hugh G. Petrie (eds.)

Textbooks in American Society: Politics, Policy, and Pedagogy—Philip G. Altbach, Gail P. Kelly, Hugh G. Petrie, and Lois Weis (eds.)

Black Resistance in High School: Forging a Separatist Culture—R. Patrick Solomon

Emergent Issues in Education: Comparative Perspectives—Robert F. Arnove, Philip G. Altbach, and Gail P. Kelly (eds.)

Creating Community on College Campuses—Irving J. Spitzberg Jr. and Virginia V. Thorndike

Teacher Education Policy: Narratives, Stories, and Cases—Hendrik D. Gideonse (ed.)

Beyond Silenced Voices: Class, Race, and Gender in United States Schools—Lois Weis and Michelle Fine (eds.)

The Cold War and Academic Governance: The Lattimore Case at Johns Hopkins—Lionel S. Lewis

Troubled Times for American Higher Education: The 1990s and Beyond—Clark Kerr

Higher Education Cannot Escape History: Issues for the Twenty-first Century—Clark Kerr

Multiculturalism and Education: Diversity and Its Impact on Schools and Society—Thomas J. LaBelle and Christopher R. Ward

The Contradictory College: The Conflicting Origins, Impacts, and Futures of the Community College—Kevin J. Dougherty

Race and Educational Reform in the American Metropolis: A Study of School Decentralization—Dan A. Lewis and Kathryn Nakagawa

Professionalization, Partnership, and Power: Building Professional Development Schools—Hugh G. Petrie (ed.)

Ethnic Studies and Multiculturalism—Thomas J. LaBelle and Christopher R. Ward

The Racial Crisis in American Higher Education (Revised Edition): Continuing Challenges for the Twenty-first Century—William A. Smith, Philip G. Altbach, and Kofi Lomotey (eds.)

Increasing Access to College: Extending Possibilities for All Students—William G. Tierney and Linda Serra Hagedorn (eds.)